HOW TO WIN

Lessons in success from the front line of performance psychology

HOW TO WIN

DR KATE HAYS

WITH MATT ALLEN

HarperCollins*Publishers*

Every person that appears in this book has given consent to their being mentioned and have approved the way in which their ideas and actions have been portrayed. No confidences have been broken; no private or confidential information has been shared without consent. Everything that appears in the book does so with the intention of improving the reader's processes via some of the greatest minds in elite sport.

HarperCollins*Publishers*
1 London Bridge Street
London SE1 9GF

www.harpercollins.co.uk

HarperCollins*Publishers*
Macken House, 39/40 Mayor Street Upper
Dublin 1, D01 C9W8, Ireland

First published by HarperCollins*Publishers* 2025

1 3 5 7 9 10 8 6 4 2

Text © Kate Hays 2025
Illustrations by Liane Payne © HarperCollins *Publishers* Ltd 2025

Kate Hays asserts the moral right to be identified as the author of this work

A catalogue record of this book is available from the British Library

HB ISBN 978-0-00-869828-7
PB ISBN 978-0-00-869829-4

Printed and bound in the UK using 100% renewable electricity at CPI Group (UK) Ltd

All rights reserved. No part of this publication may be reproduced, stored in a retrieval system, or transmitted, in any form or by any means, electronic, mechanical, photocopying, recording or otherwise, without the prior written permission of the publishers.

This book contains FSC™ certified paper and other controlled sources to ensure responsible forest management.

For more information visit: www.harpercollins.co.uk/green

For my husband Ian, and our children Coco, Rafe and Baye

CONTENTS

INTRODUCTION	ix
BUILDING BLOCK #1: WHO ARE WE?	**1**
1. DECIPHERING YOUR VALUES	7
2. PERSONALITY TYPES AND HOW TO UNDERSTAND THEM	19
3. STRENGTHS, SUPER-STRENGTHS, WEAKNESSES AND BOAT-SINKERS	35
4. ONE-PAGERS: THE SECRET WEAPON	52
5. HOLDING UP A MIRROR	65
BUILDING BLOCK #2: WHY ARE WE HERE?	**73**
6. THE NORTH STAR	78
7. MISSION BUILDING	89
8. WINNING BEHAVIOURS (AND HOW TO IDENTIFY THEM)	104
9. WALKING THE TALK	118
10. TELLING STORIES	131
BUILDING BLOCK #3: HOW DO WE PLAY?	**143**
11. GAME-PLAN DEVELOPMENT: DEFINING YOUR HOW	148
12. GAME-PLAN TRAINING: BRINGING THE BIG IDEA TO LIFE	161

13. GAME-PLAN SUPPORT: COUNTING DOWN TO THE BIG EVENT	177
14. GAME-PLAN EXECUTION: DIRECTING ATTENTION UNDER PRESSURE	193
15. GAME-PLAN DEBRIEF: PLAN, DO, REVIEW	204

BUILDING BLOCK #4: HOW DO WE WIN? — 219

16. DON'T ICE A COLLAPSING CAKE	224
17. THE PRE-COMPETITION HEALTH CHECK	239
18. STRESS BUCKETS AND SELF-CARE	251
19. PSYCHOLOGY ON THE GRASS	264
20. STADIUM SKILLS	278
21. DECOMPRESSING THE RIGHT WAY	297
ENDNOTE	309
AFTERWORD BY TOM DALEY	311
ACKNOWLEDGEMENTS	321

INTRODUCTION

Wembley Stadium, Sunday 31 July 2022
England 2-1 Germany

Chloe Kelly scored what looked to be the winning goal of the 2022 Women's European Championship, tore off her shirt and sprinted towards the bench. The noise ricocheting around Wembley Stadium was deafening, the mood euphoric. With that one goal in extra time, the Lionesses looked set to topple Germany, saving the nation from the stress of an excruciating penalty shootout. A major international tournament win, England's first since the men's World Cup victory in 1966, would also assure them a place in football history.

Well, *maybe*.

Despite the late strike, a goal poked in from close range, the Germans were an experienced side and couldn't be written off, especially as they'd already shown the emotional resolve to come back from a goal behind. Meanwhile, the England players, plus subs, were celebrating on the pitch. Chloe was surrounded by her teammates at the sidelines as Sarina Wiegman, the England head coach, attempted to instil some sense of order. At the very moment when cool heads were needed to secure the win, England were in danger of losing theirs.

It was hard not to get caught up in the euphoria, but from my position in the stands a feeling of excitement soon turned into apprehension. As the head of women's psychology at the FA, I understood the dangers of emotional turbulence all too well.

'*We haven't won it yet,*' I thought. '*Get your shirt back on, Chloe.*'

Then I looked down at my watch. Ten minutes to go, plus stoppages. '*Stay in the present. Manage the game.*'

I needn't have worried. Chloe was soon back in full kit, the team steadied and I tried my hardest to appear composed. In my job it's important to at least look like a picture of calm, even when my heart rate and rising adrenaline levels are telling a quite different story. That's because there was little doubt that the fate of England's tournament hinged on the players' emotional control during the remaining ten minutes, although if they could echo their resolve from the previous five games there was every chance that the final was over. Throughout the tournament, the team had performed with grit and resilience. There was a powerful sense of self-belief within every member of the squad. And despite them living in team hotels and training venues for the best part of nine weeks, their spirit and camaraderie remained undented. Every single player was committed and driven, even the ones who hadn't experienced a minute of competitive action. Those individuals were just as impressive as the headline grabbers. They'd showed up in training; they'd pushed the starting XI to work even harder; and they'd given 100 per cent in every aspect of preparation, ensuring they were ready if and when their time came.

Up until the final's 110th minute, the vibe permeating the Lionesses' camp had been relaxed and emotionally controlled. The team had progressed through the group stages and knockout rounds with conviction, and behind the scenes everything was calm. Sure, we celebrated the wins as they happened, but for the most part there was an air of *business as usual*. The atmosphere around the squad had shifted a few times, most markedly on the bus journey into the stadiums as the tournament progressed, and then only for a few brief moments. The roads leading to Wembley on the day of the final had been lined with tens of thousands of fans. The national mood was revved up, the country sensing that we were on the verge of achieving something special, and every now and then we caught a glimpse of what had been happening outside the walls of our team hotel. In such an atmosphere I briefly found it hard to suppress my emotions – excitement, pride and unity hit me all at once. But then, when I looked around at the players, they appeared relaxed. Their nerves had been reframed as excitement, and they accepted the emotion as a cue that their bodies and minds were ready.

This tone had been set by Sarina's final team briefing, where her delivery was characteristically calm but focused. The determination in her voice was palpable as she reiterated the fact that we didn't have to win the European Championship, *but that we really wanted to*. Achieving that feat required the players to stick to their processes and to remain engaged with the game plan. During that crazy, excited minute following Chloe's goal against Germany, the Lionesses quickly reverted to an almost default setting of composure, and the remainder of the game was pretty much played out in one corner of the pitch. When the final whistle blew after what felt like a lifetime, I became choked up with emotion. Having worked with the team for a little under a year, I'd had the great privilege of hearing their stories and I'd learned about their journey to this point, while experiencing their passion, determination and work ethic first hand. They were a special group of players and staff, and I really wanted them to achieve their dream.

But that's the thing with sport: as with any activity rooted in performance – work, personal challenges, even family life – there are no guarantees. And it's not enough to *want* to win. A team or individual must also know *how*.

The Building Blocks of Success is a framework I've developed over a 20-year career as a sport psychologist, via a series of elite-level breakthroughs and mistakes, and a number of collaborations with some of the greatest minds in UK sport. During this time, I've practised alongside some of the world's greatest athletes and coaches. While at the English Institute of Sport (later renamed as the UK Sports Institute, or UKSI), I led the psychology team through the Rio and Tokyo Olympic and Paralympic Games and worked as the headquarters psychologist for the British Olympic Association in Tokyo. Over a 14-year period I was also part of the team that supported several Team GB divers as they secured Olympic medal success, including Tom Daley. During his career, Tom won five Olympic medals and recently retired as one of the most successful divers of all time. Elsewhere, I was part of the staff behind the successful professional rugby union team Harlequins and in 2012 supported them towards a Premier League title for the first time. I also worked from 2015 to 2018 with the Cambridge Women's rowing team, who were unbeaten from 2017 to the time of writing.

Over this period, *The Building Blocks of Success* became a transformative programme for developing a winning mentality in both an individual and group setting. Comprising four easy-to-follow stages, the process, if executed correctly, has the power to transform good teams into great teams, while turning underperforming or misfiring athletes into title-winning forces. Meanwhile, I arrived at a clear idea of how to achieve success through tactics, management, instruction and reflection, and focused on the way that victories arrived. The athletes' mental health was an important consideration, every bit as important as team selection and tournament prep. Yes, it was important to win. *But it was more important to thrive.* The priority focus was creating a sustainable culture that enabled the people within our care to succeed, over and over again.

Importantly, *The Building Blocks of Success* isn't a resource solely reserved for elite Olympians or international football teams. In fact, anyone can find long-term and sustainable success using the methods contained within it because the blueprint is so simple to understand. Really, all that's needed is for the user to work through the four building blocks, while defining the very important, but often overlooked, questions contained within:

- Who are we?
- Why are we here?
- How do we play?
- How do we win?

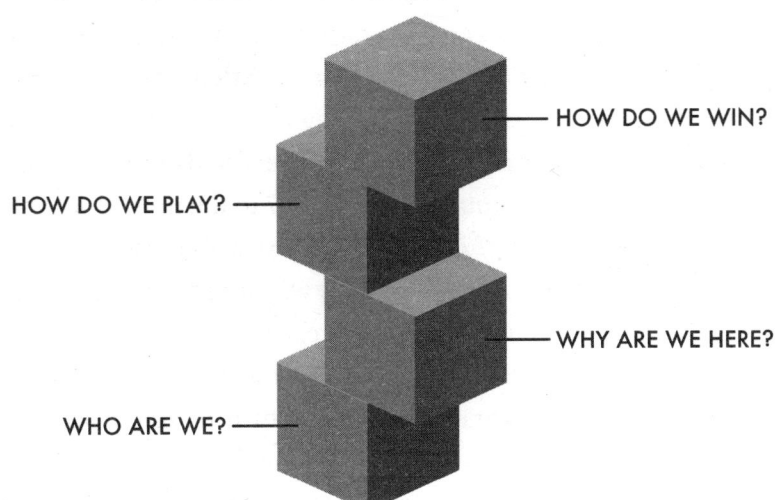

On the surface, the answers might seem painfully obvious. For example, if you were to ask a potential gold medal winner their *why* on the eve of an Olympic Games, the answer would be predictable: *To win gold*. Likewise, if you were to press a business entrepreneur, doctor, creative or charity organiser for their *why*, they might answer in a similar fashion: I want to be the best. But while these are legitimate answers, they often crumble under pressure. For example, what happens to a person's attitude and motivation when they don't win the Employee of the Year Award or if they're not the very best creative in their field? Does that crush morale and reduce desire? And if so, does that realisation then prevent the person or team from succeeding in the future?

Rather than relying on these surface-level answers, each building block motivates the participant to dig much, much deeper by working through a series of easy-to-understand psychological exercises and challenges, each one devised at the top tier of elite sport. The next step is for the participant to apply the learned lessons and skills to their environment, whether that be in sport, business, family, or any individual or group endeavour, such as a charity drive or expedition. Anyone following the processes set out by *The Building Blocks of Success* can then create a greater understanding of self and of the people working, playing or striving alongside them. That in turn will develop into a clearer understanding of purpose, identity, clarity in performance and results:

- *Who are we?* Do we truly understand who we are as a group and individually?
- *Why are we here?* Are we aligned on our shared purpose?
- *How do we play?* Do we have absolute clarity about our methods?
- *How do we win?* Do we have the tools and an environment that will enable us to perform to the best of our abilities?

While conducting this work and seeing its impact, I learned two very important truths:

1. People function at their optimum when they're valued for who they are and treated with respect. Performance environments are challenging, and that challenge should be met with support. Because of that, leaders have a responsibility to facilitate environments that are conducive to performance (the results business), but also to mental health (the life business). It's not about screaming from the sidelines, and success shouldn't come at the cost of someone's well-being. That approach leads to burnout. *The Building Blocks of Success* are all about sustainability. The aim is to perform in such a way that it's possible to win, over and over and over again.

2. Sport psychologists, as well as many coaches and support staff, don't generally have the opportunity to talk about their work or share the things they've discovered during their journey. Most often we work at an individual level and then must learn how to apply psychological principles to a team, organisation or system. I was lucky that when I first started working in professional sport I didn't need to have all the answers, because I was working in a collaborative team where the aim was to problem-solve together, and I was given space to learn how to apply my ideas and theories to both the team and the individuals working within it. This was the start of a journey of discovery about how to support an athlete or a team, and how to create systemic change – as this book strives to do. Everyone should have the same opportunity, including you. (And I would have loved a book like this to provide a framework for my thinking back then.)

Implementing *The Building Blocks of Success* is a challenging but rewarding experience, as I have discovered alongside the many staff and athletes I've worked with over the years. Together we've learned that no elite team can truly strive for their common cause without an understanding of those four building blocks. Nor will they fully support themselves in times of stress. Experience has also taught me that without an affinity for the characters and personalities within their group, athletes are unlikely to discover the confidence to call out a drop in standards. Likewise, they will find it hard to inspire a struggling teammate in tough times.

When I joined Sarina and the Lionesses at St George's Park at the end of 2021, we knew that if England were to go on and succeed in the European Championship the following year, the coaching staff and I would have to create a safe environment, somewhere the squad could work through the four building blocks in stages, a place where the players would feel comfortable enough to speak without criticism and to make mistakes knowing that they would be allowed to grow as a direct consequence, rather than fail. Together with the rest of the staff and the players, we brought this process to life.

Sarina Wiegman, Lionesses head coach

Kate and I connected in our very first meeting. When I started as the Lionesses head coach in 2021, I wanted to bring in a psychologist who shared the same vision for sporting success as me. When it was agreed that Kate and I should meet, I brought in some slides, she brought in some slides, and there was an immediate click. 'Wow,' I thought. 'I'm from the Netherlands, Kate is from England, and we share the same vision for how people can succeed sustainably.' That was important because as a coach I must make a lot of tough decisions. I want to be high-demanding and honest, but I also want to be kind, caring and supportive. Kate's ideas on sport psychology reflected that attitude.

I believe that everyone can benefit from these four building blocks, whether they're focused on their work, or a personal challenge or life moment. By working through them, it's also possible for a person or team to see progress and to know exactly where they are in their journey, which is brilliant. That's because the work is systematic, and the processes and techniques involved are easy to implement. From time to time I've checked which parts of the building blocks we've covered and where work still needs to be done, and this has provided me with structure and affirmation. That's because the building blocks give me clarity. I know how I want to coach. I understand how my workflow should be. My environment must be structured in a certain way. And I have a vision for how I want my team to play – and make the chance of winning as great as possible. Kate's ideas and processes allow me to manage these factors without taking away my spontaneity. I believe they will do the same for you too.

Exactly how *The Building Blocks of Success* can be applied to just about any person in any environment is laid out in detail for the first time in *How to Win*. Organised into four parts (every building block in the programme gets its own section), the book is made up of a series of instructional chapters. Each one consists of easy-to-follow theory and anecdotal evidence that will help you to develop as an individual or a group, all while delivering an insight into the working practices utilised by a series of elite athletes and teams. Meanwhile, every chapter carries a series of battle-tested exercises, tasks and bullet-pointed takeaways, so that anyone reading this can experience a tangible sense of progress as they commit to putting *The Building Blocks of Success* into practice.

I hope you enjoy the journey.

Dr Kate Hays, 2025

BUILDING BLOCK #1

WHO ARE WE?

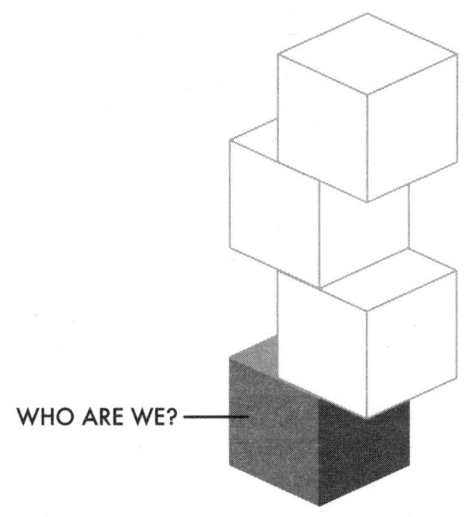

INTRODUCTION

No elite team, in any context, can truly strive for success without first answering one simple question: *Who are we?* That's because all of us carry around a system of personality characteristics and personal values – our definitions of right and wrong – as well as a subconscious hard drive of the things that matter most to us. These values vary widely from person to person, and no two individuals are the same. For example, one team member might cherish self-sacrifice, brutal honesty and team effort, while the person working alongside them might place more importance on self-care, diplomacy and individuality. There are, however, no set rules on what these values need to be or how many a person should have.

Most importantly, these personal values are intrinsically linked to our behaviours and decision-making, which means that with an understanding of our *who*, it's possible for us to control our emotions, rather than having our emotions control *us*. The knock-on effect is that we can then better understand and interact with the people we're working with. This information is particularly powerful when gathered within a team setting and then shared, because during pressurised situations like a major football tournament or a boardroom negotiation, this understanding works like a cheat code, and in three ways.

A greater understanding of *who* both strengthens the connections between individuals and reduces any assumptions. As human beings, we can be very quick to judge. We see someone crying after a minor dispute and dismiss them as being *overdramatic*. When someone is late, we brand them as *unprepared*. If a person expresses their requirements directly without sugar-coating things, they become known as *blunt* or *aggressive*. Of course, while there's a chance that some of these assumptions might be true, it's probable that there's a more deep-seated reason for these reactions. The overdramatic person values acceptance and feels judged during disputes. The late person has a sick parent at home and it's their responsibility to provide care in the mornings. The blunt person needs straightforward communication to function effectively and feels that others deserve the same.

Knowledge of *who* generates a certain level of predictability. If everyone in a group is aware of their selves, plus the characteristics and values of those people around them, it's possible to predict the responses to certain events. This information then helps to avoid any flashpoint situations. So, if there's a player who regularly ruminates after a mistake, they can be cajoled and encouraged, both on the pitch and at half-time. The individual who reacts strongly to what they perceive as unfairness can be calmed and reassured when a refereeing decision doesn't go their way. The CEO who goes quiet before a presentation can be given the time needed to reflect and prepare. This understanding and empathy within a group is incredibly important in circumstances where the stakes are high, deadlines are tight and stress levels are rising.

When differences are understood and valued – and deep connections are formed – the impact upon performance can be positive and profound. Organisations that take the time to understand their people often foster environments that celebrate difference and uniqueness. They encourage learning and growth through considering multiple perspectives, rather than being led by groupthink. Also, with high levels of self-awareness and humility, a team can make incredible demands of one another, they can hold each other to account when it's really needed, and they can drive overall standards to a much higher and more sustainable level, all while amplifying the strengths of the individual. We all know the saying: *a team is greater than the sum of its parts*. This rings particularly true when taking in the concept of *who*.

This understanding is just as powerful away from sport, although a common mistake made by a lot of companies and/or collectives is that they don't spend enough time truly learning about the people under their employ. They fail to understand the individuals in the room – the characters that make up their team, and their stories and values. By ignoring this information, these groups never fully comprehend their driving forces or effectively manage their team's strengths and weaknesses. Imagine if a mechanic failed to learn about the latest updates within a hybrid engine or the intricate advances in a new steering or braking system. The cars in their care would never leave the garage forecourt and the business would fail as a result. It's the same with any team.

I've also learned that if a group fails to understand their *who* it becomes much harder to fully support itself in times of stress. Without understanding the characters and personalities contained within, a collective of individuals won't know how to react if one person begins to struggle emotionally. Equally, by not learning about the personal values and characteristics within the group, it's much harder to call out a drop in standards, because the circumstances leading to that drop will be unclear. To avoid these scenarios, it's important to create a safe environment in which a team of very different people can work together.

Because if done correctly, learning about the *who* can establish a team's individual and collective strengths, their super-strengths and their weaknesses, so that when working at the highest level, they can amplify the positives and minimise their flaws. It also helps to brand the overall identity of a collective. With a clarified understanding of a team's *who*, the individuals working within it are more likely to uphold its values, using them as an inspiration in tough times. It's why the UK Special Forces have empowering mottos that amplify the belief they're working to a much higher standard than anyone else in the military, especially when operating from the shadows in some of the most hostile environments on earth. The SAS fight to the code of 'Who dares wins', while in the SBS it's 'By strength and guile'.

The only way of achieving this state of collective unity is to ensure that everybody striving for a shared cause knows exactly *who they are* and is able to align to the higher purpose of the group.

The path to successfully reaching that understanding is detailed over the following chapters.

CHAPTER ONE
DECIPHERING YOUR VALUES

One of our basic psychological needs as human beings is to feel a connection with others. Not only are relationships vital to our physical and emotional well-being, but in sport – and in all organisations or group settings – a healthy relationship between a team's members can provide the foundations for sustainable levels of high performance. I strongly believe that the individuals in any organisation will perform to their optimum when they feel supported, understood and valued.

This notion was put into action when I started working as head of psychology with the Lionesses in 2021, approximately nine months out from the upcoming European Championship. At the time I wasn't planning on working in football. I was also unsure if I wanted to work on the frontline of a major sporting team again, especially as I'd been overseeing the psychology team at the UK Sports Institute, an organisation dedicated to delivering 'outstanding support that enables sports and athletes to excel'. But when Kay Cossington, the FA women's technical director, called me out of the blue to talk about sport psychology for the women's teams, I was inspired by her passion and stories of the game. Kay had a clear vision for success and told me all about Sarina

Wiegman, the new England women's football team head coach, and her staff.

When I was eventually introduced to Sarina, I presented the 'How to Win' framework – and the four building blocks – to her, and throughout our discussion found that our philosophies on sustainable performance were intertwined. The way in which she managed her team felt quite different from anything I had experienced before, and from the moment we met I connected with her. The thought of bringing the framework to life together felt exciting.

Once I'd arrived, I learned that Sarina had already made one or two inroads into understanding her players and their stories, while sharing her own values with the group. As a result, the squad and its support staff were becoming aligned to the concept of their *who*. This was an incredibly important first step, because if the England women's football team were to succeed in the European Championship they would require an environment in which they could a) fully support themselves in times of stress, b) drive one another to even greater heights, and c) have the confidence to call out a drop in standards in both the group and the individual. To achieve this, the players had to come to an understanding of what was important to them – both within their own value systems and in those of the people around them.

To advance this process, the coaching staff and myself needed to create a safe environment, one in which the players would feel comfortable enough to take risks, express their ideas without criticism and to admit mistakes – all without fear of negative consequences.

But how?

I've found that one way to build connections within a mixed group of personalities like the Lionesses is to first carve out some time where everyone can share their stories on a one-on-one basis, and discover one another's likes and dislikes, preferences and values. This process, if done correctly, helps to form connections on and off the field, though it isn't as simple as gathering everyone together in a meeting room and instructing them to deliver CliffsNotes on their personalities. Instead, what's needed is an environment in which people can be themselves without feeling judged, especially when displaying vulnerability.

To get the ball rolling on this idea, I organised a value-sharing exercise where I set the team two tasks. The first was an icebreaking exercise – the players took turns to answer a set of ten questions posed to them by their teammates. Each one was taken from '36 Questions That Lead to Love' – an experiment conducted by Arthur and Elaine Aron in 1997, during which the two psychologists tried to establish whether strangers could develop an 'intimate connection' by answering a list of personal questions, such as:

> *Given the choice of anyone in the world, who would you want as a dinner guest?*
> *What do you value most in a friendship?*
> *What is your most treasured memory?*
> *What would constitute a 'perfect' day for you?*
> *Share with your partner an embarrassing moment in your life.*

Once these questions had been answered, the players were asked to partner with someone they didn't know very well at that point and work through a timeline of their life, represented by a piece of paper with a line drawn across the middle. The starting point on the left marked a person's birth, the end point on the right, the current day, and each player had to draw on any important or pivotal experiences they'd had over the course of their life. The secret to gathering this information, I've learned, is to bring nuance to the exercise. So, rather than simply writing down an event and moving on, every participant was encouraged to recall its emotional impact at the time. Why? Well, if I were to ask someone to describe themselves, they would probably provide the basic facts in short order, about who they are, where they work, what they've experienced, who they spend their time with, and some of their likes and dislikes. There would be very little insight into what truly makes them tick. However, if I were to ask that same person to retell their life story, while highlighting its highs and lows – and then dig into *why* they were highs and *why* they were lows – a distinct collection of themes and values tends to emerge.

For example, I would probably answer the first style of questioning by describing myself cognitively before expanding on the fact that I was brought up in Croydon. I'd then talk about my family, education and career path. Anyone wanting to learn about my values wouldn't have much to work with based on those facts alone, because there's not a lot of context or emotion involved. But, when working with the second style of questioning, my answers would likely reveal the peaks and troughs of that same journey, while exploring *why* those extremes were so impactful. From then on, it would be possible to draw several accurate conclusions about who I am and why I behave in the way I do: that I'm someone who values care, clarity, exploration, togetherness and family. And because of that, I feel empowered in a person-centred team environment in which positive action and solution-focused approaches lead the way.

This information can be vital in a team setting, where so many differing personalities and values are brought together to challenge for the same prize. That's because as human beings we tend to judge the people around us on their behaviour rather than their intentions. Worse, we make assumptions. We see people as being difficult, arrogant or lazy, and write them off without ever hearing the backstory to their actions. But what would happen if we were to explore the narratives informing this behaviour? We might learn that the rude person has been crippled by social anxiety; that the arrogant person feels inferior to their peers and uses standoffishness as a defence mechanism; and that the lazy person has become so stressed about their performance levels that they deflect by pretending not to care. Every single behaviour is understandable with context; we only need to discover what that context actually is. From there, powerful connections can grow.

When putting this exercise to the Lionesses, any positive events that took place were written above the timeline running across their page; the more difficult events were written below it; and everyone had total control over what they were willing to share. When the exercise began, the players – and coaching staff – were encouraged to explore the feelings attached to any positive and negative events. By doing so, everyone was able to learn of their teammates' values naturally, while gaining a deeper understanding of the context behind each one. Meanwhile, as the team workshopped, the support staff restaged the meeting room to create a welcoming, campfire vibe. Beanbags were set out on the floor and fairy lights were strung from the ceiling. Someone even projected a digitised roaring fire on to the wall.

When the squad returned, mugs of hot chocolate were passed around. I noticed that, while the players looked relaxed with one another, they seemed apprehensive about being asked to share their personal stories with the group as a whole. I pointed out that this wasn't the purpose of the exercise and that they only needed to share if they wanted to. The ideal outcome, really, was for them to enjoy the environment and to connect with one another. The response from that point on was interesting. Several team members became happy to talk and opinions were aired, although interestingly nobody betrayed a confidence; the players only spoke of their own experiences. Almost immediately, the squad felt safe and relaxed in an environment where they could express themselves without fear of repercussions or judgement.

Most importantly, the players began forming new connections with their teammates, ones that would strengthen the group in times of pressure. They understood themselves better. Everyone was on their way to finding a deeper and much stronger psychological power, and one player even commented: 'I've spent years going on England camps with the person I spoke to during this exercise, and I didn't know any of the things they told me today.' I wholeheartedly believe that robust connections on the pitch can only be made when there are connections off it. Without a shared understanding – and a sense of respect – it becomes impossible to drive standards upwards and hold one another to account. People will accept challenges from those they respect and trust, and they will hear their messages, even when they are clumsily conveyed – which is quite often the case in the heat of the moment.

Interestingly, every person involved remembers that particular session. Over the past couple of years I've heard several players and coaches refer to it, and the comments are always positive. That's because everyone shared in a unique exchange, probably for the very first time, which then created some extremely powerful bonds. What followed was a series of exercises – some of which will be detailed over the coming pages – that focused on the group having absolute clarity about *who they were*. This is something that every successful athlete, team and organisation I've ever worked with has spent time working to understand.

DESIGNING A TIMELINE

In its basic form, timeline drawing is a form of storytelling, and I was first introduced to the concept during a UKSI workshop several years ago (though it was made famous by the entrepreneur and author Simon Sinek in his book *Find Your Why*). I've since used it on a long list of athletes and staff, both in team sports and individual disciplines, and when applied in the right way, this simple technique delivers a tactical insight into the values of an individual and the emotions that can drive them forward or hold them back.

When running through the process with an athlete, their job is to be the narrator, mine is to be the listener,* and I'll ask them to create a timeline that starts at their childhood and runs to the present day, marking down the events that evoke the strongest emotional reactions. These, of course, can be both positive and negative. During childhood, it's not uncommon for a kid to walk away from their parents in a supermarket and become lost, which can feel utterly terrifying at the time. A participant might become excited when remembering their first visit to the cinema, a time they attended a birthday party or the moment they were introduced to an important person, like a partner or close friend. When noting these events on the timeline, the most positive are placed farthest away from the line, at the top of the page; those that are less impactful should be positioned closer to it. This procedure is mirrored for the more difficult events, with the most powerful events being positioned at the bottom of the page.

---

* In this context I'm working as a practitioner and not sharing my own timeline. But if you're doing this exercise in pairs, one person should be the narrator, the other the listener. You should swap roles once the first timeline has been concluded.

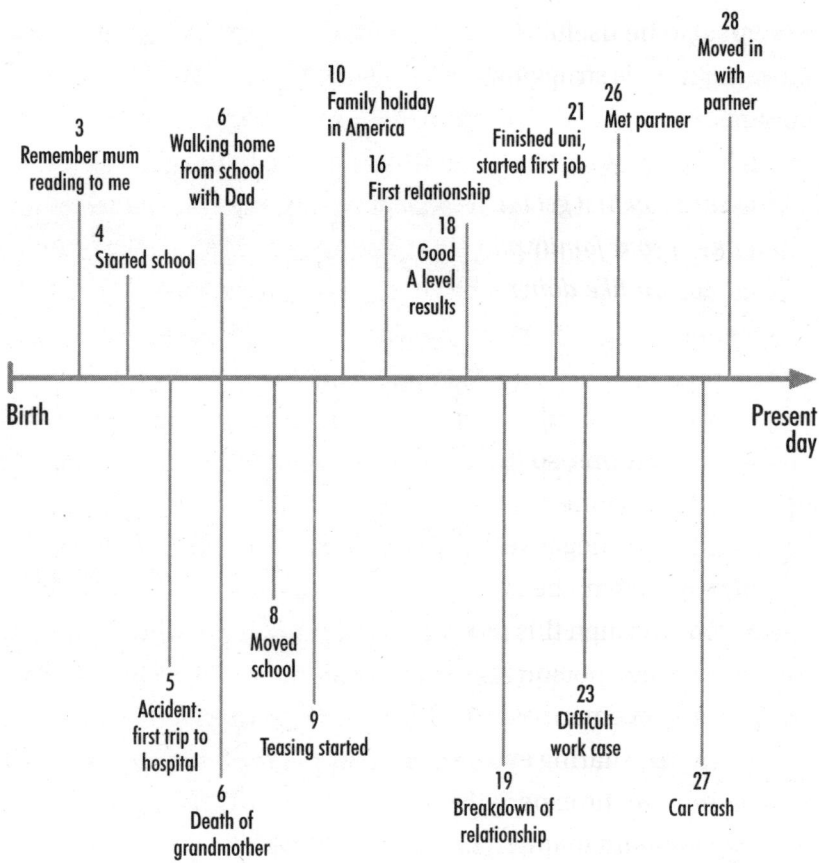

Once this process has taken place, I'll ask the individual to run through their story. My job as the listener is to dig into the key events, ask questions and explore any emotional responses that might occur. I am looking to uncover what really matters to them, what inspires them and what drives their behaviour. Lines of enquiry I like to consider when picking through a story include:

How did you feel in that moment?
Who else was there and how did they react?
Why was it so powerful, and what did you learn?

It can also be useful to ask additional questions, particularly if the participant is struggling to clarify what is important from their timeline:

When did you first get into your sport?
Did any of your family play?
What do you like doing for the sake of it (doing something just for fun)?

Every answer should be explored further and there must be follow-up questions, so it's not enough to accept a statement and move on. If someone's earliest childhood memory is overwhelmingly positive or negative, I'll explore their reaction to the event and note it down, because it's important to know how they responded. Through this process, key themes will emerge. I might notice that one person's happiest moments are connected to personal achievement, while another individual might be at their happiest when sharing experiences with friends and family. Some participants might experience shame after failing at something, others might tend to quit if they receive criticism. Quite often, the same themes will emerge repeatedly from multiple stories, and once that happens the heart of what someone is all about can be revealed.

Of course, it's possible for an individual to run through this exercise on their own, but I'd maintain that a second pair of eyes is invaluable, mainly because we're often unable (or unwilling) to identify the events that have shaped us in life, especially if they're emotionally painful. Skilful questioning often encourages people to reflect in greater depth than they have previously. Also, the beauty of doing this exercise with another person is that both participants can witness the reactions in their colleague's face as they talk. Sometimes, the answer lies not in a person's words but in their physical expressions. It's possible to see someone light up whenever they talk about a certain person, place or activity and notice that they shut down when describing situations where they had to perform in front of others, assume leadership or take financial risks. (What I find most often is that the clearest themes are not things that have previously been identified by the storyteller. It's a great privilege to be trusted with a person's narrative, as well as being deeply fulfilling to witness them learn something new and powerful about themselves.)

There is a great power in identifying themes within a person's timeline because these serve as a predictor for how they might react in future events. Values form the basis of our thoughts, behaviours and actions, and this is potent intelligence to have when approaching crunch situations. It can be applied equally well to events not associated with sport: deadlines and financial pressure; public speaking and networking; rejection and praise; and so on. I've also adapted this technique when trying to discover when and why an athlete feels at their most confident, especially if they're struggling to perform tasks in games that they ordinarily deliver in training without too much trouble. In such cases I'll ask them as many questions as I can about how they think, feel and act when they're at their most confident. Once I've highlighted the psychological factors occurring in practice, when they're able to perform comfortably, I'll help them to transfer those same factors over to higher-pressure situations. (We'll discuss this process in more detail in Building Block #3.)

When a person becomes aware of their values, they can thrive both in moments of adversity and periods of success. They're less likely to be shocked by their reactions to certain events – positive and negative – and they're able to plan and make decisions that are aligned with what's truly important to them. As I mentioned earlier, I've learned through this process that one of my key values is the importance of family, but I've often been separated from my husband and kids for several weeks in the year, due to working commitments at the World Cup, European Championship or the Olympic Games. I now know to prepare in advance so I can counteract any negative feelings that might occur during those moments of disconnection. I ready my mind by spending as much time with my family as possible before I leave, and at the event I make sure to find the space and time to connect with everyone at home during the day, via the phone, Zoom or text. I'll also foreplan self-care into my routine, so that if I do feel down about being away from the family unit, I can look after myself emotionally.

 ASK THE QUESTION

Who would you feel most comfortable sharing your timeline with?

Ideally it will be someone that won't be afraid to ask questions, or to dig into your backstory. A trusted work colleague or even a therapist would be a good someone to progress this exercise, rather than a partner or close friend. Remember: they must be trustworthy, and you must feel comfortable in showing vulnerability around them.

LIGHTBULBS

- A team that knows itself can support its members in times of stress, confidently call out a decline in standards and help the individuals within to maximise their potential.
- As human beings we judge the people around us on behaviour, rather than intention. Everyone's behaviour is understandable with context – we just need to discover what that context is.
- It's not enough to know the positive and negative events in your story. It's enlightening to explore why they made you feel the way you do. Explore these emotions by running through a timeline of key events in your life.

CHAPTER TWO

PERSONALITY TYPES AND HOW TO UNDERSTAND THEM

A team without an understanding of their *who* can stumble into one of two pitfalls: when things are going badly, their work becomes increasingly chaotic due to miscommunication and misunderstandings; if things are going well, the group is unlikely to reach their full potential because the multiplier effect between the personalities involved will have been overlooked. I have worked with teams in the past that had yet to understand the personality characteristics operating within the dressing room, and as a result their performances sometimes came apart under the greatest pressure; they didn't understand one another or have a strategy for managing their connections and communication styles.

I remember an early fixture with one such team, where they ended the first half trailing to a technically inferior side. The action on the pitch was a mess. Some players weren't sticking to the plan, others were taking unnecessary risks. As things began to crumble, several members of the group, including the captain, attempted to regain control in their own way by issuing instructions and barking orders, but because there wasn't a clear focal point or a singular voice, their commands were disregarded and occasionally contradicted one another. One or two players went missing and looked confused. Several coaches, who were sitting in the stands and communicating with the bench via headsets, gave directions, but amid the anarchy their tactical instructions became muddled when they were transferred on-field. With the team being outplayed and overwhelmed, emotions ran high.

Everything blew up at half-time. As the players sat in the dressing room, feeling frustrated and confused, the manager tore into them. Individuals were called out for their mistakes, or a lack of perceived effort, which left them feeling humiliated. I stood at the back of the room, in silence, observing the chaos.* The group looked shellshocked, as did the coaching staff, and when the second half got underway, things went from bad to worse. Without a clear plan of action or a grasp on why certain individuals were behaving the way they were, the team crashed to defeat. In the closing stages of the match some players were embarking on personal crusades, the group stopped listening to one another, there was no clarity around communication and the whole thing broke down.

But had the team developed a clear understanding of one another's preferences, of how they were likely to perform under pressure and the ways in which they could play to their strengths (while counteracting their weaknesses) the following would have been apparent:

- The shouters and the leaders were goal-oriented and solution-focused. When the pressure was on, they all

---

* As far as I was concerned, this was an inappropriate way to deal with underperformance. No athlete ever goes out and tries to underperform, so there is never a justifiable reason to reprimand someone in this way. What is needed in such moments is clarity and control, a plan of action to get behind and the confidence to execute it

independently liked to take control, but if they believed that someone else was trying to take control from them, they became frustrated and aggressive.
- The players that stepped back in the chaos were more analytical. In turbulent moments they liked to make sense of what was going on. When people shouted and yelled at them, they were unable to think clearly.
- The risk-takers were optimistic in their mindset. They took chances because they had faith they would come off, and if they could claw their way back into the game with a couple of unexpected plays, well, *everything would work out fine.*

But this also happens on an individual level too. No solo sportsperson truly works alone. Tennis players have coaches. Golfers have caddies. Similarly, sole traders in business have important allies, such as an adviser or someone else they work alongside in a close capacity. In certain situations it's helpful for these people to have a handle on their own personal *who,* so their reactions to positive and negative events can be managed.

Consider the scenario where a tennis player and their coach are having a difficult time. The athlete is underperforming, and the relationship is fraught, mainly because communication channels have broken down. The coach knows how to fix the player's problems on the court, but whenever they issue an instruction or some nugget of knowledge, the player asks, 'Why?' and then does something entirely different. This then creates an incredible amount of tension, because as far as the coach is concerned, the player is being petulant and unprofessional. Their conclusion: *Why won't they trust my instructions?* The reality, of course, is very different, and tied into the personality preferences of both individuals.

The coach likes to be in control. Rather than considering an individual's thoughts and feelings when imparting knowledge, they want them to follow their instructions unquestioningly, so that the problem can be fixed quickly. When they're at their best, they look at a situation and think: *Right, what's the best solution for this?* They then communicate their ideas assertively in their drive towards successful outcomes.

The player is more risk-adverse than their coach. They don't want to take chances unnecessarily and risk making things worse. To follow an instruction, they must start by understanding the reasons for it being delivered in the first place. They're not asking 'Why?' to be awkward. They're asking 'Why?' because they want to know the root cause of the problem, what the solution is and why it will work for them.

Had this knowledge been established in advance, various strategies could have been put in place for managing the different personality types in play. That's because most problems begin with communication: everyone sees the world in a different way and has different preferences for finding and communicating solutions. When people's opinions clash, it can be destructive. However, if a group or individual has knowledge of how they – and their teammates – see the world, any disparities with the people around them can be viewed through an entirely different lens. Friction can be managed, so that it doesn't have a negative impact, and connections can be harnessed in such a way that they create an overwhelming net positive.

And that's where personality profiling comes into its own.

If a team of different characters, sporting or otherwise, are to work together effectively, it's vital they understand the personalities contained within it, and a useful method for reaching this position is to run a profiling session. Personality profiles have become increasingly popular in recent years, particularly in the contexts of sport and business, and while they'll never provide an exact breakdown of someone's character, they can deliver some clues about their *preferences* – the style in which an individual might behave in certain situations, such as when working alongside others or operating under extreme pressure.

When pulled together, a personality profile provides a lot of valuable intelligence. For starters, the individual is presented with an insight into how they might act in certain situations, and why. They can then choose to adapt their mindset or behavioural style to manage those situations and meet any changing demands. When these profiles are conducted with a team, it's possible for everyone involved to explore the various psychological connections (and differences) at play and create a framework in which the individuals can understand one another better. For example, some footballers might feel a burning anger as they sit in the dressing room after a bad result, while others might laugh and joke around as a way of coping. These different reactions do not represent how deeply each group cares about the performance of the team, although they might be misinterpreted as such. Their responses are simply driven by different factors. If those two different groups understand one another, they can co-habit. If they don't, the potential for conflict is high.

In these circumstances, an understanding of *who* is key.

HOW TO USE A PROFILING SYSTEM

I was introduced to personality profiling several years ago and it's something I've subsequently utilised in some form with almost every team I've worked with. But while there are countless variations of the personality-profiling method available, I ask two questions when determining which one to apply:

- Does the profiling system have a solid theoretical base?
- Is the profiling system appropriately designed for its intended purpose?

Ultimately, when picking a profiling system, the decision is completely personal. What might work for one person might not be appropriate for someone else's circumstances, so I advise engaging in some research until a suitable fit (and facilitator) has been found.

The system I currently use is Spotlight, the proprietary profiling tool of a company called Mindflick. This resource was developed for elite sport by the sport psychologists Pete Lindsay, Mark Bawden and Tim Pitt, and it's underpinned by several modern theories of personality. It also focuses on the development of performance through adaptability, and has been designed specifically for people working in elite sport and across a range of other performance domains, such as business, education and health care. To use Spotlight, a person must first become accredited through Mindflick. If that feels like too much of a stretch, I've provided an easy-to-follow approach for doing a profile of your own later in this chapter, one that will give you an insight into some of the basic personality preferences and what to look out for yourself.

A Spotlight profile comprises the results of two distinct modelling systems:

1. **Mindset.** This model explores an individual's sensitivity to reward and threat. For example, when faced with a challenge, a 'contained' mindset is based on not being particularly sensitive to either. This helps a person to take a step back, look at the situation for what it is, and say: 'Keep calm and carry on . . .' An 'optimistic' mindset will view the situation positively and imagine the best-case scenarios. A 'prudent' mindset will approach the event with caution; it will imagine all the things that might go wrong and look to prevent these from happening. An 'engaged' mindset will approach the challenge in a reactive way. They will think: 'Stay alert, and get ready to respond.' Knowing the details

of these differences mean it's possible to understand how people might approach a variety of situations ahead of time.
2. **Behavioural style.** This model is based on the personality domains of agreeableness and extraversion. Individuals who are more task-focused (which is associated with lower levels of agreeableness) will be tuned in to what needs to be done, and why, while those personalities that are more people-focused (which is associated with higher levels of agreeableness) will have greater sensitivity to the harmony of the group and the way in which everyone can work together. The model then uses the extraversion dimension to describe behaviours that are a) more internal and associated with lower levels of extraversion, and b) more external and associated with higher levels of extraversion. This can be thought of in terms of where people get their energy from: extraverts lean into social interactions, whereas introverts take time out to reflect, analyse and recharge.

There are lots of personality-profiling systems to choose from, but it's my view that a reliable profiling tool, when used effectively, can be a benefit to all sorts of teams and collectives. Once identified, a series of characteristics – and the degree to which they appear in an individual's personality – can be laid out in a one-page map that details a person's behavioural and mindset preferences; it can provide insight into their drivers and strengths, their confidence sources and needs, and their stressors and pressure signs. (We'll discuss one-pagers and how to use them in greater detail later in the book.) By understanding this map – and the degree to which certain traits exist in someone – it's possible to find 'tells' for how they might behave in certain situations.

In the example of the dysfunctional team described at the beginning of this chapter, a profiling system revealed the personality traits that were causing the group to misfire. We were able to identify the senior players with a forceful behavioural style – an extraverted task focus – that all wanted to lead independently and take control, the optimists who wanted to take risks, and so on. To counteract this, a constructive leadership and followship strategy was developed so that the team could communicate effectively when under pressure. Messaging duties were designated to a single individual so that the team's instructions remained clear throughout a match, and we worked on body language techniques among the group. We also developed a mechanism for players to come together in a crisis event, conduct a rapid debrief and regroup. By maximising the differing personality types, the collective was able to pull together for the greater good.

Of course, personality profiles won't deliver a complete picture of a team or individual. But they can provide informed insights that deepen understanding and become a reliable barometer for how a group or person might act in high-stress situations. As a result, they provide a useful starting point for planning and reviewing sessions, and later, when designing tactics and procedures. It's always important, however, to 'sense check' the personality-profile information with the group and discuss which of the behaviours resonate with them, and which don't.

To implement a profiling system successfully, we need to follow several easy-to-understand steps.

1. GATHERING THE DATA

Before asking a team to conduct a personality profile, I like to run through an education session in which I'll explain 1) what a personality profile is, 2) what it measures and 3) how the profile can be used to benefit the individual or team. Then I'll ask the individuals to complete the profile in their own time. In doing so, they will answer a series of questions, and the results will reveal their personality preferences. Afterwards, they can then choose to share this information with the group.

An individual's personality profile doesn't reveal anything about their political beliefs, sexuality, age, values, life experiences, and so on. Instead, it presents the user with a scale of results that shines some light onto their personality preferences and how they might process information, communicate and make decisions. *The tool confirms what type of personality preferences they have, rather than revealing any secrets about what sort of person they are.* Of course, consent is sacrosanct and it's important to ask for permission when using this data, although I've never had an individual refuse to share their profile.

If you're unable to engage in a profiling programme, for whatever reason, there are still useful ways of learning about the preferences of the individuals within a team. For example, a lot of information can be gathered through informed discussion. It also helps to observe how a person interacts with others, and the ways in which their behaviours change in certain situations. Meanwhile, asking someone to reflect on whether they prioritise objective data (task-focused) or the feelings of the individual/group (people-focused) when approaching certain situations or making decisions will give you some insight into their behavioural style. Similarly, by asking whether a person draws their energy from being in a group or working alone, you'll learn whether they lean towards extraversion or introversion. Once this data is gathered, it's possible to gain a greater insight into the individuals within a team and then develop connections between them that can inform working relationships and performance under pressure. Questions you might like to utilise to inspire reflection or team discussion could include:

- Is it more important to keep the peace or to be correct?
- Do you like to settle disputes by relying on facts rather than diplomacy?
- Will you press ahead with projects even when there are social/relationship pressures to do otherwise?
- Do you often put aside your own comfort for the greater good?
- Where do you get your energy from? What takes it away?
- Do you prefer to work alone with minimal distraction or enjoy working when there is a lot of bustle/noise going on?
- Do you spend time considering how your action has impacted/will impact on the feelings of others?
- Do you speak to think, or think to speak?

> **Sidebar:** This information is also invaluable for someone who often works alone, especially when seeking to understand how they prefer to work and interact with other people. If you're struggling for answers, ask a trusted friend to help you reflect. But be prepared for some surprises!

2. SHARING THE DATA

There are a couple of important things to consider when discussing personality profiles. First, they're not the be-all and end-all. The data gathered through an online questionnaire is only as good as the answers given – if someone is reluctant to fill in the results honestly or accurately, their results will be skewed. Second, while a personality profile can provide a useful snapshot of a person's preferences, it's the discussions that take place afterwards, and the exploration of the profile and how it's brought to life through real-life examples, that provide the most fruitful discoveries. A personality profile won't give you the sorts of holistic insights that are gained from great discussions, although they will most likely align to what can be observed through your interactions with someone over time. But where personality profiling becomes particularly effective is when working with teams of individuals for the first time, where it's important to develop relationships quickly, such as in a training camp with a new group of players or in advance of a rapidly looming deadline, assessment or competition, where people will naturally find themselves under pressure.

Once the results have been collated, I'll go through them with the relevant individual on a one-to-one basis. I'll discuss their feelings regarding the profile and the information contained within it. Then I'll gather the team together and, with everyone's permission, place the profiles on a wall map. Each person will have a position on the map based upon their results, and it's possible by looking at it to determine which team members share similar personality preferences and which ones are very different to one another. These different perspectives can be used as 'lenses' through which to view the behaviours and communications styles of the team. It's important to remember that the results measure preferences not capability – somebody might prefer logic and reason, but that doesn't mean that they can't be expressive and enthusiastic at times. Also, all preferences are positively framed and there are no better or worse combinations; everyone has a blend of everything, and mindset and behaviour can shift dramatically across contexts, particularly when someone is under pressure.

3. USING THE DATA

It helps to hold discussions so that the team can figure out how they might work together more effectively when the stakes are high. Having these conversations enhances team connection and increases the likelihood of team members holding each other to account. Whether under pressure or in the moment, people won't always communicate in a way that's conducive to everyone, so these discussions provide a foundation for wriggle room, and for people to debrief and move on.

When I'm exploring an individual's preferences, I want to understand their strengths and any potential areas of development from their perspective, as well as the strategies they think will be helpful to their performance. If they are more internally focused, I want to figure out how they can recharge their batteries in the often-extraverted world of elite sport or business environments. I want to be aware of what they find difficult in terms of communication, as well as recognising the incorrect assumptions people might sometimes make about them. I really want to learn about *who* they are.

The reasons for this are clear: once a group understands the people within it, conflicts and disputes are more easily resolved. A sense of unity is created. It also shapes the way in which a manager might handle their team. For example, a player with an internal task focus, like our aforementioned tennis player, will want to understand why certain decisions are being made, because the details are important to them. A player with an external task focus will be results-driven and will want to move quickly and assertively. A player with an external people focus will want to enjoy themselves and the interactions with their teammates, while a player with an internal people focus will want the group to work harmoniously. All these factors will influence the implementation of new ideas, the putting into place of strategies, and the ways in which training, reviewing and debriefing sessions are conducted. How a manager or coach – in any walk of life – handles these situations can be the difference between a harmonious dressing room, or team, and an unsettled one.

Personality profiling creates self-awareness within a group of disparate characters and backgrounds. This enables the individuals involved to look at any clashes through the lens of personality preferences – they can learn how different views of the world might be at the root of any difficult working relationships. So, by bringing the tennis player and their coach together and detailing their personality types and associated behaviours, it's possible for them to see the world through the other's lens as well as their own. They'll then learn about how the other person processes information, which can lead to some interesting discussions on teamwork, including:

- How do we work together effectively?
- When do our personalities clash, and what can we do to counteract that?
- When are we at our best?
- When are we at our worst?
- What are the things that impact on us as a team?

This process was illustrated a couple of years ago when I ran a personality-profiling session with a new (non-sporting) team. After the results arrived, it was clear that the group contained a lot of individuals with an internal task focus and a preference for prudence. This manifested itself in a couple of obstructive ways. These individuals were taking way too long when analysing any new information being presented to them, meaning they were often hamstrung by a focus on what might go wrong. In contrast, there were others in the group who were people- and externally focused. These individuals were more optimistic in their outlook and often became frustrated by the slow pace of the prudent members of the group. Consequently, a rift had formed.

By discovering their different personality types and preferences, the group was able to better understand their strengths, while identifying several areas for development. Together, they developed a framework for times when they needed to consider new information, and as a group they settled on a three-step process:

1. Consider the facts.
2. Assess the opportunities and risks.
3. Consider what might change.

They then evaluated their projects around the contexts of mutual understanding, efficiency, enjoyment and collaboration. As a result, they felt less frustrated with one another in moments of pressure and worked more effectively as a team.

4. REMEMBER THE ETHICS

Once a personality profile has been concluded, it's important that people aren't put in a box or categorised harshly. If that happens, an ethical minefield has been set. It's the job of the profiling session organiser to ensure that 'typing' does not emerge because of the work. Whatever their personality preferences, people are capable of being flexible and adapting to the demands of an ever-changing world. Furthermore, sport psychologists are not involved in team selection. In the sports I've worked with, players, individuals and athletes have been selected by the coaches based upon their competence on the field of play. It's widely understood that personality profiles should be used for individual growth and to enhance team effectiveness, not to make selection decisions.

ASK THE QUESTION

Do you understand your personality preferences?

Most people think the answer to this is a resounding yes. However, we all carry blind spots and often we don't know how other people are viewing our preferences. Also, who we are on a stress-free day and how we react in a pressurised situation can be very different. My recommendation would be to consider taking a profile. If your team are agreeable to it, embark on the journey together so you can learn everybody's preferences when it comes to mindset and behaviour. It might reveal why some individuals click and why others clash. This will allow you to devise strategies to improve communication and performance.

 LIGHTBULBS

- Personality profiles such as Spotlight are useful because they help a team to gain additional insight into each other's preferences and communication styles, and how they might show up in a group context. With that information they can then explore how to get everyone working together more effectively.
- Personality profiles are most useful when used as part of a comprehensive people-development strategy. They should never replace self-reflection and team discussion, and they won't give you an insight into the experiences that have shaped

someone's personality in the way that a timeline will. They are, however, particularly useful when trying to understand a group of people in a short amount of time, or when the collective is too big to make any significant individual observations.
- Be creative with your personality profiles. Build a map on the wall to see where everyone sits and create tasks and activities to bring them to life. You might consider loading a task with those people that have similar preferences or devising groups with an even mix, then analysing their performance.
- Personality-profiling work should be principle-led and, as promoted by Spotlight, encourage:
  1. Humility – to recognise that there are other ways to view the world, and that nobody has the monopoly on reality.
  2. Curiosity – to understand other viewpoints; to learn and to grow.
  3. Tolerance – to value our differences, amplifying them to build adaptable people and an adaptable team.

CHAPTER THREE
STRENGTHS, SUPER-STRENGTHS, WEAKNESSES AND BOAT-SINKERS

Many jobs require people to perform under extreme pressure. In some cases, these roles can mark the difference between life and death; in others, it's the ability to achieve results-based targets, whether that be through monetary gain, sales figures or scientific breakthroughs. Through speaking to people who operate in such environments, I've learned that the focus of those in charge is often deficit-based: leadership figures will look to where their team is *going wrong*, rather than amplifying the things that are *going right*, even during moments of success. Attention is then focused on the team's shortcomings and failures, especially if their latest results aren't up to scratch, and this analysis then heaps additional pressure on the workforce, which can cause people to become fearful of making a mistake.

In sport psychology, the most consistent finding in our field is the direct link between confidence and performance. When an individual feels confident in their abilities, they can channel their thoughts, feelings and behaviours in an effective way. This, in turn, impacts upon performance. We will explore this idea in more detail throughout Building Block #3, but for now it's important to know that the more confident we feel, the more likely it is we'll succeed, especially if we're applying effective performance strategies. The reverse can also be true, though, and self-belief can dwindle away if a group focuses disproportionately on the things that need to be better, rather than capitalising on their strengths. People can then become afraid to take risks and are hindered by a fear of failure. As a result, the group's performances stagnate, people second-guess and their results suffer.

Instead, by applying a *strengths-based* approach – a branch of psychology that concentrates on the positive attributes of those involved – the team and its players can move beyond simply surviving, or avoiding screw-ups, and instead focus on their key skills in both competition and everyday life. It's understandable why this style of psychology has become so popular in the context of sport, where attention is directed towards using psychological knowledge to build mental strength and optimise performance and well-being. When looking to make performance gains, the biggest impact can come from enhancing an athlete's advantages, rather than minimising their flaws. As a sport psychologist, I often think of our role in terms of an 80/20 rule: 80 per cent of it is proactive and directed towards the building and enhancing of performance gains; the other 20 per cent is reactive, where we work with teams and individuals on overcoming their performance issues.

To apply a strengths-based approach to the performance of an individual or a team, it's important to identify four things clearly and accurately: their strengths, super-strengths, weaknesses and boat-sinkers. I was initially introduced to this concept by the sport psychologist Kate Ludlam, a colleague of mine at the UKSI. Positive psychology was something Kate was all too familiar with, having written her PhD on the subject, and she was well versed in the concept of the strengths-based methodology and designing strengths-based interventions to enhance performance. In the process of completing her research, Kate asked me for an interview, as well as other sport psychologists, coaches and athletes working across high-performance sport, and during our discussions, and our later work at the UKSI, Kate explained her definitions of all four terms:

- **A strength:** something that an individual is good at; as good as anyone else in their team or among the people around them. *A 100-metre sprinter's anaerobic capacity.*
- **A super-strength:** something only that person can do to an incredible level. It's their thing; no one else in their performance context possesses that same ability. A world-beating strategy for performance that gives them a unique competitive edge. *A rugby player's precision and consistency in their kicking.*
- **A weakness:** an acceptable flaw; something a person is not particularly good at, but that's OK, it's not a deal-breaker. In a team setting it's something that will not impact on their success in the context of their performance. *A footballer who is slower than many players, but is able to compensate through game understanding and positioning.*
- **A boat-sinker:** the deal-breaker; a weakness that stops a person from realising their full potential. This flaw can also hinder the progress of a team. *A tennis player's temper, which derails him or her during moments of high pressure.*

Importantly, these four categories provide a roadmap to success, because by identifying them a team can then work out how best to apply their time and attention. As I suggested earlier, amplifying the strengths and super-strengths of a group or individual can bring the greatest gains in sport, and I'd maintain that this approach would prove useful in other contexts, such as business or personal endeavour. For example, say an advertising company is uniquely witty and visually imaginative; if these areas are celebrated and time is spent considering how these unique strengths can be optimised, there's a greater chance they'll become market-leading qualities. This improvement then compensates for any minor weaknesses within the group, such as gaps in specific skill sets or outdated digital tools and technologies. That's not to say these flaws should be ignored completely. If there's a boat-sinker in play, it must be tackled, but subtly, and at the right moment. Equally, strengths, super-strengths, weaknesses and boat-sinkers must be regularly reviewed in relation to any future competitions or challenges. That's because weaknesses can develop into boat-sinkers over time, and strengths can be amplified into super-strengths with training.

As with most concepts, the proof's in the pudding. I've seen how effective a strengths-based approach can be when applied to high-pressure situations, perhaps most notably in 2015 when I was asked to help the Cambridge University Women's rowing team as they competed against Oxford University Women in the Boat Race. Initially the challenge felt huge. The sport of rowing had been notoriously slow in recognising its female athletes, and the televised coverage of the Boat Race, which is held on the famous Tideway championship course, only ever focused on the men's competition. The women's teams seemed to be an afterthought and usually competed at Henley, on a different course and away from the media fanfare and public celebrations. Meanwhile, the ridiculously outdated view in some areas of the sport was that the women were physically unsuited to a distance regularly rowed by male athletes; there was a false belief that females couldn't bring the required levels of strength or endurance levels to succeed. But that all changed on 11 April 2015 when the women's race was held for the first time on the same day and over the same course as the male event, with both events being broadcast on national television.

The first time I spoke to the coach, Rob Baker, he'd told me the work would be both history-making and inspiring. He wasn't wrong. At that stage of my career I knew next to nothing about rowing, but it didn't take me long to realise I'd taken on exactly the right challenge. Having arrived at Cambridge's boathouse for the first time, I learned that the team were high achieving and incredibly resilient. Collectively, they were unbelievably dedicated and often rose at 5 a.m., usually in the pitch black, to train in the freezing cold and pouring rain. They then went to lectures and studied, and then studied some more, before heading back to the boathouse to train again in the evening. These traits weren't unusual, especially in women's sport, where the athletes involved have often had to overcome challenges or push through barriers in male-dominated environments. It's one of the reasons I love working with female sports teams and athletes. These adversities were amplified during the build-up to the race when several female rowers were interviewed about their experiences of competing in past Boat Races – their stories were shocking. Former Cambridge rower and Olympic athlete Sarah Winckless even spoke to the *Guardian* of an era during which everyone had to change in the nearest car park before training:

> We had no landing stage, so we were singing the *Mission: Impossible* theme tune every time we got into the boats because you had to have a leap of faith, the drop was so great. We would have loved to have had the facilities the men had, the funding and support. But there was no acrimony, it was just an acceptance, to be honest. Which is maybe a very sad way to put it. It's just the way it was. We were going to make the best of it and be the very best rowers we could to win our races.

With the male and female teams suddenly competing on the same day and the same course, the event was set to be a momentous occasion. And in truth, we were not necessarily setting up to win. I was brought in to help Rob Baker and the team produce their best performance under great pressure, because Oxford had a double Olympic champion in their boat, plus other rowers with high-level international experience. The Cambridge crew, meanwhile, were not matched in terms of their rowing pedigree, although to this day I remember that 2015 team as one of the most inspiring groups of women I've ever had the pleasure of working with. For Cambridge to produce their best performance, they'd have to maintain focus on themselves and their own unique strengths, and Rob knew exactly how to instil the required amount of belief in them for the job in hand. It wasn't a lot of hot air either. Instead, everything was strengths-based.

To remind the rowers of who they were and why they were important, Rob held a brief one-on-one meeting with every rower on the morning of the race, and gave them an individual message:

The reason you're in the boat is because . . .

He then presented each one with a super-strength that was unique to them, something nobody else in the boat – or in the opposition boat, for that matter – could do. To wrap up, he explained why they were valued and told them that he believed in their abilities.

This tactic was a powerful driver. It reminded the athletes of their qualities via a strengths-based approach, without puffing them up on hyperbole. It said: *This is the reason you're here. These are the things that you're bloody good at. And this is your competitive edge.* It gave every Cambridge woman a validating truth they could lean into when the going got tough, rather than reminding them of any weaknesses they might need to be wary of. I watched all of them visibly lift in mood as Rob relayed his thoughts. They knew exactly who they were and what they were capable of, and that they had the full support of their coach.

They only had to get in the boat and do their best.

MAXIMISING STRENGTHS AND SUPER-STRENGTHS

There are multiple methods for how an individual, or team, identifies their strengths and super-strengths, and when gathering this intelligence it's important to include objective-based data, in addition to self-reflection and performance-based reviews. What's vital is that the results of this discovery process are emphasised regularly, so that that the people involved can understand their positive attributes and how they help the collective, or cause. For example, in a team of fire fighters, one individual's super-strength might be their calm persona. It helps them to settle casualties that are panicked or hysterical due to the trauma of an emergency, which is a game-changing asset in a stressful situation. Reminding the individual of their super-strength means they will be more likely to maximise it at the appropriate time, helping them to bring calm and order to moments of chaos. (A second very important point is that every member of the team needs to be aware of each other's super-strengths. That way, they can maximise them when necessary. For example, in football, if a winger possesses fantastic pace, their teammates can play the ball over a defensive line for him or her to run on to at key moments.)

The professional rugby union team Harlequins adopted this process when I began working with the coaching staff during the 2011/12 season. My role in the set-up was to work systemically with the coaches to ensure the players were able to execute their strengths on match day. We wanted them to operate without fear of failure, to compete with freedom and expression, and to perform at their natural best. In meetings we talked in strengths-based terms, and we discussed the group's power and advantages over their rivals. Whenever we sat down with the players individually, we detailed their strengths and super-strengths. We asked questions such as 'What does your best game look like?' and 'What do *we* need to do to give *you* the best opportunity of bringing that on Saturday afternoon?' Talking positively about individual and team attributes became a part of our everyday language and ensured that the players were focused on bringing their best attributes to matches, while also bringing out those of their teammates. The effect of multiple individuals working together to capitalise on each other's strengths is exponential in terms of team performance – it ensures that the team is far greater than the sum of its parts.

Talking in strengths terms isn't always easy. I've often found myself surprised by how many sport stars struggle to identify their assets when asked about them. We often think that athletes, particularly those performing at the elite level, instinctively know what sets them apart from the rest of the field, but in reality they can be reticent when putting their honest thoughts forward. This might be a result of modesty or a feeling of awkwardness, but often it's because they haven't considered their greatest attributes in the same level of detail that they've thought about their flaws – the areas that require improvement. I can't count the number of Olympic competitors that have stumbled their way through this discussion. *That's why it's so important to hold it in the first place.* And handily, there are several alternatives to presenting the slightly awkward question of 'Why are you so great?'

Among them are:

- Why do you get selected?/If you were a coach, why would you pick you?
- What was your greatest performance?
- When are you are at your natural best? What does that look like and how does it feel?
- How do we create an environment that gets you operating at your best?

These questions can apply to anyone in any field: doctors and dentists, stock market traders and bankers, film-makers and scriptwriters, scientists and explorers, and so on. When an individual knows *who they are* in terms of their values and personality preferences, plus their strengths and super-strengths, they will operate with freedom. They'll know what's needed in terms of environment and process so they can work to the best of their ability. They're able to tactically plan in such a way that they can perform optimally. When all these things are combined and they've been given permission to use their assets (and to not worry about making mistakes), their chances of success are greatly improved, as outlined in the responses below.

CASE STUDY

A landscape designer

- When are you at your natural best?
  When I'm supported by my colleagues, I'm encouraged to be creative, and I have time to think and plan.
- What does that look like?

> I'm in tune with the people working around me. I feel comfortable taking creative chances and I deliver in a way that exceeds client expectations.

- How does that feel?
  Empowering. Free. I'm inspired. It doesn't feel like work.
- And how do we create an environment around you that gets you operating at your best?
  Don't ask me to make quick decisions without giving me the time and space to think first. I need a clear brief that gives me the freedom to experiment. I like regular updates on my progress from my colleagues.

*

There is one vital caveat, however. The strengths-based approach requires everyone in a group to accept the methodology and align on a narrative. That's because people don't get things right 100 per cent of the time and must be given room for error. For example, one rugby player's super-strength might be their ability to run with the ball. When they're playing well, they tend to create opportunities for themselves and their teammates, while sowing chaos within the opposition ranks. They should be encouraged to lean into this talent when required. That said, if a mistake then happens because of that player leaning into their super-strength, and the manager or their teammates reprimands them after the event, the strengths-based approach is undermined. You can't tell a player to maximise their ball-holding talents and then scold them for doing exactly that on the one occasion they lose the ball. Inconsistent messaging will cause them to become indecisive and predictable, or worse, frustrated and reluctant to use their greatest talent at all.

SWEET SPOTS AND THE 'WRIGGLE ROOM' CONCEPT

When it comes to applying our strengths and super-strengths there's a balance to be struck. If we lean excessively into our best assets, or use them in the wrong context, we *overdo* them. If we become fearful of applying our super-strength or fail to identify the ideal moment in which to employ it, we *underuse* it. Slap-bang in the middle of this spectrum is a zone of optimum performance, or 'the sweet spot', and this concept can be mapped visually on a graph.

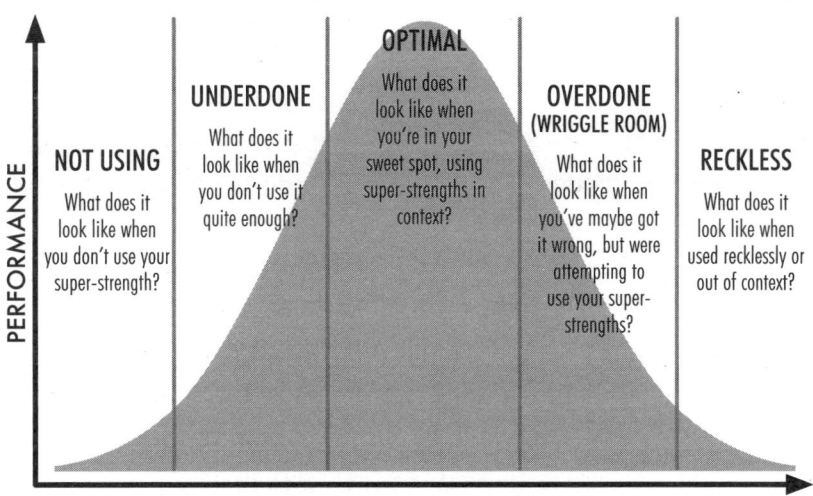

Source: Kate Ludlam, 'Super-strengths in elite sport', doctoral dissertation, Sheffield Hallam University, 2017.

For example, it might be that a pro golfer's super-strength is their mid-irons. When playing in the sweet spot, they're able to hit five-, six- and seven-irons flush to the pin pretty much every time. However, if they solely rely on these clubs throughout a championship rather than thinking their way around the course with different shots, there's a chance they'll *overdo* their super-strength, become reckless and make mistakes. On the other hand, if they play with fear and don't reach for their mid-irons at all, they'll *underuse* their greatest asset. In a non-sporting situation, it might be that a public speaker is very good at making their audience laugh when operating in the sweet spot. This makes their messaging incredibly memorable. However, if they overplay their super-strength and spend an entire speech cracking jokes, their core message will be lost; if they underplay it and fail to relax the crowd, their important points will go unheard. Knowing how to sit in the sweet spot is key.

To overcome this problem, it's important to identify the following things:

1. What does the sweet spot look like? And what must happen for a person to get there?
2. What happens when a person underplays their super-strength? What contributes to them feeling fearful?
3. What happens when a person overplays their super-strength? What causes them to become reckless?

Within the overdone zone there is an area of *wriggle room* – an area just beyond the sweet spot where a person might make a mistake when attempting to use their key attributes in context. Having this buffer empowers the individual to use their super-strengths without fear of reprimand if they get it wrong. They are given permission to make mistakes, course-correct tactically and then move on. The golfer can lean into their mid-irons a bit more. The public speaker can crack a few more jokes if the vibe feels OK. And both will know when and how to dial back tactically on their super-strength. This concept is particularly important in the context of strengths-based psychology because it creates an area of safety and stops a person or team from being governed by fear. Once these zones have been identified, it's possible to recognise exactly when a group is performing to their optimum or not, and responding appropriately.

I have a personal example of this process in action. My super-strength is my ability to get people onboard with an idea. I tend to view the world in terms of possibilities, and I engage others when getting behind a project. In this context, I know exactly where the sweet spot sits and what I must do to locate it. I'm also aware of what happens when I'm overplaying or underplaying my super-strength and I have a tactic for course-correcting.

- **The sweet spot:** I think things through, I do my contingency planning and I understand the job completely. I'll bring in the people I want alongside me because I'm able to gain their buy-in through both my enthusiasm and a well-thought-out plan. When they ask questions or make suggestions, I know what they mean and can respond articulately, which enables me to utilise their expertise. Working with others means I can get the project into better shape than I would have had I been doing it alone.
- **Overplaying:** Whenever I get too excited about a project there's the chance I'll act recklessly. I'll bring lots of people onboard without dotting the i's or crossing the t's first. I'll get people excited about the possibilities without having a clear direction of travel, and I'll fail to thoroughly consider a contingency plan. If people ask questions and I don't know the answers, I'll look unprepared for the work ahead. My ideas are undermined.

- **Underplaying:** When the project requires considerable commitment of time and effort from others, I'm fearful of putting people under pressure. As a result, I might hold back and become indecisive.
- **Wriggle room:** I need time at the start of the project to generate lots of ideas with others. It won't be perfect right away, but with the creative juices flowing I can make a solid start and I'll work on my contingency plans as I go. I've got some of the answers to some of the questions, but I feel confident enough to gather more information on the fly.
- **Tactics:** When I'm in danger of overplaying my super-strength, I take a moment or two to pause. Sometimes I'll ask a prudent friend for her opinion. Most often, most people's areas of weakness are their strengths overplayed or used out of context. Because of that, I make sure to plan in a logical and organised way, and to gather enough data to support my facts and my arguments for when the team gets together. Only then am I guaranteed to hit my sweet spot.

MINIMISING WEAKNESSES AND MANAGING BOAT-SINKERS

At this point you're probably thinking, *So, how do we address our flaws? We can't just ignore them* . . . And the strengths-based approach requires us to consider how we'll achieve the greatest performance gains, and manage our deficits, in two ways:

1. Minor weaknesses can sometimes be accepted, or outweighed, by amplifying strengths and super-strengths.
2. Boat-sinkers must be addressed and dealt with in the appropriate manner.

When deciding where to focus attention and time, it's imperative to remove the boat-sinkers, while working to transform strengths into super-strengths. The first stage in this process is to identify the big problem early on and then put a comprehensive plan in place. The next is to address the issue in a balanced manner while continuing to harness the strengths of the group, which will prevent the negative issue from working its way into a team's psyche or an individual's head. Sometimes this can be done subtly to protect the confidence of a team. For example, if the analysts of an international football side have identified that the players' effectiveness at attacking set pieces has decreased ahead of a major tournament, the technical staff might adapt training so that it places a greater emphasis on the work in that area without sharing any negative data with their players. As always, the language used, and the approach taken, will depend upon the individual or team, and their personalities. (Which is one of the reasons why it's so important to know the *who* of a team.) The proximity to an important event will also play a part: if the tournament is only a few weeks away, work will have to start very quickly.

This approach can seem like a big shift for some, and those that are more risk-averse sometimes push back on the idea of encouraging people to perform to their strengths without fear of failure, highlighting what are perceived to be the catastrophic consequences of making a mistake. Elsewhere, I've presented talks to different sectors where people have suggested that sport is an outlier. They'll say, 'That's all very well and good, but if *we* underperform or make a mistake, we get fired.' But there are consequences of not meeting performance targets in sport too. The Premier League is notorious for its high turnover of players, managers and coaching staff. In the Olympics environment, if a particular sport doesn't hit a designated medal tally, its funding can be cut, which impacts on jobs and the security of athletes. These days, many people work in an unpredictable and unstable world. However, I believe it's possible for all of us to create a culture that's not governed by fear, whether we work in sport, banking, business, big tech or even politics. Taking a strengths-based approach can be a healthy first step.

 ASK THE QUESTION

Do you know your strengths and super-strengths?

If not, take some time to consider them. If you're struggling for answers, reframe the question. Ask: *When are you at your natural best? What does that look like? How does that feel? And how can you create an environment that gets you operating to your optimum?* Also, consider the boat-sinkers that might be preventing you from being selected for a team, landing a job or getting a promotion. Work up a plan to remove them while capitalising on your strengths.

LIGHTBULBS

- All of us have strengths and weaknesses, but the biggest performance gains happen when we turn our strengths into super-strengths while negating any boat-sinkers. Doing the opposite, by focusing our time on fixing the acceptable weaknesses, rather than the big issues, can stagnate a person's development.
- When trying to perform in the sweet spot, give yourself a little wriggle room. Sometimes it's OK to over- or under-play a super-strength, but not too much, and not too often.
- We're all working in an unpredictable and unstable world. To overcome a fear of failure, we need to create a culture where people are allowed to make mistakes in the pursuit of excellence (without being reckless, which is very different). When a team isn't worried about failure, they are able to maximise their strengths and super-strengths, operate without fear, and perform with freedom and expression.

CHAPTER FOUR

ONE-PAGERS: THE SECRET WEAPON

Having run through the processes detailed in Chapters 1 to 3, it's likely that you've amassed a personality data bank* on both yourself and your team. The facts about what's important to you and to those around you have been defined, and you'll have now gained an insight into everyone's fundamentals. The most powerful memories, good and bad, have been distilled and categorised, and you will have a deeper understanding of behavioural styles, communication preferences, and the situations and interactions most likely to prove troublesome or challenging. With these notes, it's possible to say to yourself and others:

> This is who I am. This is how I behave when I'm at my best and worst. And this is what happens when I'm under pressure. (And here is how you can help me.)

---

* To reiterate: much of this information can be gathered by simply interacting with someone over time, observing how they behave in certain situations and engaging in meaningful conversations. The personality profiling work simply speeds up this process.

The same can be said to the team members in a group setting:

> This is who we are. This is how we behave when we're at our best and worst. And this is what happens when we're under pressure. (And here is how you can help us.)

The beauty of completing this work is that it removes any assumptions teammates might have, while at the same time establishing a sense of clarity. For example, it might be that Player X has gone quiet in the build-up to a very big game. Without any knowledge about their psychology, other players in the team might conclude that something's worrying them; that they're feeling anxious and in need of support. But by gaining an understanding of *who they are* and *how they behave*, it's possible to strip away the second-guessing: Player X goes quiet in the build-up to big games because it's how they behave when dealing with pressure; they like to run through their performance plan internally to ready themselves for the game ahead; and to thrive they require space and time in which to prepare.

This type of knowledge can be extended to a group of varied personalities. One player studies opposition analysis before a match. Another uses visualisation techniques. This player likes to talk about the weather, that one keeps their noise-cancelling headphones on all day. *It's what they do.* With a detailed understanding of an individual's characteristics, things that might previously have been misunderstood or a cause for concern are now both expected and normalised.

If you require further evidence about how your team will respond under pressure, arrange a trip to your nearest escape room. This is an adventure game in which a group must solve a series of puzzles to free themselves from a locked space within a certain amount of time. I guarantee that you'll see everyone's personality preferences brought to bear, especially if they're in direct competition with another group. Those participants that are people-focused with a preference for extraversion will want to crack on and experiment, and they'll encourage their teammates to join them; those with an internal task focus will take a step back to assess the situation carefully, formulating a plan individually before taking action.

If you don't have time for a trip to the escape room, design a task for your team where there's something to be won or lost, then increase the stakes by setting a deadline. By watching how everyone approaches the test you'll gather valuable insights into their response to challenge and how they interact with others. It's also possible to notice behaviours and connections, and how these might translate into success or failure.

This type of understanding is particularly interesting when managing group dynamics in a pressurised situation. I remember while working with Harlequins, the director of rugby, the head coach, skills coach and defence coach all had very different communication preferences, and we utilised them when necessary. This was especially useful when approaching half-time team talks, where there were obviously natural constraints on time, and what the players needed depended upon the specific context of that game. In such situations, it was decided the messaging should come from the coach best suited to the moment, and who this was would change every time. If the team needed a motivational pep talk, the person with a more empathetic communication style would lead; if clarity around process was in order, a different coach would drive the discussions. The bottom line: when the pressure was on and time was limited, our strategy was to play to our strengths. Rather than trying to get one coach to be flexible and adapt in the moment, we got the right person for the job instead.

Of course, with high stakes and tight deadlines – or when working with a team for the very first time – it can be very difficult to remember people's values, preferences and characteristic responses to pressure. And this is where a one-pager comes into play. A sheet of information created by an individual, its role is to define clearly and succinctly who the person is, how they behave and the environment they require in which to perform optimally. It can include any information that's useful for others to know, but as a general rule I would suggest focusing on four elements:

1. **General personality characteristics:** if you've completed the profiling work as detailed in Chapter 3, you'll have a clear idea of what these might be. For example, you'll know if you're introverted or extraverted, task-focused or people-focused. You'll also have a handle on whether you're more likely to take risks when working under pressure, or if you're more risk-adverse. When written down, these details provide a series of indicators to the people around you for how you'll behave in various scenarios.
2. **Values, of both the individual and the team:** these are a series of personal details that might explain why a person behaves the way they do. For example, someone who values togetherness generally places considerable importance on cooperation, reliability and compassion. Someone who values objectivity and fairness will believe that process, analysis, precision and discipline are hugely important. And those that value creativity and connection will thrive in an environment that places importance on openness, engagement, freedom and flexibility.
3. **A list of 'need-to-knows':** when putting together one-pagers, I always ask the individual to answer the following questions: *What are your strengths? When are*

you at your best? When are you at your worst? What are the first signs that things are starting to derail? How do you show up under pressure? And how can other people help you when things are going wrong? The answers provide vital tactical knowledge and cues for high-pressure events.
4. **A photo or picture:** this further personalises the output and is useful in large groups, where individuals can come and go at regular intervals.

When put together, a one-pager could look something like the text opposite. I'll now break down how and when to use one.

READING THE ONE-PAGER

At first glance, the one-pager might seem like an information overload, but in fact it's a cheat sheet on an individual's personality, with guidelines on how to help them reach their optimum levels. As you'll see from the example, their most dominant characteristics are taken from a personality-profiling session. So, a person might be described as leaning towards introversion or extraversion, or optimism or prudence. The headlines will depend on the personality-profiling system in place (even if it's one of your own design) and a variety of descriptors can occur here.

On the left-hand side are the answers to the 'need-to-know' questions. In the example, the person's strengths are described as enthusiasm and energy. They get people on board with their ideas and are people-focused and responsive. They work at their best when their team is connected, communicative and harmonious. They also need a healthy work–life balance to function at their optimum. Their performance slips when they act without fully considering the risks or unintended consequences, and if

Name: Jane Bloggs

General personality characteristics

I have an optimistic mindset, so will most likely focus on the best-case scenario, and I'm happy to take calculated risks. I also tend to be people-focused, with a preference for extraversion, so the harmony of the group and social interactions are important to me.

My values

Deep care • Positivity • Human connection • Clarity

My strengths

Enthusiasm and energy • Getting to the crux of a problem (cutting out noise)

I'm at my best when:

Working as part of a team that is connected, communicative and harmonious
I have a good work-life balance • I'm clear about my role and purpose •
I can contribute positively

I'm at my worst when:

I act without fully considering the risks or unintended consequences •
My team is being overlooked, undervalued or disrespected

My derailers

Lack of work-life balance, sleep and fresh air

Under pressure I...

Will be calm and rational • Will focus on being supportive to my colleagues/teammates

You can help me by...

Communicating what you need honestly and clearly with me

the people important to them are being overlooked, undervalued or disrespected. This negative tendency is exacerbated if their work–life balance is out of whack. Finally, they show up on game day by acting in a calm and rational way, and being of service to others. To help them, the other people in the group should communicate clearly.

DISCUSS THE INTELLIGENCE

One-pagers are there to spark conversations. They help a group to connect. By doing the profiling work, everyone embarks on a journey of discovery and at the end they're given the opportunity to create a document – in their own words – that lists the things they believe everyone around them should know. As much as anything else, one-pagers are in place to give people a better understanding of their teammates and how they're likely to behave. Finally, a document of this kind presents everyone with the tools to offer support. If the group sees somebody behaving in a way that suggests they're being derailed, a colleague can put their arm around them and ask, 'Are you all right?' But that only happens if the one-pagers have been absorbed by everyone in the group ahead of time. My advice is to always have these discussions during periods when the pressure is off. That way, people will know what to expect when the stakes – and the tension – are cranked up to a stressful level.

The information contained within a one-pager is by its very nature succinct, but it's important that these documents are on hand for everyone to reference. At the very least they should be shared electronically, so that everyone can have them to hand, though there have been times when I've stuck them to the walls in a team space. When I've gone away for a tournament with the England women's football team, I've taken the one-pagers with me. Each time we've checked in to a new hotel, or a training ground, they're put on the walls again as a point of reference.

It's also important to remember that a one-pager is not there to replace great discussion; it's there to facilitate it, and to provide an opportunity for people to be curious about each other and connect on a personal level. It's not enough to say, 'Oh, when Player X feels overwhelmed, they go silent for 24 hours before a match' (though that's still good intelligence). There may be other, more subtle signs that a person is beginning to struggle. People often do not ask for help when they need it most, and knowing when to step in if they seem to be finding things tough – rather than leaving someone to follow their routines – can be really useful. As we'll discuss later, storytelling is a great way of making information stick, though certain details can always be clarified and given context. I remember when I put my one-pager together with the Lionesses staff, I took a little time to explain my responses to my colleagues. In doing so, I provided a sharper view on my personality and preferences.

'If I'm doing a presentation, I will think about it a lot,' I said. 'So, in the period leading up to the event, I'll go over it in my mind and rehearse. That way I can be clear about what it is I'm delivering. It's the process I go through and it's nothing for anyone to worry about. But these moments of silence can be misinterpreted by other people. They might think: *Kate's not herself. Kate's a bit quiet today, I wonder if she's all right.* Or: *Is Kate nervous about what's going on?* What then happens is a series of people will ask if I'm OK, and that can then distract me from my preparation. In such situations, a better question would be: *Kate, are you thinking?* That tells me you've understood my one-pager, you know I'm probably fine, but you just want to check.'

These discussions can help de-escalate potential flashpoints ahead of time. Whenever I help a team prepare for a World Cup, Boat Race or Olympics, I like to ensure that anything with the *potential* to feel overwhelming appears smaller for the group, not bigger. That's because when the stakes are high, people can change, both in terms of their emotional regulation and behaviour. Without a depth of understanding of the personalities present, there's a chance that one or two inaccurate assumptions will be made about an individual or the group. That can lead to disputes and conflict.

It's the same in a non-sporting context too. For example, it might be that a specialist corporate team has been asked to give a company-wide presentation about a new product or service. This is the first time they've worked together in such a pressurised environment, and the stakes are high. If one person in the group tends to chit-chat under pressure because it helps them to calm down, their behaviour might be misconstrued as a sign of indifference. But with an understanding that their chit-chatting is a sign of discomfort, the team can help them to process it in a useful manner. That way everyone can execute the task without the potential for conflict.

A one-pager is also a great resource for when large groups are brought together and tasked with working efficiently, especially when there's very little time to get to know one another. In sport, final squad selection decisions for some staff and the athletes happen quite late on. Certain individuals might join with their colleagues at the last minute, or only have limited time together before the competition begins. In such circumstances, producing a series of one-pagers – and then discussing them – can work as a quickfire team-bonding exercise, and serves as the final piece in a complicated puzzle. During the Olympic Games, a lot of athletes live together in a designated 'village', a bit like a university hall of residence. They're away from home for weeks on end, and living and competing in an environment where success and failure happens all at once. As a result, emotions run high. Any additional information on what makes a person tick in such circumstances can help to build a greater team dynamic, and quickly.

USE THE INTELLIGENCE TACTICALLY

There are different ways to utilise the information gathered during the one-pager exercise. In the build-up to the 2022 European Championship, the Lionesses support staff put the profiles into action as quickly as possible. Sarina Wiegman had started the job in September 2021, I'd joined a month later and our first profiling sessions took place in November. At the time we only had nine months to prep for the tournament, but we wanted the players to reflect early on their personal strengths and the strengths of their teammates. To do this, we created one-page profiles and conducted some group discussion exercises on top. Part of this work involved a series of sheets of paper stuck to a wall. Each one had the name of a squad member printed on it. We then asked the group to add the following details to every person's profile in the space provided:

- Their strengths
- Their value to the team

One by one the pages filled up with positive comments. This gave everyone in the squad a 360-degree view of who they were, as viewed through the eyes of others, and it served as a confidence boost for every player as the tournament approached.

On another occasion, while working with the Cambridge Women's rowing team, we only focused upon the one-pagers once the final boat selection had taken place. Then, having conducted a series of sessions on the athletes' mindsets, strengths, values and behaviours, we homed in on *who* we had in the boat. From that point on, we were able to answer the type of questions that sometimes gives a team and their manager cause for concern on race day:

- What do we expect from each other on that day?
- How do we help each other out?
- How do we react to pressure?
- How do we communicate?

By assessing the personalities involved, and their preferences when working under stress, it was possible to take a lot of guesswork out of a situation where every tiny detail counted.

UPDATE THE ONE-PAGERS REGULARLY

One-pagers are a constant work in process. I update them whenever a tournament or qualifying event comes around, not only because there are nearly always one or two new faces in the group, but also because people are on a continual journey of growth and reflection. Their strengths evolve, and their experiences and responses to pressure alter too. In some ways human beings are not too dissimilar to chameleons: as we move in and around different environments, we learn how to reflect and adapt to that environment. What tends to remain relatively stable is a person's personality preferences. Knowing how they might react in stressful situations, and carrying a handy cheat sheet that communicates the relevant info, is a great way of harnessing our *who*.

 ASK THE QUESTION

Do you have enough information to write your own one-pager?

If so, draw one up using the guidelines in this chapter, then encourage your teammates, colleagues or staff to do the same, before presenting that information to the group. It's a useful exercise to help you learn about yourself and those around you. It can also assist you to reach optimum performance levels when faced with a great challenge.

LIGHTBULBS

- One-pagers are there to nudge conversations and help a group to connect. They're also in place to give people a better understanding of their teammates, and how they're likely to behave.
- A one-pager presents everyone with the chance to offer support. When somebody is behaving in a way that suggests they're finding things difficult, a colleague can ask if they're OK and deliver assistance.
- Make one-pagers visible by putting them up in a shared team space. Encourage everyone to become familiar with one another's preferences. Doing so removes any assumptions about a person while establishing a sense of clarity about their behaviours.
- In a large group there can be a lot of information to take in, so encourage your group to discuss their one-pagers. Expanded details can bring clarity and establish context.

CHAPTER FIVE
HOLDING UP A MIRROR

Through the process of self-discovery suggested in these pages, it's possible to understand how things can look and feel when we're performing at our best or falling short. But sometimes it's difficult to recognise *when* we're in our sweet spot because we're too close to the events taking place. On occasions when we might be overplaying things and taking chances, our inner voice can repeat a false narrative: *that this time it's going to be OK*. Or we might feel as if we're doing enough when we're actually underplaying our super-strengths. It's in these moments that we all need some outside assistance. Having encouraged several teams and groups to establish their *who*, I've learned that everyone needs a person to call them to account from time to time, what one might call a 'logical sounding board' who can hold a mirror up to the person during a pressurised situation and say, 'You're showing signs of stress. *What can I do to help?*'

This logical sounding board is a vital resource as it offers a different perspective. Too often in stressful situations the emotional brain overrides the logical brain and we catastrophise and go into a spin. Having someone acting as a logical sounding board offers us an alternative and more rational perspective because this person is coming from a neutral position, with no feelings attached. It might be that a terrifying tax bill has landed on your doorstep, giving you a few nights of intense stress. A logical sounding board can help you to focus on the steps needed to rectify the situation, rather than concentrating on the emotion of the present moment. Think of them as a rational head you can borrow during times of drama.

When looking to bring in a logical sounding board, I recommend you pick someone who shows the following characteristics:

- Trustworthy
- A good listener
- Maintains a cool head under pressure
- Asks good questions
- Encourages self-reflection

When bringing in such a person, it's important to first give them the insight needed to support you as identified on your one-pager, and then to provide consent for them to raise a mirror to your behaviour should you display any signs of stress or falling short of your optimal levels. It might be that when you become worried, you talk negatively about your situation or yourself; maybe you pick a target to take your frustrations out on. In the heat of the moment, this might feel like normal behaviour. But with a logical sounding board by your side, you'll find they can identify the things you're blinkered by and encourage change, or a course correction. To establish this relationship, it's important you give them permission to step in by telling them how you behave when you're not in a great place, and what you want them to say as they try to break your negative cycle. Something non-confrontational will work: 'Look, this is what I'm seeing . . .

Are you all right?' Then you can both take steps to improve the situation.

Giving permission to a logical sounding board in advance is very important, because it increases the chances that their help will be accepted, especially when you're up against it. Their language will trigger positive thought rather than an implosion or a backlash. If you haven't extended your permission and then someone approaches you to provide some feedback about your behaviour when the pressure is ramping up, it might not be well received. This is especially so if it's someone you've not really spoken to before and who doesn't have a solid connection to you. In those situations, a negative reaction from you would be completely understandable, but it's beneficial to neither party.

Make sure you have chosen at least one person within your environment that will hold you to account in an effective way, someone you know you can go to, and they can come to you. It's also important to have someone like this, not just in a pressurised environment but on a day-to-day basis – we all need someone with whom we can discuss the events in our life that isn't necessarily a partner or close friend. For now, focus on finding a person who you can bounce ideas around with, in a safe space, and who isn't going to judge you. More importantly, select someone that isn't going to tell you what they think you want to hear but will instead provide an opportunity for you to really engage in self-reflection. I know that when I'm working in a tournament, having a logical sounding board outside of that environment is useful, even when the work isn't pressurised or stressful. They're not mixed up in the emotions of what's going on and are impervious to the drama. That enables me to have a clear and unobstructed conversation where I'm able to get to the heart of what's troubling me. Sometimes I just want to vent and say what I need to say, in a safe and confidential space, where my thoughts aren't going to be judged, or might negatively impact upon the group.

CASE STUDY

The Covid Games

The Olympics are a phenomenal festival of sport, and each edition has its own unique story that can either derail an athlete or provide the perfect platform for them to live out their dreams. For the Team GB athletes, London 2012 brought the home advantage – or added pressure – of a host-nation event. The Rio Olympics were very nearly overshadowed by an outbreak of the Zika virus. The headlines during the preparation for 2018 Winter Games in South Korea were dominated by politics, in particular the relations between Donald Trump and the North Korean dictator Kim Jong Un.

And then along came Covid in 2020, which pushed the Tokyo Olympics back a year. Under those circumstances, there was a lot of emotional pressure on the athletes and the staff who supported them during the Games in Japan, which eventually took place in 2021. Some competitors had been seriously disrupted by a chaotic, stop-start training schedule due to the lockdowns and postponements; others were wondering if it was even safe to travel. The work of our UKSI psychology team in the preceding 12 months had necessarily focused on supporting the mental health and well-being of our staff and athletes. This included us assessing the psychosocial impact of isolation (plus the return to training, which was complex and unfamiliar), while managing a sense of uncertainty that never really went away. When the Games finally arrived, a lot of us had understandable reservations about flying around the world, especially as it was a time when vaccines weren't yet universally available.

As with a lot of things during that moment in history, the working environment was uncomfortably complicated. All Team GB support staff and athletes had to isolate for two weeks prior to flying, and when we arrived at the airport, the building was mostly deserted. We knew that we'd be tested for Covid upon landing in Tokyo, and most of us felt some nervousness about that, even though we'd done everything possible to keep ourselves, and each other, safe. A positive test meant quarantine in Japan and would also require the person to isolate, as well as anyone near the person who'd failed their Covid test; if that were to happen, their Olympic dream would be seriously compromised. Despite the meticulous preparation, planning and support in Tokyo Airport, the wait for our results felt like an eternity. But before long we arrived at our Olympic 'base camp', fit, healthy and ready to execute our roles to the best of our ability.

As with any major sporting event, the support staff are not immune from the day-to-day pressures of competition. After all, we were people who had worked for a long period of time, for a specific moment in time, and were driven to ensure that we provided our athletes with the best opportunity for success. We were about to work in an unfamiliar environment at an unstable moment, and the consequences of a potentially positive test result were a constant worry. Meanwhile, everyone was thousands of miles away from home and detached from their support networks, while working long hours and sometimes running on very little sleep. Had there not been an appropriate level of prior planning, or a series of strategies to help us manage the Olympic challenge, some of us would have fallen short in reaching our optimal levels, and others would have struggled to function effectively at all.

But that wasn't going to happen. As with the athletes, the support team spent a chunk of time in the build-up to the Games discussing the unique aspects of Tokyo 2020. We discussed mental health and the mental health continuum. We worked on values, behaviours, timelines and personality profiles, and we produced one-pagers. In doing so, our team settled on three winning behaviours (we'll discuss these further in Building Block #2), or precepts, that would help us through the event: *Take care. Stay connected. Share responsibility.* These were repeated like a mantra and were in place to remind everyone to look after themselves.

- **Take care:** Not only was this a reminder to look after myself, but it also acted as a cue to stay professional. In a working context, self-care also meant being able to do the job to the best of my ability. That meant not working 24 hours a day, seven days a week, because this would have been unsustainable.
- **Share responsibility:** When the going got tough, I had to ask for help. It wasn't acceptable to simply get my head down and work on my own through whatever might be going on.
- **Stay connected:** I had to identify a logical sounding board, someone I could talk to and share my stresses and frustrations with.

In the lead-in to the Games, all of us worked on devising a series of coping mechanisms that fell into these three categories. In the context of working with a logical sounding board, I arranged an online call with Amanda Gatherer – a clinical psychologist from the UKSI's mental health expert panel – or one of her team. As the Games got underway, I was able to use my 30-minute slot as needed, to work through any complex situations or simply debrief on my day. Amanda was the perfect logical sounding board throughout: she was balanced, she encouraged me to reflect, she was a great listener and she never came from a place of emotion or judgement. This support helped me to maintain perspective throughout the duration of the Olympics, and deliver my role effectively and professionally.

Elsewhere, I also ensured that the psychology team in Tokyo was able to link with one another through a WhatsApp group. As is the way with Olympic events, the team was scattered around the Games, as were the athletes – there were actually 33 competition venues in total – and some of us were operating out of the Olympic village. Through the group we were able to share information, offer support, crack jokes and stay connected. Communicating in this way sent out a message to everyone involved: *You don't have to have the answers to everything. You don't have to be responsible for everything. We can bounce ideas around, we can share practice, and we can utilise the help and support of other people.* In doing so, everyone had an avenue for support in a potentially stressful environment. Meanwhile, those psychologists on the team that didn't travel to Tokyo worked from home to assist those that did. We knew that sometimes when people are under pressure, they are less likely to ask for help, so we ensured that there were trusted colleagues that would check-in with them proactively to provide a supporting ear.

 ASK THE QUESTION

Do you have a logical sounding board?

If not, maybe it's time to bring one in. It will enhance your process of self-reflection and your ability to think logically, while facilitating your performance. With a trustworthy, unbiased and calm listener to bounce ideas and feelings off, you can rationalise, normalise and work more effectively.

LIGHTBULBS

- Find a logical sounding board, a friend or confidante whom you can lean upon for advice and support.
- When looking for a logical sounding board, consider someone who is trustworthy, a good listener, calm, who doesn't judge, asks good questions and encourages self-reflection.
- Provide consent, so that they can alert you to any telltale signs that you might be derailing or falling short of your optimal standards.

BUILDING BLOCK #2

WHY ARE WE HERE?

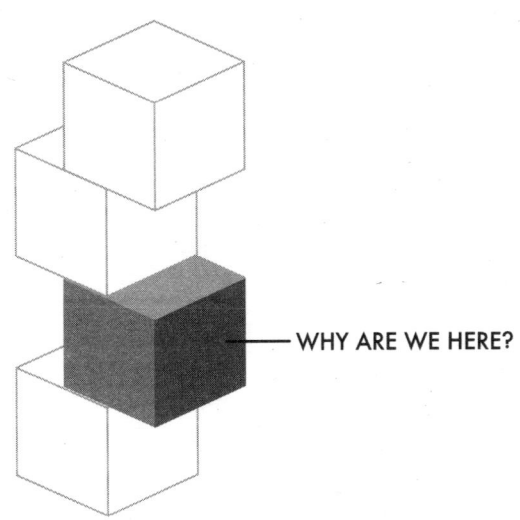
— WHY ARE WE HERE?

INTRODUCTION

The second building block revolves around a question that so many of us struggle to answer in life. In fact, defining our *why*, or purpose, is an issue some people never get to resolve, which can be problematic. It's been shown that those with a clear understanding of purpose, or a sense of working for a higher cause, have stronger personal relationships, fewer physical and mental health problems, and overall happier lifestyles, whereas people and groups without a clear sense of *why* experience the exact opposite. In a team setting, a business without a defined purpose will drift and stagnate. But with a clear sense of *why*, that same business will foster improved performance levels. This is especially so if its vision, values and expected behaviours are translated throughout the company. What organisation wouldn't want to experience that within its ranks?

In a football team's case, when explaining their *why*, an understandable response from every player would be to say: 'To win the league' or 'To win the cup'. But as we will learn in this section, while aspirational, an entirely achievement-based mission isn't usually enough to galvanise a squad of footballers, which will include individuals with differing ambitions and belief systems.

Instead, what's needed is a much deeper sense of purpose on both the collective and individual level, so that the players – and the team – can feel that they're fighting for something much bigger than a trophy, or personal gain. That way, if they fall short of achieving their goal, they won't feel as if their work has been for nothing, which can be demoralising for anyone looking to thrive in a sustainable way.

Without spoiling the forthcoming chapters in this building block, a successful team should come to an understanding of their *why* through five phases of work:

1. They first determine a holistic purpose, or goal.
2. A clearly defined mission is established.
3. The group creates a list of non-negotiable winning behaviours. These are actions that give the team a greater chance of executing their mission and of reaching the overall goal.
4. The players live their behaviours.
5. The importance of the purpose and mission are reinforced through storytelling and the personal experience of others.

This process has helped countless teams thrive and achieve, even in moments that might have otherwise seemed testing, boring or even emotionally painful. For example, when required to spend several weeks away from their friends and family, an Olympic athlete should remind themselves of their *why*. When asked to deliver 100 per cent in training, a rugby player or rower on the fringes of first-team selection can remind themselves of their *why*. And when instructed to give everything in matches, even when playing through pain, those athletes worn down by the grind of a long season can also remind themselves of their *why*. This thought process is important because there are so many uncontrollable factors that can decide a match, tournament or competition: world record-holding sprinters get sick on the eve of an important race; referees make weird decisions in hockey matches; and freaky, match-winning shots come out of nowhere in golf, tennis, even darts.

However, if a team or athlete has defined their *why*, it's possible for them to reset after a disappointing result and then approach their next challenge with unwavering levels of enthusiasm. That's because they will have a clearly defined purpose or goal. Their next mission has been established. A series of non-negotiable winning behaviours are in place (and have been lived), and through storytelling and the experiences of others they will have reinforced their purpose and mission. My aim is that by working through this next building block, you'll be able to do the same, no matter the situation you might find yourself in.

CHAPTER SIX
THE NORTH STAR

It's no secret that teams and players with a clearly defined sense of purpose, or north star, generally thrive in a more effective and sustainable way. On an individual level, people with a sharper idea of their *why* tend to be happier and more productive than those without. They brim with focus and energy; they rarely drift along in life, making do or simply getting by; they know what they're doing and understand their reasons for doing it. Most importantly, they have a direction of travel, and their everyday actions and interactions are focused on maintaining the course. As a result, they can feel incredibly fulfilled.

Equally, when considering collectives, the team with a north star is generally stronger than one lacking purpose. That's because everyone within the group is plugged into a common cause, a target that supersedes any individual values, dreams or belief systems. That common cause then directs work rate, intention and effort within the group; it helps the team to overcome any internal differences or disputes; and it sharpens the decision-making process because everyone knows what they're doing and why. Meanwhile, the 'journey' – whether that's an international tournament, company launch or community project – becomes a shared experience in which successes and failures are managed collectively, while pushing the group to overcome adversity. I don't believe that a team or organisation can sustain long-term success without a powerful north star.

It's not rocket science to claim that everyone should have a purpose of some kind, and countless books have been written on the subject. The problem is that too many of us choose either results-oriented north stars, or short-term navigation points not guided by a north star (that inevitably wilt under the test of time). On the eve of an Olympic Games, every athlete wants to win a medal. In business, every company strives to be a market leader. But these ambitions, while working as powerful motivators, run the risk of providing only limited levels of satisfaction, and a team or individual can be crushed if they fail to meet their targets. It's also worth noting that in both sport and life, so much of what takes place is uncontrollable. On the eve of important games, teams can be weakened through injury; in business, black swan events such as pandemics or natural disasters sometimes wreck financial markets and destroy previously successful companies. A powerful north star ensures people don't become defined by a singular event, particularly one that's beyond their control.

Life can become stranger still when an aspiration is *actually achieved*. Say, for example, a team's north star is to become Premier League champions, win an Oscar for best movie or compose a number one single: what happens if they're successful and the world moves on? The history books are littered with superstars that have struggled to find happiness after achieving their ultimate dream. Victoria Pendleton, for example, described feeling 'empty' and 'numb' after winning an Olympic gold medal in Beijing. Previous successes can also weigh heavy on a title-winning team and hamper forward progression. I've learned that to achieve sustainable, healthy success – while sidestepping emotional and physical burnout – an effective north star really needs to comprise two elements:

- A target that glues a person to their sense of purpose, regardless of results.
- A target that withstands the test of time.

Having helped a series of teams to define their north star, I've come to realise that this concept doesn't just work in sport, it also extends to just about any walk of life.

The short-term goal	The north star
To write a bestselling screenplay or novel.	To inspire, educate or entertain people through storytelling.
To run a successful tech start-up.	To build environmentally friendly, life-changing products.
To raise money in next year's London Marathon.	To pursue altruistic endeavours through sport.

In all three cases, consider the emotional differences between the short-term goal and a sustainable north star. By aiming to inspire, educate or entertain through storytelling, the novelist won't feel unfulfilled if their first book fails to top the bestsellers lists. By building environmentally friendly, life-changing products, the tech entrepreneur can stay on track even if their first few releases fail to impact on the market. And by pursuing altruistic endeavours through sport, the marathon runner won't experience a comedown in the wake of their first fund-raising effort because they'll already be planning for the next one. That's the additional beauty of a north star: by working to their higher purpose, while being guided by something much bigger than themselves, a person has a greater chance of hitting the next short-term goal. And the next. *And the next.*

An example of this thought process in action took place in 2015, while working with the Cambridge University Women's rowing squad during the build-up to the Boat Race. For the rowers, this was a whole new experience. As it was the first time the women's event was taking place on the same stretch of the Thames and on the same day as the men, the hype and media interest were huge, all of which presented a major psychological challenge. A lot of university athletes discover sports like rowing once they've enrolled in higher education, rather than having previously learned the skills in school. As a result, they might not have experienced the pressures and challenges that occur at county, national or international meets. Even for those athletes that had, the Boat Race was on a whole other level. On race day, helicopters hovered over the Thames, and the riverbanks were lined with thousands and thousands of spectators. Inexperienced athletes could be forgiven for crumbling under such scrutiny, and my role was to work with Rob Baker, the Cambridge Women's coach, to create an environment in which they would thrive in a sustainable way.

The Cambridge Women's rowing team seemed particularly dedicated. This was immediately apparent during our first few sessions, when, to get a handle on what was motivating them outside of the Boat Race, I asked everybody the same three questions:

1. What makes you do this?
2. What do you love about it?
3. Why are you here?

Pretty much every rower answered with clarity and consistency. Yes, they wanted to be the best they could be, and they most definitely wanted to beat the Oxford boat, but what emerged was a clearly identifiable purpose. The women's rowers were striving for equality and to challenge the status quo during a period in which the men's race had dominated the headlines. They also wanted to go down in history as the first female team to have competed in a televised Boat Race. But most of all they wanted to leave a legacy for themselves and the women that would follow. In striving for all of these goals, they were happy to get up at the crack of dawn and slog their guts out in the freezing cold. Their purpose was easily definable from there on in:

> To create a force of change that is never satisfied with the status quo and is *always* present. To leave a legacy of honour, tradition and pride through a culture of success that recognises we are stronger together.

Not only did this target serve as a powerful reminder to keep working whenever the going got tough, but it also hit the two requirements of every north star:

- The target glued the team to their sense of purpose, regardless of results.
- The target withstood the test of time.

That year, Oxford Women came out winners, beating Cambridge Women by six and a half lengths. But while the conclusion was undoubtedly disappointing, it wasn't destructive or debilitating, and that's because the team's north star had been rooted in something much bigger than the result. Had it not been so, the Boat Race, taken on its own, might have been considered a failure. (And had Cambridge won, the goal to simply triumph in the Boat Race might have bred complacency a year later or ramped up the pressure.) Instead, the Cambridge team made history. They had raced their best race under the greatest pressure, and in doing so had challenged the status quo and created a legacy for themselves. From that moment on, nobody was going to doubt whether an all-female rowing team could race the same distance as their male counterparts. Put together, the Cambridge team had followed their north star and were able to hold their performance up as a massive achievement. I felt honoured to have been given the opportunity to work with them.

The following year, Cambridge built on their impressive showing, although it might not have looked like it to the untrained eye. The 2016 Boat Race was fought in horrendous weather – high winds whipped across the Thames and the waves were worryingly choppy, with one commentator even describing the conditions as 'biblical'. By the time both teams arrived at Hammersmith Bridge the Cambridge boat was taking on a concerning amount of water and there was a very real chance that it might sink. At one point the umpire – who was following in a boat – called through his megaphone, suggesting that Cambridge should abandon the race, something echoed by shouts from the riverbanks. The team conferred and were absolutely clear that they would carry on, rowing valiantly to the finish line. Although Oxford would go on to win by 24 lengths and 71 seconds, the story across all the national news media was of how the Cambridge team had refused to abandon their boat in horrendous circumstances.

Before long, Cambridge Women had transformed their defiant spirit into long-term success by winning seven successive Boat Races between 2017 and 2024. It was yet another example of how their north star was setting a resilient streak throughout the team from one year to the next.

BECOME THE CURIOUS KID IN THE ROOM: HOW TO FIND YOUR NORTH STAR

I can't recall walking into too many team environments where the participants had already developed a clearly defined north star (the FA were an exception to this, which we will discover in Chapter 7). In my experience, many teams have been fixated on short-term ambitions ('to win the cup'), or goals that lack clarity or greater meaning over the long haul ('to be the best'). I know that this is an easy trap to fall into, and I experienced it first hand when working as the head of psychology for the UKSI, as we worked towards the Olympic and Paralympic Games.

As part of a 30-strong team of practitioners, it had been stated that our north star was to be the world's leading psychology team. While this was a noble cause, it didn't quite chime with the passion, care and creativity prevalent within our collective, and I was often left thinking: *What does 'world leader' mean?* (Because the idea of being the best didn't fully represent the team or convey what we were truly about.) In meetings I couldn't help but wonder whether we needed something bigger to strive for, such as a goal much larger than a result or an achievement – a cause that would still inspire us 20 years down the line.

To pinpoint a new north star, I worked on a three-part process that could be applied to both teams and individuals. The first step was to identify the motivating factors within the team – the events and actions that left them feeling fulfilled, satisfied or excited, regardless of results. This was particularly important in a group of wildly different people where there were varying personality types, values and experiences. In the UKSI's case, the *why* of an individual wanting to be a part of a world-leading sport psychology team could have been rooted in all sorts of characteristics, such as financial reward or reputational enhancement. To help me establish what their motivation was, I asked the practitioners around me a series of questions, including:

1. What do you love about psychology?
2. Why this team?
3. What do you believe sport psychology is here to do?
4. What really matters?
5. How would we know if the UKSI were the best in the world?

Then I asked everyone to dig into the answers by asking the same thing over and over again: *Why? How? When?* In many ways I had transformed into an annoyingly curious child – the one we've probably all encountered at some point – that seems unwilling to accept an answer, no matter what it is. In such situations, the nearest frustrated adult is usually forced to muddle through, doing his or her best to respond, before delivering a definitive, end-game response: *Because . . . it just is!* And while this experience can be infuriating, it can deliver a powerful lesson: thinking like a kid encourages us to be playful, which in turn helps us to chip away at any superficial factors masking a true north star. By doing this, we shake off our adult inhibitions and lower our barriers, without fear of judgement or failure.* And in much the same

---

* This technique can also work in a less cerebral way. On the eve of the 2023 World Cup in Australia and New Zealand, Lionesses head coach Sarina Wiegman tapped into the same spirit by asking the team to consider their inner child. 'I want you to remember the little girl that loved playing football,' she said on more than one occasion. 'The kid that just wanted to play, that just wanted to be on the pitch and kick the ball with curiosity and fearlessness.' As a further reminder, the FA brand team got photos of every player as a child in their grassroots team's football kit, put them together and transformed the resulting collage into a commissioned team painting that hung from the wall in the Lionesses' training camp. The image was designed so that a feeling of childlike

way that a kid will imagine scenarios without any limitations – *I want to be a zookeeper! How do I build a jetpack?* – a team can do the same when trying to pinpoint the thing – or things – that truly motivate them. But be careful. It's not enough to just ask 'Why?' over and over again to every single response you get. In these situations, it's important to explore what is most meaningful to a group without driving everybody nuts.

Having drilled into our responses, the next step was to identify any recurring themes within the group's answers. And in this case, two emerged:

1. Everybody was passionate about enhancing the performances of the athletes under our care.
2. We wanted to ensure our athletes remained mentally healthy – especially as the pressure intensified during the build-up to an event such as the Olympic Games – and that they left the performance system feeling enriched.

Through this three-part exercise we were able to develop a clear idea of what success would look and feel like for everyone in the UKSI sport psychology team, regardless of results or time constraints. If all our athletes medalled at the next Olympics, then wonderful. If they didn't, but every individual's performance had been maximised and their mental health enhanced, we could still consider ourselves a success. With that information, the third and final step took place, and we identified a new north star. Eventually, the group created a memorable directive: *To maximise human performance and enhance positive mental health.* Our future decisions and actions were soon driven by this clearly

---

freedom could be evoked within the team, and the players were able to recall a time when they'd performed without pressure, simply for the love of the game.

defined purpose, and as a result our psychology team became more collaborative and increasingly effective. When following this exercise and defining an inspiring and sustainable north star, you and your team will too.

 ASK THE QUESTION

If someone enquired about your purpose, or 'why', would you be able to answer them with clarity in a sentence or two?

If the answer is 'No', spend some time exploring the things that make you the happiest, or provide you with an overwhelming sense of achievement or satisfaction. That should give you a greater understanding of what truly drives you. And remember to think without limits!

LIGHTBULBS

- A north star will keep you on track when the going gets tough. It will also guide you whenever you might feel lost or directionless.
- Teams that understand their north stars, and the individuals within them, are generally happier and more productive than those who don't.
- Search for greater meaning. Results-oriented goals work in the short term, but in isolation they can also lead to burnout, stress and dissatisfaction. Instead, pick a north star that outlasts a season or a career. It's more sustainable to inspire, entertain or break the status quo than it is to win a cup or an 'Employee of the Month' award. (Though there's nothing wrong with either of those things.)

CHAPTER SEVEN
MISSION BUILDING

With a north star in view, a team or individual can expect to feel motivated and inspired. But to really get a handle on their *why*, that same group should then select a mission with a focus on the near future, because in doing so it becomes easier to align the aspirations of a team – and its component parts – to their potential. While a north star serves as a permanent guide for where we generally want to be in life in both the short and long term, so a mission provides us with a series of processes that brings us closer to our sense of purpose, helping to turn what might feel like an intangible concept into a tangible reality. *It delivers noticeable results and teachable moments.*

This is important because a north star can sometimes feel too big to manage on a daily basis. For example, a senior care worker in a nursing home might have a very clearly defined sense of purpose: helping people less fortunate than themselves to lead a comfortable, dignified and fulfilling life. *But what does that look like in an everyday environment?* Sure, there might be times where they feel powerfully connected to their north star. They'll be directly responsible for the patients' welfare or the management of care programmes and health updates. But those moments can often be disrupted by other responsibilities, such as administrative meetings, human resources meetings and meetings about meetings. The same goes for a film director filing their tax returns, the restaurateur overseeing a monthly hygiene inspection and the company owner organising a stressful relocation overseas. These sorts of events, although undeniably important, can often feel disconnected from the overarching purpose.

When taken literally, the word 'mission' has a very clear meaning: *a special assignment given to a person or group that by its very nature focuses attention towards the task at hand*. And while working with sports teams and athletes I've found that such a special assignment can be identified in one of the following three ways:

1. An achievement-based mission: something aspirational that a team and the individuals contained within it can rally behind. Unlike a north star, these missions can be results-oriented and change, or adapt, with time. For example, to win the Ryder Cup or become a FTSE 100 company by the end of the year.
2. A function-based mission: a target that aligns the aspiration of a team or an individual to their potential. For example, to play a clinical, counter-attacking game at an intensity that the opposition can't live with or to be a dynamic business that listens to the needs of its customers.
3. A combination of the two, because the team that wants to win a World Cup can strive to do so by playing clinical, counter-attacking football, in much the same way that the business working to be a market leader can also listen to the needs of its customers.

Taking option 3 is particularly useful because it encompasses a motivational – but potentially uncontrollable – driver, as well as the use of controllable processes and behaviours that are designed to reap rewards. I'll explain how you can create these behaviours and processes in Chapter 8.

To pick a relevant mission that truly connects with our north star, we must first ask one simple question:

What does success look like?

To an individual with a north star, arriving at the answer shouldn't be too hard. Consider the storyteller whose purpose it is to create inspiring, entertaining and educational narratives; their mission could be to write a book, play or poem that does just that. Things get slightly trickier in a team setting, though, because no single person shares an identical set of values to another. So, if you were to ask three carpenters working on a housing project for their definition of success, it's highly likely they'll deliver three very different answers, among which might be financial reward, pride in a job done well, and customer satisfaction.

The trick to inspiring all three drivers is to arrive at a mission that appeals to the desire for financial reward, the satisfaction of personal pride and the achievement of results. For the most part, this can be done by collating the answers and identifying the commonalities between them. From there, it's possible to arrive at a succinct, function-based mission – in this case: *To execute the project to the best of our creative and management abilities.* This one mission has the potential to fulfil everyone. The financially motivated carpenter understands that effective management will maximise profit. The creative mind is being motivated to do the best job possible. The results-oriented carpenter knows that their client will be happy if the mission is completed to the highest standards.

Of course, there will be some cases where this process seems unnecessary; certain missions arrive already pre-conceived. Sports teams often have medal targets, or perhaps need to achieve promotion to a higher league because their future budgets depend upon it. The same is true for businesses and other organisations. While these groups also have north stars that are holistic and sustainable, their missions must be achievement-based because it might be the only way for them to receive funding in the future. And then there are the missions that must be completed because they're just there, or they're chosen for us. These include house moves, marriages and divorces, driving tests, university exams and enforced lifestyle changes.

When marrying a desirable outcome to a functional objective, it can be useful to split the process into two stages. The first is to consider the dream result – to win the World Cup, for example. The second is to outline a concept that can be worked towards in the short term, one that feeds into the dream result and is controllable – to build the capacity to train and play at a greater intensity than our opposition. In the case of the Cambridge Women's rowing team in Chapter 6, their north star was clearly defined: to challenge rowing's status quo and create a legacy for themselves and the women that would follow. We then identified a mission that would bind them tightly to their new purpose and their north star, even when working on activities not directly connected to their *why*.

To get there I asked them to define Boat Race success for themselves, and the responses were interesting. The rowers talked about the performance they wanted to execute, and what would be required from them to achieve this. They talked about the dynamics of the crew, and their desire for excellence in both body and mind. Through these answers, we constructed a function-based mission to sit alongside their dream of beating the Oxford Women: *to be a strong, resilient and tough team that's prepared to perform under any circumstances.* It was a mission they focused on during every aspect of their day, no matter what they were doing – competing, training or representing Cambridge in media or university commitments. By sticking to a short-term mission they stayed true to their north star, even during tasks that might have felt detached from their target of challenging some of rowing's archaic attitudes. By working to their vision of what success looked like, they were constantly motivated by their achievements, even after finishing second on the day.

CASE STUDY

How the Lionesses designed their mission

During the build-up to the 2022 European Championship, Kay Cossington, the FA women's technical director, brought the senior technical team together to answer that very same question. *What does success look like for the Euros?*

In advance of the meeting, a shared north star had already been agreed upon, which was to unite the game and inspire the nation, and we understood that winning a major tournament would significantly contribute to this. In many ways, this process wasn't too dissimilar to what happens in a business or non-sporting organisation. At the head of a global company, the CEOs generally decide what the overarching mission for their brand should be and the different components of the business will then settle on relevant missions that feed into the bigger goal. In our first discussion, our brief was to settle upon an overarching group mission, and this was done by first considering what our individual achievement- and function-based missions were.

Among the technical group were head coach Sarina Wiegman and her assistant Arjan Veurink, alongside our performance analysts, additional coaches and key support staff, including myself. We were given Post-it notes and asked to write our idea of what a successful tournament for the Lionesses might look like. My answers were, as always, both function-based and controllable, with a heavy nod towards mindset. *For me, a successful tournament would be our players understanding Sarina's game plan and their role within it, and having the confidence to execute her instructions under pressure.* As far as I was concerned, completing that one mission would help the team and the players to compete to the best of their ability, while also giving them the best possible opportunity to win football matches. If that then contributed to the fulfilling of a greater dream, like a tournament win, then brilliant.

Typically, everybody was different. As we stuck our ideas to the wall, I noticed that some people had selected an achievement-based mission, whereas others talked about the beauty of the game in general, and the beauty of *our* game. Several people delivered answers that were even more directly aligned to our north star than mine. As we looked over the collated answers, Sarina called everyone together. 'OK, let's discuss this,' she said.

We kicked around the ideas and made suggestions, the group talking through the things that were important to us individually, and what we wanted to achieve as a collective.

'Our dream is to win the Euros,' said one of the coaching staff. 'But if we do everything within our power and we don't win, does that mean we've not been successful as a team?'

We explored this as a group and talked about maximising our strengths. Then we dug into the team's advantages. It was decided that we also needed a mission we could control. Eventually we landed at an agreed objective: *to execute our best game under the greatest of pressure.*

At the next camp, after the coaching team's mission had been shared with the squad, we tasked them with the very same exercise: *what does success look like for you?* Naturally, the players talked about a very understandable dream: to win the Euros. But they also wanted to focus on a more process-focused target: *to maximise the squad's strengths and stick to our playing principles.* With these objectives in mind, the players and support staff rallied around clearly defined missions that, if completed effectively, would give the group a shot at winning the tournament. It was an incredibly productive step.

EVOLVING YOUR MISSION: THE RIO CHALLENGE

While north stars can remain in place throughout the entirety of a life or career, missions by their very nature are temporary. We complete one challenge and move on to the next. And if we're able to manage our emotions in a sustainable way, this process can seem straightforward – we succeed and push on to another test, or we fail and learn any number of lessons before moving forward again, guided by our powerful north star. But problems can arise when a team or person fails to commit to a new, inspiring mission. Sporting history is full of stories of athletes that have won a golf or tennis grand slam, or achieved their Olympic dream, only to struggle in the aftermath.

This downturn in performance sometimes happens because the people concerned haven't yet found a test that fits with their new champion status, or because they have forgotten *why* they pursued their dreams in the first place – they have lost sight of their north star. Getting up from one challenge and moving on to the next in an inspiring way is vital when striving for sustainable success, but it also needs to be managed correctly. *Just Do It (Again)* wouldn't be the most inspiring of slogans. Instead, the first thing to do after every mission – when the dust has settled and the post-mortem has been completed – is to ask another question: *Is our mission still relevant?*

This seems particularly important in team environments where there's often a constant churn in place. In football clubs, new faces arrive to replace the old guard; big characters leave NBA or NFL teams and different personalities arrive in the locker room; managers and coaches are fired and hired. These events can contribute to a sense of transition, and missions that might have seemed entirely appropriate for one group suddenly feel out of place for another. This is also true outside of sport. People rarely stay in their jobs forever and team environments are constantly in flux, especially in cut-throat industries. All of which makes mission-setting even more of a priority. To get an understanding of a collective's *why*, any new arrivals should be immediately introduced to the north star and then attached to a team mission. It's even better if that team mission feels new or exciting for everybody. Human beings crave novelty. Without an inspiring goal, the process of *doing* can become boring and uninspiring, maybe even unsettling.

This idea became apparent to me after the phenomenal success of the London 2012 Olympics, where Team GB's athletes won a total of 65 medals (29 gold, 18 silver and 18 bronze) and finished third in the medal table. Not to be outdone, the ParalympicsGB team also finished third with a whopping 34 gold, 43 silver and 43 bronze medals. Part of this success could be attributed to the fact that the group was competing on home turf, which can have its advantages. That and the fact that a host nation usually invests heavily in their athletes, so they can put on a show and create a party vibe at home. Because of this, no nation had ever improved their medal tally in an Olympics following a home Games and statistics tell us that performances naturally drop off. But unbelievably, Team GB managed the feat in Rio 2016, scooping two more medals than their 2012 total (27 gold, 23 silver and 17 bronze) and finished second in the table behind the USA. The ParalympicsGB team also made history by finishing second behind China with a combined total of 147 medals.

The results filled me with pride. During the 2016 Olympic and Paralympic Games I'd led the psychology team at the UKSI, but there was very little time to rest afterwards. Almost from the moment Rio had concluded, our attention turned towards the Tokyo Games in four years' time, and as we began our preparations I remember thinking, 'Flipping heck . . . *Where do we go from here?*' The answer was to set a new mission for ourselves. Shortly afterwards, I sat down with my colleagues Lara Barrett and Jonathan Riall, both of whom had been working for British Triathlon. We discussed the Rio Olympics and Paralympics and what was next for psychology and the UKSI team in Tokyo. Then I asked the most important question of all when planning a mission: *If psychology support was to be even more successful in next Olympics, what would that look like?*

Jonny's answer was inspiring. He argued that it would see our athletes thriving in elite competition. 'Not simply coping,' he said. 'Not just managing the event and any related anxieties – but *thriving* in the context of an Olympic or Paralympic Games.' He went on to explain that he believed some of our athletes hadn't adjusted to the concept of competing and flourishing at such a high level. They had coped rather than thrived. It was his theory that Great Britain could have won even more medals in London and Rio as a result. *Bingo!* We immediately combined an achievement and function-based mission:

- **Achievement-based mission:** to win more medals than at the previous Olympiad.
- **Function-based mission:** to help Team GB's athletes thrive under extreme pressure.

We called the work 'Project Thrive', and before long our psychology team had united behind a revolutionary goal in elite-level sport psychology. To build upon this concept I questioned several coaches, athletes, performance directors and support staff on what they thought needed to happen if Team GB's athletes were to succeed in a sustainable way during the Tokyo Games. This new project galvanised me. But even better was the realisation that this new mission had re-energised our UKSI psychology team following the highs of Rio. Rather than feeling frustrated at what would likely be a gruelling battle against the statistical headwinds, the group became incredibly motivated.

We immediately began looking beyond our small working silos. The very next time we came together as a team, I excitedly told them of my meeting with Jonny and Lara and the project we were going to get behind: 'This is Project Thrive,' I said. 'We need to figure out, as a team, the answer to this big, bold question: How do we ensure that every athlete in our care can get into that Olympic or Paralympic environment and thrive?' At the time, the UKSI sport psychology team comprised 30 working practitioners. All of them were brilliant, but none of us had worked together so closely before. Traditionally, we had been set apart in smaller groups, individual practitioners working within a specific sport, and as a result our ideas and processes had become self-contained and were rarely shared across the larger group. But by drawing everyone together, barriers were broken down; people who hadn't previously worked with one another rallied to create our function-based mission for the next Games.

Through this work we were able to land at a succinct mission for ourselves: *To facilitate the creation of psychologically underpinned and sustainable high-performance environments that enable the person as well as the performer to thrive.* This focus also stayed true to our north star: *To maximise human performance and enhance positive mental health.* In the end we arrived at ten principles that every member of our team could hang their hat on. Each one helped us to facilitate the creation of sustainable high-performance environments in which an athlete could both develop and thrive under extreme pressure.

PRINCIPLE 1: THRIVING IS EVERYONE'S BUSINESS

Individuals don't thrive in isolation. Sustainable behavioural change can't happen through one individual intervention or by targeting one person. It requires everyone to promote attitudes and behaviours that will allow the group to thrive.

PRINCIPLE 2: SUCCESS IS DRIVEN BY A PROCESS FOCUS ALIGNED WITH A HIGHER PURPOSE

When an athlete or team is under pressure, emotion can win out over logic and results become distracting. This can be problematic. But with a clear north star and mission, that same emotional drive to win becomes a strength rather than a weakness.

PRINCIPLE 3: PERFORMANCE ENVIRONMENTS REQUIRE APPROPRIATE BALANCE OF CHALLENGE AND SUPPORT

As they prepare, athletes need a combination of challenge and support so that they can safely push past their comfort zones in training and competition. By doing so they'll grow, learn and trust in a sustainable way.

PRINCIPLE 4: SHARED UNDERSTANDING – AND LANGUAGE – PROMOTE CONSISTENT COMMUNICATION

It's good to talk. A team that understands its individual members through shared connections and a common communication style will problem-solve and work effectively when under extreme pressure.

PRINCIPLE 5: PERSONAL VALUES DRIVE BEHAVIOUR

A person's values will determine their intentions and, in turn, drive their behaviour. By understanding these factors we can help an athlete or team to connect with their own north star and mission.

PRINCIPLE 6: UNIQUENESS AND STRENGTHS SHOULD BE EMBRACED AND OPTIMISED

Results at the top tier of sport are settled by small percentages and fine margins. A team's strengths – and those of the individuals within it – should be embraced and optimised to gain a competitive edge over their rivals. Meanwhile, uniqueness and perceived differences in the group should be viewed as assets rather than weaknesses.

PRINCIPLE 7: PURPOSEFUL EXPERIENCES AND REFLECTION EVOLVE HUMAN PERFORMANCE

To reach high-performance levels, a team (or individual athlete) needs to assess any progress by evaluating their performances. If they are to evolve, they then must plan their next steps, execute them effectively and self-reflect on the process.

PRINCIPLE 8: PSYCHOLOGICAL SAFETY PROMOTES COLLABORATION AND RISK-TAKING

When an athlete feels psychologically safe through collaboration, communication and engagement, they are happier to take risks, embrace innovation and learn from mistakes.

PRINCIPLE 9: THE PERFORMANCE CULTURE IS DETERMINED BY CLEAR AND UNAMBIGUOUS STANDARDS

A collective hoping to reach the status of 'high-performance' needs to embrace a culture of clearly defined behaviours with an emphasis on elite standards, decision-making and self-governance.

PRINCIPLE 10: FAILING SMART ACCELERATES LEARNING AND PROMOTES GROWTH

Overcoming the fear of failure at all levels allows a team to learn from their mistakes, no matter the circumstances. Growth lies on the other side of disaster, but only if approached correctly.

TOKYO 2020

Team GB went on to win 64 medals in Tokyo – 22 gold, 20 silver and 22 bronze. This total, while falling a little short of the achievements in London 2012 or Rio 2016, was incredible, especially considering British athletes were winning medals across a wider number of sports than ever before. Later, the ParalympicsGB team finished as runners-up in the table for the second successive Games, and while their overall haul wasn't enough to beat their Rio total, they also rewrote the history books by medalling in more sports than any other nation at a Paralympic Games, winning medals in 18 out of the 19 sports they competed in. This was the 'Covid Games', don't forget, so history had been made on the back of the most complex, challenging and difficult competitive environments in recent times. As far as I was concerned a four-year Olympic cycle wasn't measured in medals. We were in the business of earning sustainable success. Together with a team of exceptional people, we had not only created the blueprint for our north star but had also clearly articulated what sport psychology looks like at the highest level, both for the greater good of our discipline and for the athletes we support.

 ASK THE QUESTION

Do you know what your next mission is?

If not, pick a challenge or target for yourself. Make sure it's both achievement- and function-based and guided by your north star.

LIGHTBULBS

- To align your team to their north star, set a relevant mission with a focus on the near future.
- Missions can be either achievement-based (*to make more profits than the previous financial year*) or function-based (*to disrupt the market with technologically innovative products*). My preference is to combine results with controllable outcomes.
- To pick a mission, ask the question: *What does success look like?* If the answer leads you to a specific goal or target, make that your priority. Don't forget to ask the people working alongside you for feedback. By spotting common themes in their answers, you'll likely find a mission that energises the group.
- Constantly evolve your mission. Don't pick one and stick with it for the long haul. Success and failure should encourage you to assess whether your mission is relevant, and whether it's still leading you towards your north star.

CHAPTER EIGHT
WINNING BEHAVIOURS (AND HOW TO IDENTIFY THEM)

No matter the clarity of your north star or the importance of your mission, a team's sense of purpose can become exposed without a set of non-negotiable winning behaviours to work from. In their basic form these are expected standards of performance and actionable attitudes that can lead both a group and the individual to success, especially when delivered without fail (or excuses). Often, businesses, teams or organisations fall into two traps. The first is that while they have a vision, plus a mission and a set of values (that have been broken down into strategies and tactics for the business), they fail to consider how these concepts can be brought to life through the behaviour of their team members.

The second is that too much time is spent on nebulous sloganeering or wordsmithery of company values. It might sound bold or exciting to state that one of your company's values is to 'think big'. But how does a team leader ensure that their workforce is following through on such a promise? Trying to coerce a group of disparate personalities to agree on the same values is often futile. What we discovered in Building Block #1 is that more time needs to be spent understanding people, and then aligning them to both the north star and the mission of their organisation, before really exploring the behavioural standards that will result in success. Most importantly, these behaviours must be observable.

Some practical examples might include:

- Be punctual.
- Communicate any issues to the individual concerned or to the team as a whole. And don't discuss in small sub-groups (and challenge others for doing so).
- Be prepared to provide constructive, well-intended feedback, and be open to receiving it.

Taken individually, actionable winning behaviours are useful but not necessarily game-changing. However, when combined with a north star and a coherent mission, they become powerful drivers and will pin a team to their course, in much the same way that a series of fixed ropes will lead an expedition to the summit of a mountain. Most importantly, they are generally actions that *everyone* in a group can get behind, regardless of their individual values, because they should be identified and agreed upon by the people involved through deep discussion, rather than being forced on them by a senior figure or external influence. It's the conversation around a team's behavioural code that's often the most powerful piece of the puzzle.

This is because some sporting squads consist of up to 50 athletes, plus coaches, technical staff and supporting members. Every person in a group of that size will have a unique belief system; no two individuals will ever agree entirely on politics, religion, social cues or their favourite football team or band. But when asked to construct a clear set of guidelines for themselves that will optimise the opportunity for success, it's likely that these same disparate personalities will bond around a shared sense of commitment. In that context, a list of winning behaviours acts like a charter of expected standards – a contract that holds a team to their cause and maintains a consistency in behaviour and, in turn, performances. Anyone failing to live up to the standards set by the group will usually find themselves being corralled into change.

When beginning the process of defining a list of winning behaviours for a team, it's important first to consider the circumstances of the group and the conditions that need to be met for them to be at their most productive. For example, some companies feel that taking their staff to a hotel for an away day delivers the best responses; others conduct their meetings in the pub, or in nature. It all depends on the vibe of the people involved. What I will say is that a consistent set of steps should be followed so that a well-defined list can be pieced together.

STEP 1: REVIEW YOUR POSITION

Sports, by their very nature, have a natural point at which assessments and reviews take place. Seasons come to a close, tournaments wrap up. There are Olympic cycles, Ryder Cup cycles and Six Nations cycles. At the end of each of these – once a period of physical and emotional recovery has taken place – there's usually a window during which to reflect on what has worked and what hasn't. It's just as important to do this behaviourally, *on feel*, as it is to review objective, performance-based targets. This is the point where everyone should take a moment to remember their north star and assess their next challenge. (Don't forget the question: *Is our mission still relevant?*) Once that has been defined, register the required winning behaviours that could sit underneath the overarching goal and will help the group or individual reach their next target.

STEP 2: SET THE SCENE

If a group is to live a list of chosen winning behaviours, it's important they have a hand in shaping them. A team with a set of rules and conditions enforced upon them is more likely to fall short (and find excuses) than a group that creates that same list for themselves. To run through this phase with the Lionesses during the build-up to the Women's European Championship in 2021, Sarina and I brought everybody together at a training camp and laid out our objective:

> We want to have clarity over what success looks like for us as a group, and establish the things that are absolutely non-negotiable if we're to give ourselves the best opportunity of success.

We stressed how success could be defined by the way in which we were aligned around a shared purpose and the importance of non-negotiable winning behaviours. Finally, we presented back to them their own stories and quotes, captured by the media in the preceding weeks, among them:

> I can't wait. The Euros will be unbelievable, I think a successful tournament would be to make the nation proud and inspire a lot more younger children to play. As individuals, all we ever do is aim to be our best. I don't think it's fair to set a specific goal because there's so many stepping stones along the way. There are so many top teams there too. We are equally one of those, but our aim is to deliver our best on the biggest stage and see where that takes us.

By reminding the group of their north star and the choices ahead, we allowed them to dictate their immediate future.

STEP 3: ASK QUESTIONS

The squad was broken down into groups. Each one was asked to consider the following questions during their time in camp:

- What excites you?
- What does Euro success look like for you?
- What are the most important winning behaviours that align to success?
- What must we stop, start and continue doing as a team?

The final question, as the words suggest, was a fact-finding mission based around three categories.

- **STOP:** What does the team need to stop doing to move forward? (Or: What is getting in the way of success?)
- **START:** What are we not doing that we need to start doing if we're to give ourselves the best chance of success?
- **CONTINUE:** What is really working for us and needs to remain in place?

By the end of the training camp a week later, the players were asked to talk through their decisions – and the answers were inspiring. Some members of the squad revealed their own experiences of tournaments to date and were honest about how their behaviours may have contributed towards, or negated, the success of previous teams. From these meetings it was clear that communication, on and off the pitch, was going to be critical to any future successes. There was also a desire to engage in difficult conversations, so that any individuals not living up to the Lionesses' high standards could be called to account, but in a positive and empathetic way.

Noticeably, the players had recognised that their focus must be on the entire squad, rather than just the starting XI. This was critical. A club or country can only win a tournament when the whole group is engaged, so it's important for the players *not* in the starting line-up to contribute to the overall strength of the group. It was acknowledged that the Lionesses comprised starters and finishers: players who were involved at the first whistle (the starters), and those that might be required to step in at any stage as impact players (the finishers). Who was in which category can change from game to game depending on tactics, form and injury. It was the finishers' role to support the starters by pushing them to higher standards in training and to challenge for their place in the team. Likewise, the starters had to ensure the finishers felt valued by showing their support when they were training the day after a game (while the starters were recovering) or when dealing with the emotions associated with missing out on match time.

STEP 4: PROCESS THE DATA

After sessions of this kind, it's important to process the gathered information as quickly as possible so that any key themes can be identified. In our case, Sarina and I went away with the team's answers and grouped them under what became three distinct headings: *Team first. Be in the moment. No regrets.* From then on, everything that was discussed with the squad – and every decision that was made – needed to be viewed through the prism of these three ideas. The words became a mantra.

- **Team first:** The greater good of the collective should be the driving force behind decisions, actions and behaviours.

- **Be in the moment:** The group, and everyone in it, had to be present, whether they were playing, training or engaged in team duties.
- **No regrets:** It was agreed that team members would do everything within their power to ensure that at the end of the tournament they could look back knowing they had given it their all.

By collating the team's ideas, a succinct list of winning behaviours was drawn up – actions and behaviours that a) fell under one of the three headings, and b) would help drive the team to success. So, for example, when it came to the concept of being in the moment, there were clear rules surrounding social media use, and strategies to ensure that media and public scrutiny would not penetrate our immediate squad bubble. If there was ever any doubt as to whether a certain behaviour was appropriate or not, a player only had to think back to the headline statements: *Team first. Be in the moment. No regrets.*

STEP 5: REVIEW YOUR POSITION (AGAIN. AND AGAIN)

As I stated earlier, there are natural breaks in a sporting calendar, especially at the end of a competition or league campaign, although it's also possible to reset after matches or in the period between events. In the sporting world people relentlessly review their performance levels and behaviours in an attempt to gain a marginal advantage. This is very different to what sometimes happens elsewhere, where team- and individual-based results are only assessed when a project is completed or at the end of the financial year. On an individual level, employees might only receive a performance review every 6 or 12 months, if at all. So much can change in that period of time.

This would never happen in an elite sport setting. At the end of every training session, for example, a technical team analyses player performance, fitness levels and the response to any new techniques or tactics. Then the behaviours of staff and players are discussed. It's a constant process. And while I'm not saying that everyone should adopt the same granular approach to their day-to-day practices (unless, of course, it's necessary), I would recommend that a team takes time to constantly re-evaluate their winning behaviours, and at a higher frequency than, say, every six months. That's what we did with the Lionesses.

Following on from the European Championship, the idea of resting on our laurels was a non-starter. Instead, we immediately assessed what had worked and what hadn't, on and off the field, and evolved a new list of non-negotiable winning behaviours relevant for the 2023 World Cup in Australia and New Zealand. These winning behaviours were then re-evaluated regularly, sometimes on a daily basis. As before, they were placed under three distinct headings, but had evolved slightly from before. In this case they were:

- **Team first:** The group had reflected on the role of every individual player in the 23-strong Euros squad. Putting the collective before the individual had paid dividends for them and they were keen not to lose sight of this important anchor.
- **Stick together:** There was a recognition that we would be performing on the other side of the world and would need to create our home away from home. Unity was vital.

- **Thrive in the moment:** It was important to be present, as before. But the squad had recognised that, rather than simply *being*, they had to *thrive*. This was a World Cup, after all.

STEP 6: REMEMBER CLARITY IS A SUPERPOWER

When defining winning behaviours, it's important to ensure that there's absolute clarity about what these behaviours are. If they are vague then they won't properly direct behaviour because people will not know precisely what is expected of them and will be unable to hold themselves and others to account. Winning behaviours should always be clear and observable within the environment, for example: 'always arrive at a meeting five minutes before it starts with a notepad and pen'. This is clear, it's observable and seeing people living that behaviour encourages others to do the same. Winning behaviours need to become 'just what we do' so that there is consistency in how we go about our business when the stakes are low and everyone feels relaxed and when the pressure is increased.

I've found that any kind of winning behaviour, even a poorly defined one, is easily remembered when the stakes are low and everyone feels relaxed. In those moments, decisions are made easily, without too much conflict; people function as they should. When the pressure is cranked up, however, a poorly constructed winning behaviour can be harder to remember, especially when lightning-fast thinking is required. On an everyday level, such moments can typically occur ahead of a looming deadline or when an unexpected chaotic event catches everyone off-guard. In a sporting context, these clutch events tend to happen in the build-up to big events or games, when the staff and athletes involved must understand how to operate, even when the psychological load has been cranked up.

Putting easy-to-understand behaviours in place is the answer. Clarity takes the pressure off, and it gives everybody an understanding of what it is they're supposed to do; it enables people to work to the best of their ability without anxiety, and it creates a sense of familiarity, even when the unexpected takes place. It's one of the reasons why kids respond so well to structure: in familiar environments where they know what to expect, and what is expected of them, they're able to regulate their emotions more evenly. The same goes for people working in stressful circumstances. If you don't believe me, think back to a time when you might have felt frustrated at home or at work, and you've reacted emotionally. I can almost guarantee that this response will have taken place because you were expecting one outcome, only for another entirely random thing to occur instead. My advice: if you want your winning behaviours to stick, keep them simple.

*

Interestingly, this six-step process isn't solely confined to the sporting arena. In fact, in can work in just about any group setting, where progress and high standards are required. Let's take the example of an imaginary secondary school with a clearly defined north star and mission, and imagine a set of observable winning behaviours the teaching staff could create for themselves . . .

RAVENSWOOD SCHOOL

OUR NORTH STAR

To inspire the next generation, show them that anything's possible and shape future pioneers.

ACHIEVEMENT-BASED MISSION	**FUNCTION-BASED MISSION**
85 per cent pass rate of grades A to C.	To ensure our staff have the tools, environment and confidence to impart knowledge and empower the children.

OBSERVABLE WINNING BEHAVIOURS

- Be approachable.
- Run an open-door policy to facilitate communication and problem solving.
- Go out of your comfort zone – invite observation and feedback of your work.
- Trust positive intent in others; check in with the people around you, rather than making assumptions or judging.
- Engage in CPD to maximise strengths as well as evolve development areas.
- Collaborate with colleagues to create innovative and effective teaching materials.

Drawing up a list of this kind might sound like common sense, but so many organisations fail to implement a series of observable winning behaviours for their 'players' or staff to follow. The focus tends to remain on what needs to be done, rather than how to do it. As a result, their north star fades from view and their missions are less likely to be successful.

CASE STUDY
The Team GB hockey team

Establishing a set of winning behaviours is an important process for any team, not least because in my experience a slip in performance on-field is usually preceded by a slipping of standards off it. This was demonstrated when I invited Helen Richardson-Walsh into the Lionesses camp during the lead-in to the 2022 European Championship, as she had a powerful story to tell regarding the observable winning behaviours of the GB hockey team. Helen was an incredibly experienced player who had won her first senior cap at the age of 17 and competed in four Olympic Games, winning a bronze medal at London 2012 and a gold at Rio 2016.

I'd first met Helen in 2014 when the team were experiencing a difficult period after winning Olympic bronze in London, having just finished 11th out of 12 teams in the 2014 World Cup, two years out from the Rio Games. The team needed to move forwards, and their performance lead asked me to drive a series of discussions with the squad. Tellingly, the group had requested to talk to someone from outside the team as they wanted to work through their grievances, without the presence of any support staff. I really had no idea what I was walking into, but I was impressed by the willingness of the players to take control of their destiny and to work together. It was also a credit to the coaching team, who were happy to respect the players' wishes.

To kick off the meeting I presented everyone with a series of ground rules. 'Everyone has to leave their thoughts and feelings on the table today,' I said. 'If you're not prepared to say something or put your feelings out there, you'll lose the opportunity to say your piece. Once we've walked out at the end of the session, a line is going to be drawn in the sand. After that, the team moves forward.'

What followed was one of the most challenging but powerful meetings I've ever been a part of. In detailing their experiences, the GB hockey team were willing to hold a mirror up, not only to themselves but to one another. As a result, they found a way to come out of the other side stronger and more connected. Typically, emotions ran high at times, and we were in that meeting room for many hours. But by the end we'd dealt with the flashpoints and challenges that were causing so much frustration within the group. Then we began the process of carving out the winning behaviours that would allow the group to move forwards, paving the way towards a new mission for the Olympics in Rio and the set of winning behaviours that would guide them towards success. I felt privileged to be in the room with people who were prepared to be so vulnerable and navigate extremely difficult conversations head-on. For the rest of the day we drew up a list of actionable behaviours that would restore team unity. As is always the case in situations such as these, it's the conversations between teammates within teams that have the greatest impact.

The work we started that day laid a foundation for the team of players and staff to forge a new vision towards Rio. Along with Danny Kerry, the GB Hockey head coach, and the new sport psychologist Andrea Furst, the squad continued their vital conversations about team culture and how they wanted to be remembered. They even created an online form that was filled in by the players every three weeks to keep this work alive on a constant basis. It gave agency and ownership to the playing group and comprised two questions: 'Did we live our performance culture?' and 'Was our training environment effective?' Danny later described this process as one of the most important pieces of work the team had conducted during their four-year build-up to the 2016 Games, where the team won gold. Their commitment to winning together – even if it meant holding one another to account and engaging in some incredibly vulnerable conversations – put them on a pathway to success, as did their commitment to a series of distinct and observable winning behaviours. They had found their fixed rope to the Olympic mountaintop.

 ASK THE QUESTION

Do you, or your group, have a list of winning behaviours?

If not, conduct a 'Stop. Start. Continue' exercise and draw up a list of actions that will improve your performance. Remember to make them observable. That way there can be no hiding place.

 LIGHTBULBS

- Without a set of non-negotiable, winning behaviours to work from, a team's sense of purpose will weaken. These performance standards act like a series of fixed ropes leading an expedition party to the summit of a mountain.
- Non-negotiable winning behaviours can unite a team in which no two individuals will ever agree entirely on politics, religion or social cues.
- Run through a six-step process to determine your winning behaviours:
    1. Review your position
    2. Set the scene
    3. Ask questions
    4. Analyse the data
    5. Review your position (again. And again)
    6. Remember, clarity is a superpower

CHAPTER NINE
WALKING THE TALK

Winning behaviours act as a framework through which a person or group can grow stronger, evolve their performance and make decisions quickly, even when under pressure. That's because they will have gone through the processes detailed in Chapter 8 and, as a direct result, understood what will likely make the difference between success and failure. But while it's great that a team defines their non-negotiable winning behaviours – and then comes up with a punchy mantra or three – to truly succeed, any agreed processes must be *lived*, otherwise the preparatory work that went into defining them will have been wasted. It's one of the reasons why winning behaviours should always be observable. A group must both witness the results of their practices when they go well, and feel the consequences of failing to live by them when they don't.

For example, if a team were to adopt a list of vague and intangible behaviours – *Think positively. Consider your teammates. Visualise success* – there would be no way of truly telling whether they were being implemented or not. How would you know if someone was thinking positively, considering their teammates or visualising success? This then makes it almost impossible to hold one another to account. A more visible set of winning behaviours – *Optimise recovery. Ask for help. Challenge others positively and directly* – can be noticeably brought to life in the following ways . . .

- **Optimise recovery:** Post-training and post-competition, is everyone taking care to eat well and hydrate effectively, while readying themselves for the next event? Or are they under-fuelled, rushing to their next commitment and ill-prepared?
- **Ask for help:** Are the team taking ownership of their personal development and asking for help when they're not sure which way to turn? Or are they shying away from showing vulnerability and struggling to move forward?
- **Challenge others positively and directly:** Are the players being supportive of one another, on and off the pitch, and are they having difficult conversations with those members of the group not operating to the agreed standards? Or have opposing cliques formed within the group?

It's so much easier for a group to plan a way forward in tricky moments if their winning behaviours are clear and visible. To make progress they simply have to put them into action. Meanwhile, those individuals not walking the walk can be identified and called to account if necessary.

Psychologically, when encouraging a team to live by their winning behaviours, it's imperative that they're given two things:

1. Ownership
2. Self-governance

The first is vital, because when an individual or group is handed responsibility for determining their agreed actions, they're much more likely to stick by them and hold themselves or one another to account against them. By having defined a clear plan for themselves on how to execute a mission, they'll only have themselves to blame if that plan isn't adhered to and they let their teammates down. That alone can be a very powerful motivator.

Self-governance is equally valuable when actioning winning behaviours. Having created a framework with boundaries in which to act, teams will instinctively know what to do and are more likely to respond positively when faced with challenging decisions. The knock-on effect is that everyone becomes confident and comfortable when making the right calls, which then creates a greater sense of connection between the differing personalities within the group – even those individuals that might ordinarily feel more secure when being told what to do and when to do it.

The power of lived behaviours, ownership and self-governance came into play during the build-up to the 2022 Women's European Championship semi-final against Sweden. At that time the England women's football team had a tricky decision to make. With only ten days and two matches standing between the Lionesses and tournament glory, the number of Covid cases across the UK was soaring. The virus had even infiltrated the England women's football team camp, despite there being a series of strict health measures in place, and a couple of weeks earlier Sarina Wiegman was taken ill and had to sit out the group match against the Republic of Ireland. But the squad's emotional well-being was an important consideration too. The Lionesses had been locked down in a tournament bubble for several weeks, with limited opportunities to see their loved ones. To maintain social connection and psychological recovery, a friends and family day had been arranged, but given the circumstances, this event began to feel increasingly risky to the mission of the team.

Shortly before the planned event, I sat outside on a picnic bench with Ritan Mehta, our team doctor, and Anja van Ginhoven, our general manager. Within this contained group we discussed the concerns we were having. The three of us felt that by opening our camp to the outside world, we were taking a risk with the squad's health and our tournament dreams. From across the courtyard, Sarina had spotted us talking.

'What's going on?' she said, walking over.

Wanting to open up the discussion, I repeated our concerns. While a little social connection with the outside world would have a beneficial impact on the England staff and players, inviting friends and family into our environment felt like a risk with the rise in Covid cases across the country, especially when maintaining the health of the team on the eve of a semi-final, and quite possibly a final. Sarina listened to what we had to say and was clear about a course of action. But she then set an important condition.

'I think we should cancel the friends and family day,' she said. 'But the players must agree to it. We can't just tell them what to do.'

I understood her reasoning. We were asking the squad to first take ownership of the situation, and then self-govern in such a way that they stuck to their observable winning behaviours. Not wanting to waste time, Sarina immediately called everybody together for a meeting. The sun had just gone down as the group assembled on the grass outside our hotel, and I looked at the time. It was 9 p.m. and some of the players had clearly been asleep. Sarina immediately explained our predicament, and then reiterated our mission and the team's three categories of winning behaviours, as defined by the squad. *Team first. Be in the moment. No regrets.* Finally, she outlined the decision facing everyone.

'We have a real opportunity to win this thing,' she said. 'But only if we make the right choices for us as a team. What do you want to do?'

The group decision was unanimous, and unsurprising. *Let's cancel it.*

With hindsight, this had been a simple choice to make because everyone in the squad clearly understood their *why*. Ever since our early training camps in which a north star, mission(s) and a series of non-negotiable, winning behaviours had been defined, these three categories had been repeated over and over. *Team first. Be in the moment. No regrets.* Every decision was viewed through their prism. They informed every action, on and off the pitch. And if anyone was in doubt as to whether their responses were appropriate or not, they only had to consider the team's winning behaviours to understand why cancelling the event was the correct choice. Some of the players and staff hadn't seen their parents, partners or kids for weeks, and while the separation was emotionally challenging for some, the Lionesses' success to date gave them three very good reasons for sticking to their guns:

1. Cancelling the friends and family day meant that every individual had placed the interests of the team first.
2. By evaluating the circumstances and considering the new information in relation to the task at hand, the squad focused on the present. Their choice then set a clear direction of travel.
3. By not seeing their loved ones for a little while longer, they could look back at their efforts at the end of the tournament, knowing they'd done everything possible to win.

The team were so driven towards their dreams that, thinking about it today, I'd have been shocked had they decided to press ahead with the friends and family day. They were winners, fiercely determined and committed to living by their principles, although had they surprised us and opted to risk mingling with people outside of our immediate bubble, their decision would have been respected. Sarina felt the same way: she also trusted them to make the right call, but rather than telling the group what to do and how to behave, she recognised the power of them arriving at the decision for themselves.

THE WINNING BEHAVIOURS PLAYBOOK

To ensure your winning behaviours are both actionable and 'sticky', consider the following tactics:

MAKE WINNING BEHAVIOURS PART OF THE EVERYDAY LANGUAGE

Write down your winning behaviours and stick them everywhere. Put them in your work bag. Fix them to your car dashboard. Have a list on your phone, so you can always refer to them. *Allow them to inform your every decision.* While working with Harlequins rugby team, two huge posters were placed either side of the wall where the coaches and players addressed the team during our performance meetings. One poster featured a list of the team's priorities – performance, excellence, respect and commitment. On the other was a list describing Harlequins' style of play – their tempo, unpredictability, ruthlessness and enjoyment. Whenever the players and coaches planned their tactics with the squad, or reviewed the latest match or training session, these two posters were constantly referred to. By pointing to them, incorporating them into game planning and reviewing the team against them, the importance of these concepts was reinforced and brought to life whenever the players were working together. You can apply this same tactic to your winning behaviours.

It's vital your chosen actions are regularly dropped into conversation as a reminder of the group's overall targets. Make them a part of the everyday language. Use them to inspire and to hold people accountable for the things they've agreed to do (such as, for example, Sarina referring to the Lionesses' winning behaviours just before the planned friends and family day). This idea becomes particularly powerful once a group has become familiar with *who they are*, as laid out in Building Block #1, especially if someone is unable, or unwilling, to live up to the standards set by the group. If that individual and their values are known to the people around them, it becomes much easier to understand *why* they're struggling to execute their agreed winning behaviours. From there, it's possible to come to a compromise on what do next.

This is important because people are more likely to approach situations with empathy when those involved have established a connection and understand one another. For example, with awareness of self and others, it's possible to say, 'We agreed on a series of winning behaviours. But you're not doing them . . . *Is everything OK?*' But when these discussions are made without any knowledge of the values of the individuals concerned, or when connections between the two are weak or have become fractured, this language can become accusatory and confrontational. Assumptions are more likely to be thrown around and, as a result, frustration and resentment kick in on both sides, which is a million miles away from the optimal result – unity and progress. The takeaway: a little knowledge and human connection can go a long way when aligning people to their winning behaviours.

ACCOUNTABILITY IS EVERYTHING

We've briefly touched on the importance of ownership and accountability, and how taking responsibility for falling short and/or letting teammates down can drive a person on. But sometimes the results of our actions are tricky to quantify, and, as a result, it can be hard for the important but difficult conversations to take place – the type that can shock an individual into changing their ways. From my experience, however, asking an individual or group about the changes *they* can make to hold themselves, and each other, accountable often results in some ingenious and effective strategies.

A good example of this took place during my time with the Cambridge Women's rowing team. The rowers came up with the idea of a marble jar, so two jars were placed on a table in the meeting room. An Oxford ribbon was tied around one, a Cambridge ribbon around the other. Each of the rowers was given a Cambridge-coloured marble, and at the end of every training session they put their marble in the jar of the team they felt they'd contributed to most that day. Had they not given it their all, or if they'd experienced a bad day at the office, their marble would go into the Oxford jar. Had they been on point and lived up to the winning behaviours set by the group, their marble went into the Cambridge jar. There was no hiding place, and it forced people to reflect honestly and accept responsibility for taking positive action.

This routine was particularly powerful in the early stages of the season when the selection process – known as 'trialling' – took place, a brutal time on the calendar. There were only eight seats in the boat, in addition to the cox, but at the beginning of trialling a much larger squad was involved. Through a series of performance-related events, the squad numbers were cut and cut, and then cut again, until two teams of eight remained: the first crew (the Blue boat) and the reserve crew (Blondie), both nicknames originating from the colour of shirts worn by each team.

Everyone in the group was in direct competition with one another; each rower wanted a seat in the Blue boat. But for the greater good, all the rowers needed to put their emotions to one side and action the agreed winning behaviours so that Cambridge's overall aims could be achieved. They knew that if they individually lived their winning behaviours, they would enhance the performance of themselves and the team. Consequently, they aligned to their *team first* ethos and worked hard to create an environment that was open, honest, positive and motivational. Everyone actioned the agreed winning behaviours so that Cambridge's overall aims could be achieved. For example:

- Be prepared to give and receive constructive feedback.
- Group practice is non-negotiable unless an academic commitment or a family crisis excuses you and is agreed in advance by the coaching team.
- Mentally and physically prepare for every session – meet with the coxes (the member of the boat who steers the boat and co-ordinates the team) pre-training, agree focus for the session and travel in crews.
- The whole team must engage in planning and review sessions for races, and implement any agreed changes.

This clarity delivered a structure for them to follow, and a logical focus of attention even when the going got tough. It wouldn't have helped anyone had a simmering sense of bitterness crept into any of the Blondie rowers or if the Blues had become fuelled by a sense of superiority. For starters, if a rower was thinking about the performance of their nearest rival, they were unlikely to be 100 per cent focused on their own, nor were they going to be relentless in bringing a race-day intensity to training. Both these outcomes would only be beneficial to the opposition. Instead, the Blondie and the Blue boat rowers had to accept that they needed one another to succeed. This approach was emulated by the behaviour of the coaches – Rob Baker and Patrick Ryan – who worked tirelessly together to ensure all the rowers were motivated, supported and appropriately challenged.

Set against that backdrop, those two jars of marbles worked to send a very clear message to the group. They reminded everyone of who the real rival was. *By battling against each other, we're helping Oxford. By working together and pushing each other's standards, we help ourselves.* This shift in mindset was very important. While the Cambridge squad were competing against one another during the trialling phases, they were still able to stick to their winning behaviours and pull together in the same direction.

VALUING OTHERS

One final note: it's particularly important that winning behaviours are actioned by *every* working person within a group, regardless of their role or perceived importance. As mentioned, a sports team generally features a line-up of starters – those individuals selected to begin the match, or race. But there's also a team of reserves in the background – athletes with the skill sets to step in, should they be required to do so for one reason or another. Elsewhere, players on the fringes of selection are vital in training when running small-sided games or set-piece drills. It's common knowledge that a squad of exceptional people is needed to win a tournament, and every one of them has a vital role to play, not only those that line up on the day.

But sitting on the sidelines can be a lonely and frustrating experience, so it's important that everyone feels psychologically supported, especially if they're being asked to live by winning behaviours that might feel challenging. That way they can perform to the best of their abilities if called upon. The same applies for any team effort, whether that be in industry, community work or the creative arts. Yes, there's no doubt that on a film set the director and their actors are the headline figures in play. But without a camera crew, special-effects designers and catering team the production will fall apart. It's vital that these people, while not in the glare of the spotlight, are as in tune with the collective's winning behaviours as everyone else, because when a group of different personalities feels psychologically connected and safe, performance levels soar.

Within this context, meaningful gestures are everything. Business manuals are packed with information on why it's important that company leaders engage with their staff at every level, from the cleaners to the CEOs. The thinking behind this is clear: when everyone feels as if they're being seen and valued, regardless of their role, they pull together and become more determined to succeed. Sadly, too many collectives overlook this reality. They fail to mention obvious but potentially energising facts, such as the positive impact a person has made in their role or the appreciated efforts of a team during a recent project. These people then feel ignored, unvalued and demotivated. As a result, they become less inclined to stick to their winning behaviours. But really, it takes only one sentence to motivate a person:

I value you because . . .

I noticed the power of this first-hand during the 2022 European Championship when the Lionesses invited the entire non-playing group to a meeting towards the end of the tournament. Led by Jill Scott, every member of the 23-woman squad stood up, one by one, and called for a member of the support team. They then presented them with their shirt and explained why their hard work was so important. This was an incredibly powerful gesture. It created an environment in which everyone working within the non-playing staff felt valued. It also left them feeling even more determined to work to the best of their ability and to stick to their winning behaviours. In the intense environment of a major tournament, this delivered a psychological boost.

 ASK THE QUESTION

Do you, or the team you're working in, have ownership and self-governance over a series of winning behaviours?

Look to bring both into your daily practices.

LIGHTBULBS

- Winning behaviours will act as a framework in which you can make decisions quickly, even when under pressure. They should become a part of your everyday language.
- To be successful, winning behaviours must be lived – no excuses. Making them observable means there's no hiding place for those people not wanting to commit.
- A group or individual with ownership over their winning behaviours is more likely to stick by them. A group or individual that self-governs is more likely to respond positively when faced with challenging decisions.
- Remember to ensure that everyone in your group feels valued. Bring junior or less experienced members of the team into important meetings and encourage everyone to pull in the same direction during moments of high pressure.

CHAPTER TEN

TELLING STORIES

When aligned to a set of winning behaviours, a group can be guided to success by one well-defined north star and a clearly outlined mission. But even the most focused of collectives is vulnerable to distraction, especially when pitted against the day-to-day stressors of life.

Interestingly, I've often found that when the going gets tough, many people become less likely to ask for help. Instead, they tend to work harder than necessary, or silo themselves away. They grind through a difficult or stressful period alone and become lost in the problem-solving process. During these moments they barely have the time or capacity to step back, look up and remember why they got into the thing they were doing in the first place. To extend our north star analogy, it's like a heavy fog has drifted in, temporarily masking the night sky, and with it all the navigational reference points mapping the way forward. But this disappearance might only be temporary. Our north star is still up there, *somewhere*, and in confusing moments like these it can be useful to lean into an alternative form of guidance, in much the same way that a ship's captain will use GPS when sailing through a heavy storm.

An influential or powerful narrative – *a cracking story* – can be considered such a navigational device, especially a relatable case study that shows us it's still possible to thrive and rediscover our purpose even when the odds seem insurmountable. I'm not talking about a fairy tale or some fictitious adventure. Instead, I'm referring to those hard-lived narratives where the core message is of finding a way forward in tough or unusual circumstances. These sorts of stories can help people see their world through a different lens, find inspiration in moments when their creative juices might have run dry or connect with people who share a similar sense of purpose. (We also take huge comfort in knowing that we're not alone, that the highs and lows and moments of self-doubt are a common part of the tapestry of life.) Delivery is everything too. It's one thing for a psychologist like me to remind a group of players that it's possible to upset the odds or to build an unbreakable team spirit. But if that same message is conveyed by the protagonist of the story, everything becomes much more tangible. It's one of the reasons why guest speakers are in demand at corporate events.

The reason for using this technique is simple: for centuries humans have shared stories. The act of communication has often helped disparate groups to connect. Through storytelling we learn valuable lessons, share groundbreaking ideas and formulate opinions. Similarly, a good story can help a collective to align themselves with a cause or shared theory. I've found this to be particularly useful when preparing a team for high-intensity moments such as an overseas tournament, or a potentially life-changing test like an Olympic Games. Faced with such a challenge, I've connected the individuals involved to stories that say, '*Yes, you can*,' so that they're able to find inspiration, with the evidence that anything is possible, and then push past any barriers. Psychologist Albert Bandura has termed this process as *vicarious learning* – the idea that the attainments of others, when modelled by ourselves, can influence our beliefs in what we can achieve.

An oft-told example of this theory in action is Roger Bannister and his famous sub-four-minute mile. Up until May 1954 the idea that an athlete could run a mile in less than four minutes seemed impossible. But the barrier to breaking this mark turned out to be as much psychological as physical, and when Bannister eventually achieved the feat in Oxford by clocking a time of 3 minutes 59.4 seconds, his effort showed the world what was humanly possible. Athletes had been failing to crack the four-minute barrier since serious efforts to do so started in 1886, but once Bannister had achieved the unthinkable and his story was told around the world, the general consensus of *it can't be done* turned into one of *yes, it can*. Less than two months later an Australian runner called John Landy bettered the time, and since then well over 1,700 athletes have run the distance in less than four minutes.

Many theories have been floated as to why it took so many talented runners, including Bannister, so long to crack the landmark time. One argument suggests that, had it not been for the Second World War, any number of elite athletes might have progressed to such an extent that the four-minute target would have been broken much sooner, though that doesn't account for the fact that runners had been trying, and failing, for 70-odd years. My feeling is that the news of Bannister's record-breaking time allowed a generation of athletes to believe that they could do it too. Having been shown that a sub-four-minute mile was possible and not some flight of fancy, a slew of runners and coaches were then freed from self-doubt. That, in turn, pushed them towards greater successes.

I experienced the power of storytelling first-hand in December 2021, shortly after starting work at the FA. The women's technical division organised an away day at Warwick Castle so that the support staff could spend some time together and formulate a foundation of working practices ahead of the European Championship the following year. Leading one of the sessions was the renowned women's football historian Professor Jean Williams, who detailed the history of the women's game. She was joined by players from the unofficial Women's World Cup in 1971, including Leah Caleb (who was compared to George Best by the British media at the time) and the midfielder Chris Lockwood, as well as ex-players from the official Lionesses team – Kerry Davis (previously the Lionesses' top goal scorer) and Carol Thomas (the first woman to win fifty caps for England). Together they talked us through the sport's backstory while recounting the challenges faced by previous generations of female footballers. It still stands as one of the most thought-provoking and powerful presentations I've ever experienced.

Through the talks we learned about a lost generation of footballers – a group of brilliant players who had been denied the honour of representing their country because the FA banned women from playing football at professional grounds in the early 20th century. These restrictions on the women's game lasted for around 50 years but were lifted in 1971, the same year that a representative football team from England played in front of a record 90,000 crowd at the Azteca Stadium in an unofficial Women's World Cup in Mexico. Although only six sides competed that year – England and the hosts, plus France, Argentina, Denmark and Italy – the tournament hype was still huge, and the 14-strong English squad were mobbed wherever they went. There were even police escorts and autograph hunters. We heard about how the team were forced to play in men's kits and boots – there was no other equipment available in those days – and how the FA's refusal to endorse the tournament created a lasting stigma for the women involved. Some of them kept their experiences a secret, even from their own families. Instead of celebrating what was a wonderful experience, these young women experienced a sense of guilt.

'We felt like we were on the naughty step,' said one squad member afterwards.

This group would go on to earn the nickname 'the Lost Lionesses'.

I found our history lesson incredibly moving and was mesmerised by the stories,* probably because prior to joining with the England women's football team set-up I hadn't cut my teeth in a traditional footballing background. Yes, I'd followed the teams in World Cups and European Championships. Like most people I'd watched the big games in the pub or at home, and I knew about the legacy of the nation's better teams: the great goals and the big wins, the missed penalties and the heartbreak. But I understood embarrassingly little about the history of the women's game. The pioneers we'd had the privilege of meeting – and the many more we learned about that day – were unfamiliar to me, as were the hardships they'd endured. *Generations of women had to fight for the right to play the game they loved.* Some of the players in Mexico had only been 13 years old at the time of the unofficial Women's World Cup, an age my daughter was rapidly approaching at the time. I wondered how she might have coped playing in a foreign environment without the support afforded to most travelling athletes today, like round-the-clock professional care.

As soon as the presentation was over, I turned to Kay Cossington, our technical director. 'The players have got to hear these stories,' I said.

---

* I could have listened to their stories all night, and in actual fact I very nearly did. On the way back into the hotel, our team manager Will and I bumped into Leah and Chris and spoke with them until 2 a.m., as they relived their past experiences and patiently answered the hundreds of questions we threw their way.

My hope was that the modern-day Lionesses might experience a range of emotions like the ones I'd felt at Warwick Castle that day – pride and anger, awe and sadness. That's because when we hear an inspirational or powerful story, we're often able to compare the narrator's experiences to our own. We put ourselves in their position and imagine our responses. We see their struggles, achievements and actions, and picture a way forward for ourselves, in much the same way that a runner in 1955 would have judged their likelihood of breaking the four-minute mile in the wake of Roger Bannister's successful time.

By hearing the experiences of the Lost Lionesses, I suspected the modern England women's football team would become glued more tightly to their north star, precisely because previous generations of women had been denied the opportunity to unite the nation. In fact, some of Sarina's players had also fought hard to play football as kids and pushed past a lot of resistance when doing so, having grown up in a world where becoming a professional football player seemed far beyond their wildest dreams. Their mission to perform to the best of their ability under the greatest pressure in the forthcoming Women's European Championship, would also seem more achievable – because the Lost Lionesses had attempted something similar in Mexico. And the consequences for failing to meet the group's expected winning behaviours would be felt more acutely – because of the sacrifices made by so many players before them.

This hunch was proved right a few weeks later when Kerry Davis and some of the Lost Lionesses came to visit the senior squad at one of our training camps. When Leah and Chris were joined by their teammate Gill Sayell and told the squad of their unofficial Women's World Cup experiences, the atmosphere in the room shifted, just as it did when Kerry Davis spoke about her 16 year international career with such honesty and humility. The players were as moved by the stories as we'd been, and they asked questions and swapped stories of their own.

Then I heard one of the players whispering to the person in the next chair. 'Bloody hell, we've got no right to complain about anything... *Ever*,' she said.

We decided to maximise the mood by dividing the squad into small groups of five or six so that they could reflect upon what the stories had meant to them personally and as a team. I wanted the Lionesses of 2022 to process the experiences of their predecessors and to analyse how they might inform their behaviours going forward. The players were able to appreciate the sacrifices of the past, which helped them to put their future challenges into perspective. The group then decided that nothing should be taken for granted – on or off the pitch.

'We have to celebrate our successes,' said Jill Scott in the debrief meeting afterwards.

As hoped, the Lionesses had unified even more tightly around a mindset that would later drive them towards European success. And all because of the power of an inspiring story.

FIND YOUR STORYTELLER

Bringing an influential storyteller into your group environment can be a powerful experience, no matter what endeavour you happen to be involved with. *But it must be the right person.* A character of importance or notable achievement might initially seem like the ideal narrator to inspire a team (or yourself), but if their experiences aren't chiming with the circumstances ahead of you, the procedure can often fall flat. It might be that you've introduced your inexperienced netball team to a famous athlete ahead of a do-or-die match. But if the speaker's career took place in an individual sport and their story focuses on the joys of personal endeavour, the chances are it won't amount to much.

The connection will probably not be there. Yes, success stories can be inspiring, as are tales about navigating challenge, but only if they're relatable. A better idea would be to invite a former champion in a team sport, one who can speak about the power of unity when striving for first-time success.

In the world outside sport there are plenty of examples to choose from too. In business, a suitable pioneer in your field could deliver a speech that galvanises the team around a new concept or working practice. During an altruistic endeavour, a beneficiary of the charity you're working for might arrive to express their gratitude for your team's efforts. In these situations, the right story from the right voice can teach, motivate and empower. It doesn't have to be someone who's directly related to your context either. A scientist can teach an art class about creativity. A soldier can teach financial advisors about resilience-building. A computer hacker can teach a police unit about case-cracking. Abstract ideas encourage us all to think differently, especially if the accompanying anecdotes are memorable and thought-provoking. The Lost Lionesses and England Legends were a case in point. Although they were from a completely different era, playing under entirely different circumstances, they had a lot to teach the modern footballer about fighting for the right to play and overcoming resistance in a male-dominated environment.

Circumstances change, so it's important that we change the stories we cling to for motivation. It's for this reason that I invited the Olympic diver Tom Daley into the Lionesses camp following their successful European Championship campaign in 2022. At that time they had achieved their aims of uniting the game and inspiring the nation, and some of them might have been wondering, *What next*? It was important we re-evaluated our mission and adjusted our expected behaviours, given we would be competing thousands of miles from home during the next World Cup in Australia and New Zealand.

Tom was the perfect person to speak. He'd travelled around the world to dive in numerous Olympic and international events, and he'd also experienced the highs of winning a medal during the London 2012 Olympics, a success that left him drifting. In the aftermath he felt overwhelmed. The spotlight trained on him had become inescapable and he felt under tremendous pressure to repeat his performances. His outlook only improved once he'd aligned himself to a sense of purpose beyond simply winning, and he changed his missions and expected behaviours accordingly. Through storytelling, I wanted to emphasise to the Lionesses the emotional importance of this process.

Simply absorbing a handful of anecdotes told from a unique or interesting perspective, however, isn't enough. Following on from a storytelling event, it's important to maximise the moment by reflecting upon the experience and for the listening individuals to share something of themselves, such as which facts or opinions resonated with them most powerfully – and to explain why. This process often works best when a team is divided into smaller discussion groups, as that way everyone's opinion can be heard. In larger gatherings, people can be drowned out and conversations are generally superficial. Sure, there will be a certain amount of task-related dialogue, plus some light-hearted banter, but when dozens of people are involved, how often do discussions really focus on what matters most? By talking through the emotional responses to a powerful moment of learning, a small group can immediately connect, and maximise any new lightbulb moments. People are more likely to become vulnerable in front of others as they're more comfortable when opening themselves up to a smaller audience. As a result, the group finds new ways to learn about one another.

Storytelling doesn't just come into play when encouraging a team or an individual to follow their north star, mission or expected behaviours. It can also be used to create cues or reminders, because powerful narratives are much stickier than a series of slogans, especially if they've been expressed in an imaginative way. I've known teams to write songs that underline their core values; before matches, the All Blacks rugby team performs the *haka*, a war dance that reminds those involved of their team's power, unity and pride. When the Great Britain women's hockey team were preparing for the 2016 Olympic Games, they invited an artist to create a painting that defined their mission – *we are one team; we are winners; be alive*. And in advance of Euro 2022, Jill Scott wrote a poem inspired by the team's winning mentality.

To amplify this message even further, we later made a short film in which Jill read her poem over a highlights reel of goals, key moments and training footage. Her words were reprinted in a team manual so that the players could have them to hand whenever their north star, mission and winning behaviours needed to be referenced. Most importantly, the poem reinforced the very real idea that the Lionesses were connected and fighting for a shared cause that was much bigger than themselves. As I learned during this process, there are no real rules when using storytelling to strengthen a group's mindset. Poems, paintings, inspirational videos: your idea could be something completely different. The medium doesn't matter. The important thing is that the narrative is sticky and unforgettable. Because if done correctly it will guide you from Point A to Point B, even when the clouds roll in.

ASK THE QUESTION

What stories do you, and your team, need to hear?

If you're seeking creative inspiration, find a speaker who can articulate their work and process. If you're looking to build team morale, bring in an expedition leader to talk about connecting individuals to a shared cause. You don't have to invite a person to meet with you either – books, films and podcasts can prove equally inspirational.

 LIGHTBULBS

- Stories make for powerful navigational devices in moments of chaos or extreme pressure. This is especially so when the narrative tells us it's possible to succeed when the odds are heavily stacked against us.
- Storytelling can help a team to connect around a common cause or shared theory. Through it we can learn valuable lessons, share inspirational insights and formulate ideas.
- When inviting an influential storyteller to communicate with your group, make sure to pick the right person. Success stories are powerful motivators, but only if they're relatable.
- Having listened to a storyteller, reflect upon the anecdotes being told, and share your thoughts and feelings afterwards in a small group. This will help to maximise the teachable moments and connect.

BUILDING BLOCK #3

HOW DO WE PLAY?

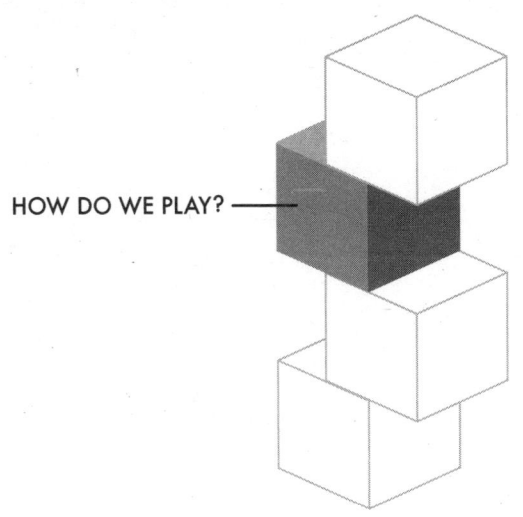

HOW DO WE PLAY?

INTRODUCTION

Having worked through Building Blocks #1 and #2, you'll have a clear idea of your *who* and *why*. You'll know what your mission is, you'll understand the strengths and super-strengths of the people alongside you, and your route towards a successful outcome will have been mapped out through a list of winning behaviours. The next step is to bring these details together in a constructive and coherent game plan – a strategy for reaching your target with a clearly defined method of play.* Throughout my career I've worked with all sorts of teams and athletes, and I've come to an understanding of what it takes to achieve this clarity. In this case, it's a five-step process that, when taken proactively, can build performance levels within a team while giving its component parts, or team members, the confidence to operate under pressure.

STEP 1: GAME-PLAN DEVELOPMENT

In sport, every coach has an idea of how their team or athletes should perform. This will be based on several factors: their

---

* The word 'play' in this section works as a catch-all term: it could refer to many different contexts, such as business, personal projects and fitness goals. Feel free to interpret it as you see fit.

management philosophy; their technical and tactical prowess; the way in which the sport is being played at home and abroad; the strengths and limitations of the players involved; the overall experience of the team or individuals. Using this information, a clear game plan can be developed so that the people involved will know exactly what to do – and when.

STEP 2: GAME-PLAN TRAINING

Every member of the team – playing and non-playing – must commit to the game plan before aligning their work to it through training, preparation and analysis. This aspect of the process should connect the players to the game plan physically, mentally, technically and tactically.

STEP 3: GAME-PLAN SUPPORT

An organisational structure must be created so that players and support staff can prepare for the game plan in both the short-term (day to day) and long-term (week to week; month to month). All aspects of training, analysis and the environment are co-ordinated so that players can perform at their best in key moments.

STEP 4: GAME-PLAN EXECUTION

In order to execute the game plan it must be broken down into key areas of focus and accompanying strategies. An analysis of self (*what we're doing*) and the opposition (*what they're doing*) takes place and adjustments are carried out if necessary. Processes that give the team – and the individuals within it – clarity about what to focus upon 'in-play' are identified, trained and delivered. Meanwhile, the overall game plan can be tweaked in accordance with any issues that might have arisen, such as playing conditions, injuries or suspensions to team players.

STEP 5: GAME-PLAN REVIEW

After a fixture or competition it's important that the performance is analysed thoroughly and effectively. New intelligence will then inform future communication, training and game planning so that the group's strengths are built upon and any weaknesses addressed. All necessary adjustments should be put into practice immediately. The motto here is: *plan, do, review.*

*

The goal in any team or individual sport is to have absolute clarity about these processes while building the confidence to execute the best game plan under the greatest pressure. That's because during any extremely tense event, such as an Olympic final, a person's emotions can override their logical thought. In these moments the outcome becomes a distraction – or noise, as I like to call it – and the individual generally reacts in one of three ways: they fight, take flight or freeze. It's one of the reasons why footballers sometimes miss penalties in cup finals, but also why first-time homebuyers chop and change their minds over perfectly suitable opportunities and theatre actors forget their lines onstage. The only way to control these moments of high stress is to go to a place of logic. And the only way to locate a place of logic when the brain is flapping and the adrenaline levels are soaring is to live in accordance with the team's sense of *how.*

Regardless of your situation, working through the five steps in Building Block #3 will give you the resources to get there.

CHAPTER ELEVEN

GAME-PLAN DEVELOPMENT: DEFINING YOUR HOW

During the build-up to the 2022 Women's European Championship, the Lionesses figured out their north star. Through timelines, team activities and group discussions they connected with their teammates, all while building a picture of what success might look like for England. Then, in a team meeting that took place during the final international window before the tournament began, one of the players made a breakthrough point: 'We all *want* to win the Euros,' she said. 'And we all believe that we *can* win the Euros. But all we really need to focus on is *how*, because essentially that's the thing that's going to get us over the line and make the difference.'

Behind the scenes, Sarina and her technical team had arrived at the same conclusion and were working on a game plan that every player could get behind. The head coach had spent her entire career building a deep knowledge of football, which meant she understood where the game was tactically, and where it was likely heading. These insights were supported by a mass of data. She'd also spent a great deal of time studying the individuals who were available to her, so she understood the team's strengths and areas of development. There was a recognition of where the

Lionesses had been successful in the past, how they could be successful going forward, and the issues that generally impacted them when things didn't go to plan. With all this information to hand, Sarina became laser-focused on the team's *how* and alongside her assistant coach Arjan Veurink she formulated a game plan that brought together team strategy, principles of play and game tactics. Under her guidance, England followed one of the great rules of sporting success: process is king.

While I can't tell you what those team strategies, principles of play and game tactics were, I *can* reveal this: every great team will have a game plan in place, a definition of how to play, which, when applied consistently, will drive decision-making while increasing the group's chances of becoming habitually and sustainably successful.* The trick to making a game plan work is by aligning it to the *who* of a group (their beliefs, values, superstrengths and so on) and the *why* (their north star, mission and winning behaviours). In doing so, every tactical decision will chime with the collective's identity and belief systems. In other words, the people involved will understand the reasons behind every decision. For example, let's say the owners and staff of a popular café have a well-defined set of beliefs and values, plus a clear north star and mission:

---

* The game plan of every team is unique, just as the people within it and their higher purpose will be unique too. Consequently, the principles that guide a game plan in one context might be destined to fail in others. The game plan of a nationwide bookshop chain will be very different to that of a local independent bookshop, for example. I can't define your game plan for you. If you're running your own business or leading a team, make sure you have a clear strategy for reaching your target. If you're working within a large group, become familiar with your team's processes. If the game plan is unclear in either context, then this is the time to devise one for yourself by marrying a strategy to your *who* and *why*.

- The café's *who* is based on altruistic and environmentally aware values, community spirit and hard work.
- The café's *why* is to provide a highly rated and welcoming establishment that makes coffee with a conscience while supporting and connecting local people.

With these two building blocks established, it makes sense that the café's *how* would be to support fair trade, prioritise customer service, and set a visible example of diversity and inclusion in the local community, all while making a profit. The owner can then create a suitable game plan for the working day:

- Every item sold in the shop must be eco-friendly and sustainable. Customers should be rewarded for environmentally aware actions, such as bringing along a multi-use cup.
- At no point should customers wait longer than five minutes before being acknowledged. In busy moments, be quick, efficient and polite.
- Throughout the day, staff will maintain a friendly rapport with all the customers. It's important that they know their regulars by name and everyone is made to feel welcome.
- The café should encourage a community vibe by involving itself in local events, partnering with other ecologically friendly businesses, and supporting local artists, charities and social groups.

By setting out this game plan, everyone working in the café will know what to prioritise. As a result, the business should operate like a well-oiled machine, with everybody working to the best of their ability, even when under pressure.

The development of a clearly defined game plan proved to be a key moment for the Lionesses. Through Sarina's work, and with the help of her support staff, the squad were able to grasp the outlined tactics, and they trained and prepared accordingly. This was important because the players were about to compete as the home nation in front of crowd attendances as big as 87,000, as well as millions of fans watching on TV. At times the hype and media attention on them was immense, but when wandering around the training camp it rarely felt as if anyone was feeling the strain. The players were relaxed, and they laughed and joked with one another and played games. They weren't focused on what the media might have been saying, or taking in the opinions of a Twitter troll. They only had to focus on sticking to Sarina's *how* – everything else was just noise.

When done well, a game plan brings clarity to a pressurised event such as a European Championship, a high-stakes financial trade or a dangerous military operation. That's because the individuals involved possess a clarity about what to do and when, which creates a certain level of calm. (Remember: *in stressful moments the emotional part of the brain can override the logical part*.) However, a poorly thought-out game plan will have the opposite effect. All too often, teams are driven by *hows* that feel vague or ambiguous to the people charged with working to them. Or worse, they're so complex that everyone feels lost when trying to understand the many nuances in play. This is particularly the case in large groups, where different personalities can push and pull on one another. A team without clarity regarding their game plan will struggle to make the right decisions at the right times. In key moments they'll move in different directions, when an almost telepathic unity needs to be in place. And because of confusion and frustration, flashpoints can occur. Every successful team, whether it's competing on the playing field or in the stock market, requires clarity of thought to succeed.

As with everything, putting theory into practice is much easier said than done and I've worked in a few settings where the complexity of a game plan hasn't been fully understood. This was apparent, for example, at the beginning of the Covid-19 pandemic in 2020, just as everything was set to pause during a series of lockdowns. At the time I'd been working with the England Women's national union rugby team – AKA, the Red Roses – for about a year. Together we'd moved through the first two building blocks and gained an understanding of *who* we were and *why* we were there. The players knew what it meant to be a Red Rose and what success looked like. But sitting in on their discussions, there was a sense that for certain players something was missing, especially when it came to distilling the team's game plan.

Meetings that focused on the Red Roses' principles of play, and the individuals' roles within them, were extremely detailed and thorough. There seemed to be lots of moving parts, but I was unsure of how they all fitted together. Disclaimer: I certainly wasn't the rugby expert in the room, but some of those that were, the less experienced players perhaps, appeared unclear about what was expected of them within the complexities of training and match play. I put this assessment to Simon 'Midds' Middleton,* the head coach, and asked him if he believed that his full squad knew their processes. His answer was a solid 'Yes'. Then, when I pushed back on his response by saying that I thought some of them were

---

* Midds is a fantastic leader and was England head coach between 2015 and 2023. By the time he stepped down in 2023 the Red Roses were drawing record crowds of over 50,000, which had much to do with his approach to the game, and the phenomenal talent and work ethic of his players and support staff. Midds's record was impressive too. He led the Red Roses to the 2021 Six Nations title and three Six Nations Grand Slams (2017, 2019 and 2020). He also guided Team GB's women's sevens team to fourth spot in the Rio Olympics in 2016. In 2021 he was given an MBE for his work in the sport. He cared deeply about his players and was open to challenge, which was one of the many reasons I enjoyed working with him. I always found that he was prepared to look at scenarios from a different angle and think creatively if ever tactics needed to change course.

unclear, he suggested we ask the group, but only when the time was right. Lockdown gave us that opportunity.

With the country at a standstill for several months, I knew that the Red Roses would likely have the time to reflect, review and plan. In addition to phoning around the squad and checking in on their mental well-being, while making sure that everyone felt connected and supported, I put a series of questions to each player during an hour-long call, including the following:

- How would you describe our style and principles of play?
- What are our strengths and super-strengths as a team?

The answers, when they returned, confirmed my fears. Generally, the leaders in the team understood the concepts of the Red Roses' strengths and super-strengths, but some of the others couldn't really distil what they were into a sentence or two. A handful also struggled to provide clarity about the team's principles of play, and not everyone was able to articulate the exact game plan Midds and his team had been trying to convey. (While the senior leaders in Midds's squad were able to articulate the playing philosophy clearly and succinctly, they thought that perhaps it could be simplified for those that didn't fully understand.) Finally, when rounding up, some of the squad mentioned that clear and objective feedback was important to them, and that they needed support when putting tangible goals and processes in place.

Midds was somewhat shocked by this new information and quickly set about rectifying the situation. Having considered everybody's feedback, he devised a way of clearly communicating the guiding principles of play to the squad – clear tactics they could lean into during matches, while ensuring that they still had the autonomy to make decisions for themselves. Midds produced an easy-to-follow presentation, in which his game plan was broken down in the following categories:

1. Principles of play
2. A definitive performance model
3. In-play alignment of winning behaviours

PRINCIPLES OF PLAY

According to Midds, rugby was a momentum game in which the result was generally determined by pressure: the amount that could be placed on the opposition versus the amount that could be absorbed when defending. His theory was that if a team was able to withstand the maximum amount of pressure in defence, while exerting their maximum in attack, they would more likely win the game than not. There was a caveat, however. 'Pressure is not about how much time you spend on the ball,' he explained. 'It's about how much time you spend on the ball in your opposition's territory, *and how you use it*.' The game plan, and its principles of play, were about *position*, not *possession*. They had to spend minimal time in their half, and maximum time in the opposition's.

A DEFINITIVE PERFORMANCE MODEL

To bring further clarity to the players' understanding, Midds created a visual aid designed to remove any doubt as to what was expected of them while working in certain areas of the pitch. The field of play was separated into four zones – red, amber, green and gold – and the players were given clear instructions on how to perform in each one.

HOW DO WE PLAY?

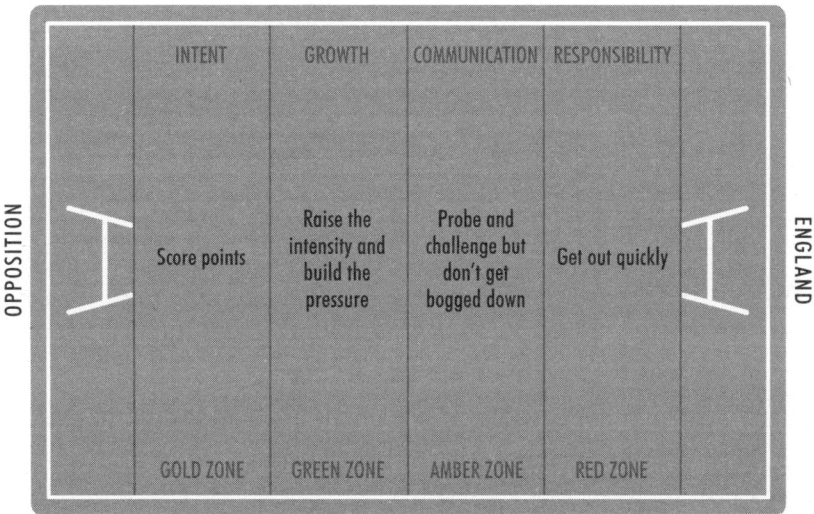

Source: Simon Middleton MBE, Red Roses head coach

This was an important development. When it comes to relaying ideas of this nature, the issue isn't the number of times a manager or leader delivers the game plan but that the message is received clearly. If the individuals involved don't all have clarity on the principles of play (and the markers of success that come with them), then it becomes impossible to make appropriate choices when under pressure. It's a real skill to take something complex and articulate it in a way that everyone understands, before building up the team's competence levels in that area, step by step. This provides a solid foundation for what I believe team sport psychology is all about: preparing players to develop clarity in the game plan, and the confidence to execute it under the greatest pressure. Team sport, like a business or family life, is a complex mix of targets, tactics and decision-making. Having a clear set of guiding principles that tells a person what to do – and when – is imperative, as it provides the foundation upon which a team of individuals can forge their own creativity.

Midds's definitive performance model did just that. He then succinctly explained the four zones and what was expected from the players in each, viewing everything through the lens of position versus possession. 'There's the Red Zone, which is nearest to our end,' he explained. 'Then there are the Amber and Green Zones, which both represent the middle of the pitch; and finally, there's the Gold Zone, the area nearest to the opposition's goal line. We want to spend the most amount of time in the Gold Zone – so we can score – and the least amount of time in the Red Zone – so we won't concede. Our whole game plan is built around exiting the Red Zone quickly, moving through the Green and Amber Zones to reach the Gold Zone.'

With these principles of play in mind, training was organised so that the players could deliver the game plan through each zone. Midds devised a series of succinct and simple performance cues, so that all the players knew exactly what was expected of them when moving up and down the pitch. Not only did these instructions give the players confidence in what they were doing, but they also created a high level of autonomy so that everyone could make decisions for themselves when performing under pressure. (Because there were multiple ways in which a team like the Red Roses could create chances or gain possession or position.) Within this framework, Midds's players were given licence to operate according to what was in front of them, but only if their decision-making matched the principles of the four playing zones:

- **Red Zone:** get out as quickly as possible by playing what's in front of you.
- **Amber Zone:** stay calm. Probe the opposition for weaknesses.

- **Green Zone:** build momentum; create chances.
- **Gold Zone:** score tries; win points.

Before long, the entire team was on the same page.

IN-PLAY ALIGNMENT OF WINNING BEHAVIOURS

As I mentioned earlier, I'd already spent some time working with the Red Roses on their *why* and *who,* and four key themes had emerged while defining their winning behaviours: intent, growth, communication and responsibility. To strengthen the definitive performance model even further, Midds took these themes and assigned one to each of the four key zones, as follows:

- **Red Zone:** the area of responsibility. A time for anchoring. The players must take responsibility and get away from their own goal line quickly and securely. *You can kick, you can do whatever you need to do, but you must get out – and fast.*
- **Amber Zone:** the area of communication. The players must move towards their opponent's half. In doing so they should probe the opposition for weaknesses. Effective communication is key here. *Look, challenge, but don't get bogged down.*
- **Green Zone:** the area of growth. Having moved closer to the opposition's goal line, it's important to increase the pressure by raising the intensity of play. *Work harder and faster – and be more aggressive.*
- **Gold Zone:** the area of intent. It's time to score. At this stage the players needed to compete at an incredibly high

> intensity. *Go for the jugular with tries, kicks, or through the scrum.*

Midds knew that if a team's winning behaviours were matched to their game plan, those behaviours would become even more tangible. As a result, the players were more likely to live them on and off the field, and grow stronger as a result.

It's my experience that when the pressure is on the rise, simplicity is crucial, especially if super-fast thinking is needed. With clarity and easy-to-understand processes, pressure is reduced, because everybody understands the game plan and what it is they're supposed to do. That's when people tend to work to the best of their ability, even if the unexpected takes place, because a sense of familiarity has been created (and it provides a basis from which to assess, reassess and make adaptions as required – we will explore this in more detail in Chapter 14).

In short: the best game plans are those that are easiest to understand.

MISTAKES ARE INEVITABLE

A game plan like the one devised by Midds ensures that the players involved have a healthy level of autonomy as they perform. They're not robots, plugged in to a mainframe of tactics and philosophies. They're decision-makers, attuned to the principles of play on the pitch, with the opportunity to act or react whenever they see fit. Within this model, mistakes are inevitable, and when they happen the individuals must be encouraged to learn and move on rather than be reprimanded. I know Sarina shares my opinions on this. As far as she's concerned, errors are a vital part of the game-plan development process and should be embraced because they encourage learning and inspire progress.

I clearly remember a pivotal moment shortly before the 2022 European Championship, when England played the Netherlands in a pre-tournament friendly. Netherlands were then the reigning European Champions, and during the build-up to the game Sarina and her staff devised a plan that incorporated a detailed analysis of the opposition's strengths and weaknesses, as well as their preferred patterns of play, key players and known strategies. But the game did not start well. The Lionesses were a goal down early in the game, the first time they had gone behind under Sarina. The players seemed constrained, even when Lucy Bronze equalised after 30 minutes. Sarina told them as much at half-time, saying that they seemed to be playing with fear. There was a weight on their shoulders, and she wanted them to shake it off.

'Don't be frightened to make mistakes,' she said. 'Actually, I don't give a shit if you make mistakes. Right now, we're playing not to lose. Let's play some football and go for the win.' Of course, she and Arjan – with support from their technical team, which featured Darren Ward, Geraint Twose and Thomas Murray – then provided the detail on *how*. This was one of only a handful of times I have ever heard Sarina swear, which probably made it even more impactful. But her approach worked. Confident that they wouldn't be reprimanded for getting it wrong, the team performed with a sense of freedom and ran out 5–1 winners. Afterwards the players spoke positively of how they'd been encouraged to play without fear and to express themselves on the pitch. The clarity with which Sarina delivered her game plan (and her approach to mistakes was very much part of that) released the pressure on the Lionesses. That then enabled them to play free-flowing football, which they later took into the tournament itself.

ASK THE QUESTION

Do you know your game plan?

If the answer is 'No', seek clarity on your processes and principles of play and figure out how they can best be put into action. If the answer is 'Yes', make sure everyone around you is as familiar with it as you are.

 LIGHTBULBS

- Most successful teams have a game plan in place. This comprises strategies and techniques that can guarantee a high level of success over a sustainable period.
- When figuring out your principles of play, look to your winning behaviours for ideas. If strong communication is something the group values highly, make that a part of your strategy.
- Mistakes are a vital part of the game-plan development process. They encourage learning and inspire progress.
- Clarity is vital. Too many teams and organisations lose their way because of poorly communicated strategies, or ideas. Clarity takes the pressure off. With it, everybody knows what to do, and when.

CHAPTER TWELVE

GAME-PLAN TRAINING: BRINGING THE BIG IDEA TO LIFE

With a game plan in place, a team, sporting or otherwise, will have clarity on what it is they're supposed to do. The next step is for the group to be trained in such a way that it can improve the technical, tactical, physical and psychological capabilities required to execute the plan, while proactively building confidence. That's because, in all walks of life, performance relies on so much more than pure skill. A brilliant doctor won't make a difference if they can't gain the trust of their patients. A brilliant stockbroker will never develop a successful portfolio if they can't make decisions under the greatest pressure. A brilliant teacher won't impact on their class if they can't control the troublemaker at the back of the room. A brilliant student won't pass their exams if they can't manage their anxiety. To perform effectively, a person needs a multitude of skills across multiple areas, which is why the technical, tactical, physical and psychological sides of training are so important. *They cover all the bases.*

For a football team such as the Lionesses, these might involve the squad working on passing drills (technical), transitional play (tactical), strength and fitness work (physical), and scenario-based training designed to replicate stress (psychological). In a non-sporting context such as the hospitality industry, a bar owner might train their staff to make a variety of cocktails (technical), share methods for handling customer overload (tactical), give staff the opportunity to rest and recover so that they're able to work long shifts into the early hours (physical), and provide techniques for dealing with troublesome customers (psychological). By working on the component parts of performance, the individuals involved can deliver on game day in a way that feels almost second-nature.

It can often be difficult to know how and what to train, especially in an environment that's fast-moving, unpredictable and prone to upheaval such as a sporting season or tournament, or within a company or organisation. A good way of getting round this problem is to first separate a game plan into its component parts, before setting goals in the areas that require improvement or focus. The team can then train against those goals. For example, when working with the Red Roses, Simon Middleton's game plan was built around the idea that his team could play at an incredibly high intensity, moving quickly from the Red Zone to the Gold. For this to work the players had to be supremely fit, and throughout the campaign Midds worked collaboratively with Alex Martin, the squad's strength and conditioning coach, to devise a schedule of day-to-day work that pushed the group towards their target performance levels. (They were also given individual training and nutritional plans to work to.) In doing so, the Red Roses were able to stick to their principles of play in the Red, Amber, Green and Gold Zones, yet at a much higher tempo. The methodology was gruelling but effective, and before long the team were playing at an unbelievable intensity. Their opponents simply couldn't cope.

From a psychological perspective, training in this way requires a tangible sense of progression so that the people involved feel rewarded for their hard work. It can take a long time for a training programme to yield results, such as the one implemented by the Red Roses. Performance gains rarely happen overnight, and sometimes people can become disillusioned, especially if they're working to their maximum capacity and results aren't yet improving on the pitch. Meanwhile, winning – the optimal outcome in sport – isn't always within a group's total control due to unmanageable external circumstances. Their opponents might have a freakishly impressive performance, poor weather might lead to an event that goes against them, injuries and suspensions can affect team selection, and so on.

To give a team a better chance of victory, it's important they establish two types of objectives in training so that their performances improve and they increase the likelihood of meeting an achievement-based mission:

1. **Performance-focused goals:** a medium- to long-term performance outcome that can be achieved by a team or competitor independently of the actions of other performers, such as a rugby team aiming for a 90 per cent tackle completion, or a diver in an Olympic final aiming at a score of 9 for a particular technique. These goals encourage the team or individual to perform to their potential.
2. **Process-focused goals:** a medium- to short-term target (or targets) that can be trained by the people involved, and aligns with the performance-focused goal. A process-focused goal generally looks at technique and behaviours. For example, a diver hoping to achieve a score of 9 in an Olympic final must break down their technique into manageable targets. They need to generate great height out of the board so that they can execute complex movements mid-air before hitting the water vertically. To achieve this physical state they might require greater leg strength,

meaning that building leg strength becomes the process-focused goal. This target is then broken down into a set of daily, weekly and monthly training goals alongside schedules for nutritional, technical and psychological work.

To achieve any long-term targets, it's important to first concentrate on the medium and short term – the process-focused goals – and this concept really comes alive in training. Football teams trying to become more counter-attacking will work on drills that yield results throughout the season. Boxers looking for more stamina often double down on their cardio work until they're able to finish strongly in the final rounds. Golfers aiming to shave shots from their scores focus on their short game and improve their putting and chipping numbers. The techniques developed when working on process-focused goals become weapons when applied to a game-day scenario.

I really noticed this concept being put into action while working with Harlequins FC. At the start of every season Conor O'Shea, the director of rugby, along with his technical team, established a series of key performance indicators (KPIs) – statistics that the team needed to hit in attack and defence throughout the campaign if they were to deliver on their game plan. These included tackle completion, possession, pass completion and time spent in the opposition's half. For each game, a minute-by-minute mindset focus that aligned to the game plan was also identified, for example 'tempo' or 'discipline'. The KPIs were trained, applied and reviewed every week in the following way . . .

After the weekend's match, the staff came together to review the team's KPIs and asked three questions: *Did we do what we set out to in attack? Did we defend in the way we'd planned? And did we keep to our mindset focuses for the duration?* The coaching staff then figured out the best way to assess the game with the players, with either Conor or one of the other coaches taking the meeting. Sometimes a player was asked to deliver the review alongside a member of the management team. This decision was based upon which person was best suited to the circumstances. In addition, the variety and different presenting styles kept the meetings fresh despite them following a similar format from week to week.

With the review completed, the senior players then went through the footage of their forthcoming opponents with the team's analysts. Together, they created a game plan for the next match based around the KPIs and those three questions: *What are our process targets in attack, in defence and in mind-set?* The players presented their game plan back to the coaches, a discussion took place, and then a collaborative strategy was agreed upon. The players were given the autonomy to review and plan, and encouraged to present their ideas so they could be discussed. The coaching staff had recognised that to develop decision-makers on the pitch it was vital that players took ownership of analysing their opponents and developing the game plan. They were the ones responsible for delivering it, after all, so it was important they had their say.

The following morning, the senior players presented the agreed game plan to the rest of the squad. For the duration of the week, that game plan was broken down into process-focused targets. By matchday, every player in the dressing room knew exactly what the game plan was, the KPI targets required to win and their role in terms of executing that plan.

Alongside their process- and performance-focused goals, every player in the Harlequins squad had an individual development plan (IDP) to work from, so they could improve themselves technically, tactically, physically and psychologically. Supported by the coaching staff, it was on the player to take responsibility for preparing and training in such a way that they would improve throughout the season and over the course of their career, all while ticking off a series of process-focused goals and action plans as determined in collaboration with the coaching staff. I've found that when setting goals in this way, it's important to follow a strengths-based approach, as established in Building Block #1. As we've already learned, all of us have strengths and areas of development, but the biggest performance gains happen when we turn our strengths into super-strengths while negating any boat-sinkers. Doing the opposite, by focusing our time on fixing the acceptable weaknesses, rather than the big issues, can stagnate a person's development. This is important to consider when we determine our goals and subsequent processes. An example of an IDP might have looked something like the example opposite.

By working to this programme – as well as training a series of process-focused goals – a player or team can direct their attention to the stuff that makes a difference in terms of performance. Distractions are removed, so it's possible for a group to see themselves achieving a series of process-focused targets, and when it comes to reviewing a match or event it's possible to do so in non-emotional terms. That's because in this context, performances aren't assessed solely on results – they're assessed on the process-focused goals set out in advance and the execution of the game plan. If the team's overall process-focused targets worked, then great; the group has tangible evidence they're able to deliver on their promises. If they didn't work, it's on the group to discover why.

This same process can be applied to just about any context, as shown on the following pages.

INDIVIDUAL DEVELOPMENT PLAN

Player name	Player X	Date created	06/08
Position	Scrum-half	Review date	06/11

General goals: Become a regular first-team player.

Super-strengths: Organisational skills in attack and defence, general work rate and attitude.

Core area	Goal(s)	Action plan(s)
Technical	90 per cent tackle completion.	Aim to identify correct tackle choice as soon as possible and execute. Keep straight-line posture through hips, spine, head.
Tactical	Get into position earlier – improve game understanding and awareness.	Analyse training and match performances with coaching staff – identify in-play focus cues.
Psychological	Maintain emotional control after errors.	Develop refocus routines to incorporate breathing exercises and refocus cues.
Fitness	Improve acceleration.	Targeted sprints work, with particular focus on sprint mechanics.

RAVENSWOOD SCHOOL

INDIVIDUAL DEVELOPMENT PLAN

Teacher name	Teacher X	Date created	6/08/2025
Position	Head of year	Review date	06/11/2025

General goals: To make the students more comfortable with exam-related pressure and enhance personal confidence.

Super-strengths: Communication skills, general work ethic and attitude.

Core area	Goal(s)	Action plan(s)
Technical	Enhance students' exam performance.	Develop 'mindset education' to help the students understand their responses to pressure and teach them exam-room skills.
Tactical	To engage students in the learning process.	Encourage students to think outside of the box with cultural trips, guest speakers and a range of experiences.
Psychological	Maintain emotional control after making errors.	Develop refocus routines to incorporate breathing exercises and refocus cues.
Physical	Improve general health.	Use the school gym before or after school.

Regardless of whether or not you decide to complete an IDP for yourself, it's vital you at least ask a very important question of yourself: *How much time do you spend developing the different component parts of your role?* If you're struggling to work out what these component parts actually are, check in with the four categories listed above – technical, tactical, psychological and physical. If you can identify any areas in need of improvement, prioritise them.

BUILDING EVIDENCE-BASED BELIEFS

The type of training you bring to a game-plan development programme will be unique to your situation. Firefighters practise for all sort of scenarios once their basic training has been completed. The same goes for people in the police, military and ambulance services. Some companies like to prepare their staff for advances in technology, such as artificial intelligence, while others encourage their group members to take on media training or presentation skills, should ever they be called upon to use them.

What's important is that a team builds up a healthy reserve of evidence-based beliefs: facts about themselves as a team and/or individual that gives them the confidence to succeed in challenging circumstances – examples might include the long-distance runner who has previously completed a marathon, the mountain climber who has scaled Mount Everest or the start-up owner who has launched other successful businesses. These people have an evidence-based belief that they can succeed because they've done so in the past. When the pressure cranks up, as it does on the start line of a major competition or in the boardroom when a big deal is about to go through, it's easy for a person to become overwhelmed by emotion. That's because the limbic system kicks into action – the part of our brain that activates our fight, flight or freeze response, none of which are useful in a competitive situation. When faced with a stressful event, such as taking a penalty in a cup final, our emotions change in much the same way as they would have done for a caveman who came face to face with a sabre-toothed tiger. Our brain is continually scanning for threats and has three responses if one is detected: we can run for the hills, take aggressive action or simply shut down.

The best way of dealing with such an event – and we all deal with them from time to time, no matter our circumstances – is to plan for it, because prevention is better than cure. And this is where evidence-based beliefs become such a powerful tool. If we can reassure ourselves with facts that tell us we can succeed in situations that appear fraught with risk, it's possible to remain calm, focus our attention effectively and compete to our optimum. I've had the pleasure of hearing Professor Steve Peters speak many times (Steve is a psychiatrist who has worked extensively in sport as well as other settings). I always remember him saying:

> If you want your blood supply to go to the stomach, you eat something. If you want it to go to the legs, you move. But if you want it to go to the logical, rational part of your brain, then you must think logically and rationally.

A solid game plan, twinned with an evidence-based belief that you can succeed, delivers that logical and rational mindset.

Place yourself at the start line of an Olympic 1,500-metres final, with the watching world analysing your every move. Without an understanding of your *who* and your *why* – plus a comprehensive game plan and a set of evidence-based beliefs – there's nowhere for you to turn for psychological support. However, if you've formulated a solid game plan and a set of evidence-based beliefs in training, and if you've considered every eventuality and given yourself an answer, you'll be able to access the rational and logical part of your brain when you need it most. That will help you to think clearly and calmly.

- Yes, I feel sick with nerves, but I knew I would. It's a sign that I'm ready to perform.
- I've done all my preparation and I'm in prime shape.
- I've consistently hit my split times in training, which means the four-minute-mile pace is possible.
- I delivered the same race plan perfectly in my last meet.

From there, it's possible to build a secure springboard to success.

In 2009 I was the lead author of a paper based on my doctoral research entitled 'The role of confidence in world-class sport performance.'* In the paper I analysed the mechanisms that underpinned the relationship between confidence and performance, and I made a key discovery. Confidence isn't just about positive thinking. It's derived from a series of evidence-based beliefs, and they impact on a person's performance through their A, B, Cs – their affect, behaviour and cognition (in other words, their feelings, actions and thoughts). Through my research I was able to draw several interesting conclusions:

- Confidence is synonymous with performance. Confident athletes can remain appropriately focused on the task, whereas less confident individuals become distracted and are unable to control their nerves, think positively or maintain focus on their usual routines.
- People have multiple sources (where they get their confidence from) and types of confidence (what they are confident about).

---

* K. Hays et al., 'The role of confidence in world-class sport performance', *Journal of Sports Science*, 27:11 (September 2009), pp. 1185–99.

- Confidence is context specific. Someone might be confident about their ability to deliver a fantastic after-dinner speech, but they feel anxious about delivering a sentimental piece at a wedding.
- The more sources you draw your confidence from, the more robust it will be. If an athlete only gets their confidence from winning, they will be negatively affected when they lose. However, an athlete that takes confidence from their preparation (physical, mental, holistic), performance accomplishments, coaching, social support, experience, competitive advantage and self-awareness will fare much better in tough times.
- It's not true to say that you are either confident or not. Confidence must be built.
- The bottom line is this: when people are confident, they think in a way that's beneficial to their performance. Their behaviours mirror what is needed to perform effectively, and they feel in control. The prepared 1,500-metres runner knows exactly what they must do on the track because they've already put in the hard yards during training and have a race plan that maximises their strengths. During the race, something unexpected might happen, such as an unknown rival athlete delivering an elite performance, but because they have a high level of confidence, a solid game plan and the ability to run a race-winning time, they won't panic. Instead, they'll readjust and kick on.

Interestingly, my research also suggested that if an athlete were to arrive at a major competition lacking in confidence, there's very little that they could do on the day to bring it back. Instead, it must be built up in advance through the proactive creation of evidence-based beliefs, and through multiple sources. This mindset, twinned with a coherent game plan, is a massive driver towards success.

Precisely how you train your evidence-based beliefs will depend on your circumstances, but a good way of starting out is to think of a time in your career or life when you've felt most confident. Then consider the conditions that fed into that moment.

- What were you confident about?
- Where did that come from?
- What did it look like?
- What did it feel like?
- What were you focused on?
- And what happened in the weeks and months leading into that moment that might have contributed to your confidence?

With those answers it's possible to see from where you've previously drawn your confidence, and then plan accordingly. For example, some people get their confidence from the opinions of others, which is an unstable source because it's beyond their control. Others take confidence from moments where they have previously shown resilience, bravery, strength or solid morals. Examples might include:

- The person who overcame serious injury to run a 10k or marathon. Evidence of this resilience can be applied to a future physical or emotional challenge.
- The person who stood up to a bully or acted as a peacemaker in a physical conflict. These actions can be used as evidence that they're able to represent themselves during a contract negotiation or business dispute.
- The person who overcame a crippling phobia. This work is proof that they're able to hurdle the toughest of psychological challenges and can do so in the future.

- The person who displayed moral character by defending a vulnerable individual or admitting to a wrongdoing when the consequences were high. These acts show they can make clear-headed decisions in the face of adversity.

Ultimately, drawing confidence from multiple sources will help improve its robustness. While writing my PhD I interviewed an Olympic swimmer who told me that her coach had brought an old-school piggy bank to training one day. Every time she perfected a technique in training, hit a personal best in the gym or shaved a fraction of a second from her race time, he scribbled the achievement down and stuffed it into the piggy bank. The wins mounted up. The ceramic pig was stuffed full of paper. When the Olympic Games came around, the coach instructed the swimmer to crack open the piggy bank on the eve of their first race and read through the notes. By the end of it, the athlete was brimming with confidence. This was an effective strategy because confidence isn't about thinking positively. It's not about being unrealistic or bluffing either. It's about knowing you have the capacity to do something because the evidence proves that you can.

This a multi-faceted process, however, and evidence-based beliefs can be constructed in all sorts of ways. So, ready yourself for a big work presentation by delivering a talk at the local library or a charity event. Steel yourself for an important debate or negotiation with some boxing or martial art classes because sports of this kind teach us how to think clearly under pressure. These training sessions, some of which might seem abstract, teach us that *we can* in situations where the first reaction is to think that *we can't*. And in doing so, we turn to our logical, rational brain, rather than our fight, flight or freeze response.

ASK THE QUESTION

How can you train a game plan and create the confidence to deliver it?

Start with the end in mind. Break your game plan down into a series of performance- and process-focused goals. Then design a training programme that brings you closer to them. Keep a record of your progress because evidence will enable you to build confidence along the way.

 LIGHTBULBS

- Train your game plan. Ensure that everyone has considered the component parts of their role and is prepared to deliver to the best of their abilities physically, technically, psychologically and tactically.
- To give yourself a better chance of success, it's important to establish two goals in training, both of which are within your control:
    - performance-focused targets
    - process-focused targets
- Training well creates confidence. It's not true to say that you're either confident or you're not. Confidence must be built. Consider your sources and types of confidence, and how you

might proactively develop your confidence base. This will have a positive impact on your performance.
- Evidence-based beliefs are a secret sauce: when created through training they tell an individual they can succeed in challenging circumstances

CHAPTER THIRTEEN

GAME-PLAN SUPPORT: COUNTING DOWN TO THE BIG EVENT

All of us work towards deadlines, whether they're fixtures in a sporting schedule, the countdown to a creative or financial target, or a month of school exams. With a game plan and a training programme in place, the chances of us succeeding in these areas are greatly increased. However, to really prepare for a key event, or events, it helps to build a *game-plan support programme* – an organisational structure in which the right things are done at the optimal time to best prepare for game-plan execution. This strategy was evident during the Lionesses' campaign in the 2022 European Championship, when a countdown was established for every match and the days between fixtures featured a set timetable of events. Before a ball had even been kicked, a sense of stability and order had been established. This ensured that every individual was able to perform their role with confidence, and the team were ready and prepared to adapt to an ever-changing environment.

This structure was important for several reasons. A clear daily order of events breeds familiarity and, in turn, reduces anxiety. Staff and players knew exactly what to expect and they prepared accordingly – they were able to focus on the task in hand, without distraction. Because the days felt organised, the squad concentrated on the *right things at the right times*, and switched off in between, which helped them perform to their optimum. Within this framework, any intense, tactical training sessions were conducted early in the schedule, giving the players more time to recover, whereas confidence sessions were held closer to matchday, so the work felt fresh in their minds. Finally, the game-plan support programme, established by Sarina and her team, encouraged growth and development. Players were given space to try new things, make suggestions and ask questions about their roles and the game plan. In doing so, they understood exactly what was expected of them on and off the pitch, and came to feel increasingly valued.

The team were together for the best part of two months, considering the preparation camps that took place immediately before the tournament phase. The planning that went into a tournament of this nature was meticulous, and each step was carefully crafted to meet the needs of the players. Given that during this period the players were staying in a hotel – an environment where a Groundhog Day atmosphere could sometimes kick in – it was important to tether them to a calendar where every meeting, workshop, training session and team-bonding session had clarity and purpose, so the players, coaches and support staff could execute their best game under pressure. In doing so, the key dates in the schedule – in this case, the games – were marked on the team calendar as 'Matchday'. The preceding days were referred to as Matchday −2, Matchday −1, in a countdown format, establishing a sense of order, while the rest days after the game were referred to as Matchday +1, Matchday +2.

This scheduling tactic was incredibly important. In busy and stressful circumstances, it's sometimes easy to lose sense of where we are. We clear one hurdle, but rather than resetting and steadying ourselves for the next, we relax and lose momentum. Before we know it, another challenge has reared up at us and we feel underprepared. In the environment of a hectic and pressurised international tournament, England's game-plan support programme ran as follows.

MATCHDAY –2

Every single member of the team was hellbent on winning the Euros. Some of them had been trying to win a major tournament for their entire careers and had experienced a lot of near-misses and heartache. They were determined to put that right by taking full advantage of the game-plan support programme on offer to them. In advance of the tournament, so much data had been collected on our opponents: we knew every single detail about how the other teams played, where they got their success from, the key players, their vulnerabilities and how we compared with them. This database proved invaluable.

With two days to go until matchday, assistant coach Arjan Veurink gathered the squad together to discuss England's next opponents. He outlined the team we were facing, where they were potentially dangerous and how the Lionesses could counteract their threats. He then listed the opportunities England might find in attack, defence and moments of transition. Arjan always led the meeting in a way that encouraged interaction from the players as he was keen for them to share their views or offer solutions to any potential threats we might face. At that stage, Arjan, Sarina and the rest of the technical staff would have already established their game plan. However, they recognised the importance of the players taking responsibility for their own performances.

Once the squad had discussed their opponents, a training session took place in which an 11 vs 11 game was conducted, with one team playing in the style of whoever England were facing next. This gave the Lionesses a chance to practise the game plan ahead of time. To further support their preparation, the players were able to access video clips of their opposing number from Thomas Murray, the team analyst, and his colleagues. They could also request additional video footage of the opposing team from the technical coaches. Once training was completed, the players were given additional downtime to rest and refuel appropriately.

MATCHDAY −1

Training on Matchday −1 was designed to give the players a high level of confidence. Sessions were quick and targeted. In the evening Sarina conducted a team meeting and announced the starting line-up. Mentally it was important not to overload the players with too much technical detail as the team had already done the hard yards on the training ground. A strategy had been distilled and understood, so all that remained was to remind the group of the game plan.

Even though we were the host nation, Sarina and her staff didn't allow anyone to get swept up in the hype. Social media guidelines had been drawn up to protect the players, and matchday was a social media-free space, with any content being distributed through the official Lionesses and England accounts. Our environment was controlled in such a way that nobody could be distracted by the outside world. It wasn't uncommon for people to know they were working on Matchday −1, without knowing what day of the week it was. This structure allowed the team and the players to smoothly navigate what could have been an emotionally turbulent experience.

MATCHDAY

Other than the game itself, and the player's individual preparations and routines, there was very little for the group to do within the context of the game-plan support structure. Goalkeeping coach Darren Ward led a set-piece meeting in the morning to remind the players of their roles at corners, free kicks and so on, and of any key tactical and psychological notes that had been set out by Arjan and Sarina in the preceding days. After the match, regardless of the result, Sarina usually said a few words to the team during a huddle on the pitch. The players were then encouraged to connect with the fans before beginning their individual recovery programmes and giving media interviews. If the game had gone well, as it did throughout the Euros, the players celebrated their successes together, usually by singing and dancing in the dressing room. The adrenaline levels on those occasions were so high that very few people managed a good night's sleep.

MATCHDAY +1

After a later start time, Matchday +1 was dedicated to the various treatment options provided by the medical and performance staff. These included ice baths, stationary bike sessions, mobility training and gym work. Sarina would lead a tactical debrief after lunch, where any areas of improvement were identified and team strengths consolidated. The clock for the next matchday was reset, and both players and staff were given the afternoon off to ensure they felt mentally refreshed. This was especially important when individuals were spending extended periods of time together during tournaments. It was vital that the group had the opportunity to remove the player/staff hat without experiencing guilt, and to connect with friends and family. This mental decompression was just as valuable as the physical recovery programme.

MATCHDAY −2

The players and staff went again.

*

While a game-plan support programme of this nature might seem like a niche idea that only works for an elite sports team, it can be applied to any situation where a deadline/performance is involved, or for multiple deadlines/performances over time. A fun runner preparing for a 10k, an entrepreneur preparing to launch a new company, the cast of a musical preparing for opening night, and so on. Another good example would be a student – we'll call her Laura – who's caught up in the middle of exam season and faces several tests over the course of four weeks. Her game-plan support programme might look something like this.

LAURA'S GAME-PLAN SUPPORT PROGRAMME: MAY–JUNE

EXAM DAY −2

Morning: complete revision sessions for Maths and Geography. Afternoon: do a one-hour mock Maths exam. Spend the evening checking in with friends and family, or do a fun activity such as playing a sport or going to the cinema.

EXAM DAY −1

Geography revision session in the morning, then shift focus onto a light Maths revision session in the afternoon. Get ready for the next day by packing the school bag that evening. No excuses. Relax at home with a family meal and a favourite TV show or film.

EXAM DAY

After completing the Maths exam, debrief with friends or a teacher, then try to unwind by going for lunch with mates. Do a Geography revision session in the afternoon. But keep it light!

EXAM DAY +1

Make sure to take healthy breaks, eat well and stay hydrated. Do a little exercise and spend some time outside.

EXAM DAY −2

Morning: complete revision sessions for Geography and History. Afternoon: do a one-hour mock Geography exam. Try to unwind in the evening with some people you love and/or fun activities.

EXAM DAY −1

You know the drill by now: a History session in the morning, then switch focus to a light Geography session in the afternoon ahead of the following day's exam. Get ready for the next day and practise some self-care to ensure you get a good night's rest.

And so on . . .

*

By using this style of preparation, the days and dates almost become irrelevant, although I wouldn't dispense with them entirely. I don't want anyone missing an exam or key event! But if several key days within a schedule are identified and a countdown created for each one, it's possible to plan our actions and reduce the overwhelming sense of pressure that can build up during a busy time at work or while studying. A schedule of this kind also ensures a student doesn't 'burn out' through overexertion. I remember an athlete discussing this concept during my PhD research. 'You can't get any fitter in the week leading up to a race,' they said, 'but you can get more tired or injure yourself. The training should be done in the weeks, or months before, so that you're easing down during the final week.'

A solid game-plan support programme should echo this principle. As a person prepares immediately before The Big Event, their schedule should allow them to rehearse their technical and tactical knowledge, reinforce their evidence-based beliefs (see the 'confidence piggy bank' in the previous chapter), debrief appropriately, and then recover physically and mentally. That way an individual can work to their optimum and then go again, whatever they're doing.

BUILDING THE BUNKER MENTALITY

There are moments in life that require us to shut ourselves away so that we can prepare and then subsequently perform – or play – at our optimum level. Usually, they are high-stakes events that demand our complete concentration, such as school exams, a sponsored charity event (an Ironman), a live performance in

HOW DO WE PLAY? 185

music, comedy or acting, or the deadline to a very important career project. In terms of sport, they tend to take place before a defining competition, event or tournament such as Wimbledon or the Olympic Games, or during the build-up to a crunch fixture, like an end-of-season match that might decide promotion, relegation or the winners and top-placed finishers in a championship.

When such moments arrive, the people involved often find themselves in a 'bubble' – a self-governed lockdown in which they can focus solely on the game plan while distancing themselves from the outside world and any distractions like media scrutiny, family and social pressures, or domestic issues. For example, Olympic athletes generally move into a specialised housing facility near to the stadium, and they'll stay there for the duration of the Games. In the run-up to title bouts, some professional boxers will enter a 'fight camp' for a month. They'll leave their homes, so as not to be disturbed, and then eat, sleep and spar at a specialist facility until the contest takes place.

Working in this way, while beneficial to performance, can bring a whole raft of challenges. Some individuals feel uncomfortable locking themselves away in a training camp with a group of people they barely know. Others might have pre-existing disputes with members of their group, meaning that spending an extended period of time with them has the potential to create an uncomfortable emotional tension. Then there are the individuals who use their alone space for energy; the athletes who suffer from homesickness; and the personality types that hate feeling constrained. (There are also athletes who love being away from home in a preparatory or tournament environment, and who thrive in such conditions.) However, if a group or individual has worked through Building Blocks #1 and #2, and come to know their *how* and *why*, a bubble can be a harmonious and productive environment. With an understanding of the people in the room, it's possible to use the differing personalities to support one another and head off any clashes before they begin. Meanwhile, with a clarified sense of purpose, the hardship of being away from home – sometimes in a completely alien environment – can feel like a worthwhile sacrifice or an adventure.

After I joined up with the Lionesses I knew that our first major challenge was the 2022 European Championship, which was being held in England. During the tournament phase, the squad was cocooned away in the Lensbury Hotel in Teddington, which was equipped with two football pitches, a state-of-the-art gym and two swimming pools. This was the perfect location in which to create a home away from home while optimising the team's performances. Within the bubble, Sarina and the team were able to focus without being distracted by journalists and fans. They could eat to the specifications set by the team's nutritionist and ready their minds and bodies for the task ahead. And because everybody understood the *who* of the group, any potential personality disputes, or the type of office politics that can arise in such a large collective, were curtailed.

After establishing a location, it became the shared responsibility of the players and support staff to address any issues that might arise, such as homesickness, boredom or loneliness. Within the bubble, the players were made to feel welcome and safe. Any exercises conducted off the pitch were done in such a way that everybody felt comfortable, as we built on the campfire vibe first introduced several months earlier when the squad talked through their personal timelines. If there were group discussions, the support staff worked hard to make sure that every team member was understood and heard. *The players connected.* Creating this atmosphere depended upon trust: everyone was encouraged to be open about their struggles and problems, especially when playing in such a high-profile event, where the attention was bound to be high given England were competing at home.

Prior to the European Championship we asked the Lionesses (and the staff) to reflect on their individual and team challenges, both during the preparation and tournament phases, so we could understand any concerns they might be experiencing about the tournament and being away from home. I supported the players as they developed personal self-care routines and introduced them to the importance of decompression (we will explore this in more detail in Building Block #4). This attitude ran from the top down and was led by Sarina. I remember a couple of occasions when staff were working late. Having stuck her head into the office, Sarina suggested they pack up for the day.

'You've done enough,' she said. 'Time to switch off.'

All of us knew that if a group of players in a bubble, of the kind set up at the Lensbury, were to feel unstable or out of sorts, their performances would likely suffer as a result. Also, any negative emotions would be exacerbated when their various coping mechanisms were taken away, which happens when working in a new, contained environment. For example, one player told me that her preferred technique for managing stress was to walk through the woods with her dog. That sort of relaxation wasn't going to be regularly available during the tournament. *So, what was she going to do as a coping mechanism instead?* It was our job to devise a similar type of pressure release while she lived in the bubble.

To help the players prepare themselves for what lay ahead, a booklet was distributed to everyone prior to their arrival as a reminder of all the work we'd done as a team in preparation for the tournament. Designed to help the group acclimatise to the enclosed environment, which would have felt doubly challenging given that the UK had been in and out of Covid lockdowns for the best part of two years, this 30-page document was accompanied by a welcoming note from Sarina. In it she reminded the players of the opportunities ahead and how the European Championship was a once-in-a-lifetime experience. She also expressed her faith in the group and how she believed they were going to succeed throughout the tournament. Finally, she stated that a lot of work had been put in to creating the 'optimal circumstances' so that the squad could do their bit to make England proud. It was their obligation to maximise the opportunities provided by those circumstances and to enjoy the experience.

Elsewhere, the booklet carried reminders of the team's values and behaviours – *Team first. Be in the moment. No regrets* – and recapped the way in which the group had arrived at those ideas. It also included tips for sleep, the ways in which individual and collective strengths could be amplified, and how stressors could be spotted and nullified – it was explained how, during big sporting events, athletes often ran through a wide range of polarised emotions, among them euphoria and low mood; a shared sense of purpose and loneliness; satisfaction and frustration; and love and anger. All of these feelings were valid. But if everyone in the bubble focused on the Lionesses' *who*, the squad would be able to support one another. Finally, the booklet reminded the players to celebrate any differences within the group and encouraged them to be open by sharing their emotions during tough moments. By becoming comfortable with being uncomfortable inside the bubble, the hope was that they might overcome the awkwardness associated with asking for help, or giving and receiving feedback. These processes were incredibly important if England were to sustain their performance throughout the competition.

DESIGNING YOUR BUBBLE

All of us can benefit from the principles behind going into a bubble from time to time. It might be that our department at work is approaching an intense period of activity or we're facing a series of tests that will determine our career progression. Maybe exam season is approaching or we've got to make a lifestyle change for health reasons. All these events, and the way in which we manage them, can benefit from a focused environment, although they don't have to be as rigid as the ones set up for an elite football team or championship boxer – I'm not expecting you to lock yourself away in a hotel for a month. The important thing is that a series of boundaries are drawn up in advance.

For the England team, this meant a period spent away from home in a suitable hotel. A university student studying for their exams might create a bubble in which they 1) turn off all social media as they revise, 2) cancel any parties, gigs or weekends away, and 3) only spend time with close friends and family until the job is done. A number of famous authors and scriptwriters go away for a few weeks when they're on deadline so they can free themselves from any distractions, while some software developers and start-up owners lean into a bunker mentality during the countdown to a new product launch. The specific environment is a totally personal choice, but the important thing is that a series of conditions are established and then committed to.

Of course, there must be some flexibility. A bubble like the ones created by Sarina and her staff at the Lensbury and the following year at the Women's World Cup wasn't supposed to be a maximum-security prison. Such an environment would have been detrimental to the players' mental health and their performances on the pitch. To create a home-from-home vibe, we brought in dartboards, table-tennis equipment and other sporting activities for the players to occupy themselves with between games.

In advance of the tournament we discussed a series of set techniques and processes for the players to consider when operating away from home. And while these were originally designed for elite athletes, I see no reason why anyone can't apply them to their own lives and circumstances. Some people love to have a solid daily routine, whereas others are less keen on the thought of a predictable plan. But even if you don't typically thrive within a strict schedule, maintaining some semblance of structure and routine can help create a sense of control, particularly in times of unpredictability, uncertainty and stress.

For example, although bubbles at major football tournaments are, by their very nature, areas in which the people working within them are separated from the outside world, we knew that to cut the players off from the most important people in their lives for a month might have a detrimental effect on their well-being. Even those people that enjoyed their alone time would likely struggle at some point, especially as the pressure cranked up. To overcome this, a farewell barbecue was arranged before the team moved into the Lensbury Hotel, so that everyone's friends and family could get to know one another. A WhatsApp 'Friends & Family' group was also established, and friends and family moments were also facilitated at the appropriate time throughout the tournament, although towards the latter stages these were cancelled due to concerns about Covid.

When a person commits to a period of more isolated working, life is made a lot easier if those left outside of the bubble are understanding of the *who* and the *why*. A person studying for a very important exam or assessment should tell their mates ahead of time so that they know not to disturb them or to not feel slighted when certain social offers are declined. The same attitude applies when people are working hard to meet a deadline or trying to reach a health and fitness goal. If the motivation for their sacrifice is made explicit, and their boundaries are clearly communicated, it's more likely that those people left temporarily waiting on the sidelines will feel appreciated rather than slighted, and their actions will become more supportive thereafter.

 ASK THE QUESTION

Can you spend your time more wisely during the build-up to high-pressure events?

Consider a structure that enables you to work without distraction, and rest and recover appropriately. Establish boundaries. Alert loved ones to your *why* and *who*. Then involve them in your journey so they can feel engaged and connected. And set a calendar to help identify a tangible roadmap to success.

LIGHTBULBS

- Establishing a game-plan support programme, with a calendar countdown marking key events, focuses us on the work that lies ahead and the areas where we might need techniques to cope with mounting demands. With an appropriate schedule in place, it's possible to see a potentially overwhelming task as a series of smaller, more manageable events.
- Game-plan support programmes enable people to focus on the right things at the right time. For a marathon runner this could include moments of intense training, moments of active recovery and moments of self-care. When organised correctly, they enable growth, learning and clarity.
- A bubble is a protected environment in which we can shut ourselves away to perform, or *play*, at our optimum and with zero distractions.
- Before entering one, a team or individual should check in on their *why* and *who*. A person with purpose will understand the rewards waiting for them outside the bubble once their work has been completed. Meanwhile, someone with self-knowledge can prepare for any potentially derailing events.

CHAPTER FOURTEEN
GAME-PLAN EXECUTION: DIRECTING ATTENTION UNDER PRESSURE

In the build-up to any fixture, competition or challenge, it's not enough for a team to have a clear game plan in place. *They must also know how to execute that game plan.* This is done by staying focused on the right things at the right time during moments of pressure. While this requires a set of psychological skills, which we'll discuss in Building Block #4, it's also important to develop a series of *focused processes* with every individual involved, to direct their attention when the stakes are high. These are techniques or strategies that have to be applied at specific times, such as the tempo at which an athlete runs during a long-distance race, and those moments in which they have to pull away from their rivals or stay in touching distance of the leading pack.

An understanding of focused processes helps to draw the emotion from an event, and encourages an athlete to think about *what they're doing,* and *what is within their control,* rather than becoming distracted by the crowd, the ref or the occasion. As we'll discuss in the next chapter, focused processes also come into play when analysing a result. If an athlete or team has lost, it's easy to feel upset afterwards, while if they've succeeded, an emotional high can kick in. Following on from a result – good or bad – it's easy to let feelings take over, which can then cloud a person's judgement. But this reaction is both short-sighted and short-term, and in addition to looking to the result, a team should always analyse whether they delivered against their focused processes, and indeed whether their focused processes were the right ones.

When I was working at Harlequins, this style of work assumed a very clear shape:

1. Evaluate the opposition.
2. Reset the focused processes; train accordingly.
3. Create clarity for the team and individual: execute the game plan.
4. Evaluate the game according to the focused processes, *not* solely the result.

This type of work is universal across all sporting contexts. I remember the Cambridge University Women's rowing team operated in a similar way during the build-up to their successful Boat Race in 2017, albeit in very different circumstances. Before the race, the coach Rob Baker broke down the course – which ran for 4.25 miles from Putney to Mortlake – into stages, with focused processes for each one. In some sections he wanted the boat to 'hold', in others they had to 'push'. He explained his plans to the crew over the weeks and months leading up to the race, then wrote his instructions in a final summary document that was distributed to the team with a motivational note:

You are strong and powerful. You have resilience and tenacity. You row very well and row very well together.

HOW DO WE PLAY? 195

You have supported each other in the boat, and in every type of race situation. We have prepared for every eventuality, and you can cope with all of them.

You are an exceptional crew and should aim for an exceptional race. You may not have it, though. And whether up or down, or if something goes wrong, you can win in any situation. This is all that matters.

I have full faith in you all and can't wait to see you unleash your potential on Sunday.

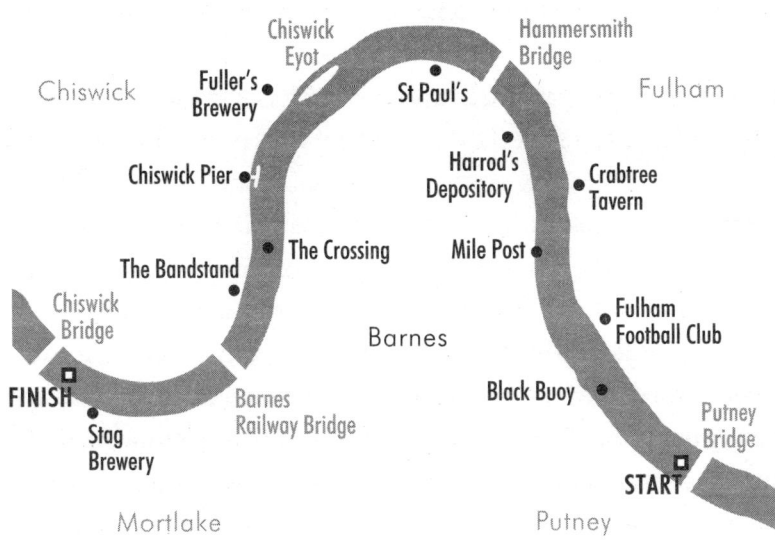

Source: scihi.org

As they studied the course, the team had a clear idea about what they needed to do and when. For example, from the start the boat had to race towards the Fulham bend, either by holding their position or moving ahead of Oxford, if possible. At Hammersmith

Bridge and the Chiswick Steps they had clear directions to push. When reaching the Chiswick Eyot it was important the team reset themselves. At Barnes Railway Bridge they had to push again, resetting and restarting if they weren't already in the lead. To execute their game plan, there were technical processes to consider for when working inside the boat. For example:

- Move through the feet and keep the mass moving with good timing and quickness out of the front.
- Punch the last quarter of the stroke.
- Straight-arm drive.

Finally, there was the directive to think like a freight train: 'If you want to be one,' wrote Rob, 'commit to that second minute and keep on it. It's all about momentum. Get it, keep it and don't let them have any of it. If they dare to try . . . *then make them pay.*'

With these focused processes in place, the team had a clear idea of what to do and when – the race had been broken down into sections. For the most part, this information was retained and relayed by the cox in the boat. But Rob had also given every rower an understanding about what they had to concentrate on technically within these sections – the motions that had to be performed to bring success. The Cambridge team practised them during training, over and over, until they happened instinctively. This step-by-step approach of taking a bigger, daunting whole – competing in the Boat Race – and breaking it down into smaller, manageable, focused processes gave the Cambridge Women all the information needed to execute the game plan. By so doing, it massively increased their chances of success because it gave the rowers a process to focus their attention on and prevented them from being distracted by things that didn't really matter on the day, such as the crowds lining the course. All their attention was directed towards the stuff that was going to make a difference.

There's another more pressing reason for implementing focused processes: they create clarity, and clarity creates confidence, which – as you're probably sick of me pointing out – is the greatest indicator that a team or individual will be successful. Rather than the individual rower thinking, *What am I going to do? What if we can't do it? All these people are watching* . . . they simply had to recall the techniques laid out by Rob during his instructions. *Move through the feet. Straight-arm drive* . . . and so on. With everything stripped down in this way, the rowers were in control and had the confidence to execute their processes under pressure. This was proved to me, when, in the week leading up to the race I asked the crew what they were feeling confident about. Their answers were overwhelmingly positive.

- 'We know that we can perform under pressure.'
- 'We know that we've got an advantage in our physicality.'
- 'We know that we can make changes quickly and be reactive to what's happening.'
- 'We know that we're stronger, which gives us an advantage in a long race.'
- 'We know the course, we've visualised it, we've worked on it. We know what we've got to do to win.'

When I asked them how that knowledge made them feel, they answered: *Excited. We're smiling, we're relaxed, and we're having fun.* When I pressed them about how that feeling might show up in their behaviours, they responded: *We're motivated. We're aggressive. We're going after it.* Finally, I wanted the team to identify their focus: *It's on the game plan. We know our roles and responsibilities and what we need to do. It's about being relentless and remembering our focused processes every single time. And trusting in them, because that's what's going to give us our performance.* (Interestingly, this is a perfect example of how a person's

ABCs – their thoughts, feelings and behaviours – are influenced by confidence.)

The idea of setting focused processes could apply to just about any walk of life, but let's look at the game plan of a touring musician and some of the focused processes they might implement around a performance. If, before a show, they tend to visualise the events of a bad gig, such as a stony-faced audience, they should instead train their attention on some of their more successful concerts from their past. Perhaps there's a track they play backstage that gets them in the right headspace. It might be that they perform better with or without a beer before walking on for the first song. Then when the show begins, they could have two or three focused processes that generally bring success, such as a moment in the set where they interact with a member of the audience, play a crowd-pleasing song or introduce the members of the band. Possessing clarity about these processes is the first step to executing the game plan. And having a game plan increases the chances of success.

It's essential that a team not only has absolute clarity about their strategies, but also understands the focused processes required to put these strategies into action. If a group can come to an understanding of what it is they're trying to do, with the knowledge of how to achieve their aim, they'll arrive at any crunch moments with absolute clarity. And with absolute clarity comes a greater chance of success.

IN-GAME MANAGEMENT (AND HOW TO MAKE IT WORK FOR YOU)

A team with a series of focused processes can be given autonomy to play with freedom, providing they adhere to the overall game plan. An excellent example of this would be the Red Roses, and Simon Middleton's zone management system. With its four playing areas – Red, Amber, Green and Gold – the team were given definitive instructions on how to direct their play in certain positions. But they were also encouraged to make their own decisions on the pitch, providing it matched the zone's principles of play. This autonomy is important because with it a team can react to any moments of adversity or triumph with 'in-play management', a term used to describe a series of strategies or actions that, when trained effectively, can help a group to reset or adjust when things aren't going to plan, or to build momentum when they are. In moments of high stress, groups can use in-game management to draw breath and recalibrate. When working under high-pressure deadlines, they can come together to identify immediate priorities or support a teammate that might be struggling under the strain. When a project is going well, they can implement a motivational tactic to ensure that everyone stays on target and finishes on a high.

There are many sporting examples of in-play management, and when implementing these strategies, trigger words often come into force – cues to get everyone in the group pulling in the same direction to meet the demands of the game. On a basic level you'll hear them on every five-a-side football pitch or netball court. As the ball is pinged around and the players move at speed, there will be commands to keep possession of the ball ('Hold'), take a second to assess the play ('Time') or move quickly to avoid an opponent approaching ('Man-on'). This language is useful not only because it directs behaviour, but also because it helps a group to stay process-focused under pressure. Without the command to *hold*, a player might release the ball too early. By not alerting a teammate that they have *time,* he or she could panic or make a hasty decision. If a player doesn't know there's a *man-on,* they might relax unnecessarily and find themselves dispossessed in a sticky area, putting their team under pressure.

In-play management was employed while I was working at Harlequins. In collaboration with the players, the coaching staff created a list of trigger words for the team to use during training and matches. Each one had a different meaning, and every player had to commit them to memory. These trigger words helped the team respond to the natural momentum shifts in the game.

For example, to regain momentum when it had gone away from them:

- **Ice:** a lost ball; react to the mistake immediately and get back into a defensive line.
- **Fix it:** respond to a mistake much faster than the opposition.

Or, to capitalise on momentum when it was with the team:

- **Chance:** a turnover opportunity; turn defence into attack.
- **Sixty:** raise the intensity; maximum effort for the next minute!

These terms, or something similar, can be applicable to any fast-moving environment where there's an emphasis on quick reactions and team effort. For example, it might be that a team of A&E doctors want to improve their communication skills and efficiency so they can better deal with the frenetic nature of their workplace:

- **Next job:** forget the last cleared patient; refocus and concentrate on the next.
- **Stay present:** if a dispute has taken place, or if you witness something distressing, try to stay focused on the task at hand. *Other patients need you.*
- **Positive:** no complaining on shift. Get on with the job. Save your thoughts for the debrief.

As always, simplicity is vital. In a fast-paced environment, one- or two-word triggers, like 'Next job', can convey a lot of information, and quickly, while encouraging the team to take action through a shared understanding of the unfolding situation. It's also vital that these words come from a place of necessity rather than simply being plucked out of thin air. If the A&E team has established that they tend to dwell on mistakes, become distracted by distressing incidents or disputes, and complain during busy shifts, these cues will have a focus and can be used effectively. The group can then turn their attentions to the positive. They will clear patients more effectively, remain 'on task' and stay in tune with the work rather than voicing their opinions. However, if a series of random or inappropriate cues are used, they will ultimately prove ineffective and exacerbate any underlying problems.

These cues are important because several things can happen to a team when working under pressure. One is that they tend to communicate ineffectively – criticisms might be thrown around, when what's really needed is information that can direct attention in the right way. The other is that communication breaks down entirely and the various individuals within the group focus on their own thing, which ultimately proves destructive. Having a set of instructive words or phrases creates a shared language. Under pressure, the team can then come together rather than drift apart, and they'll likely stick to their game plan more effectively. It also tells each person in the team that their colleagues have their back. When a mistake is made, the call of 'Next job' ensures that the team moves on. Nobody dwells on the negative or plays the blame game.

Trigger words are just as useful for the individual, either when functioning as part of a team or as a solo operator. For example, in most team sports, elite competitors will have two or three mental processes to execute once a match has begun. Some footballers in the opening minutes like to have a good first touch of the ball, get stuck in to a positive tackle and drive the tempo of the game. In this case, the trigger words *touch*, *tackle* and *tempo* would be applicable. You might have seen athletes attach a piece of tape to their wrist; the fabric is often marked with a brief list of important tactical reminders and triggers: *Cover #8 at set pieces. Press high. Maintain position when OOP (out of possession).* During the match, when there's so much to take in, or after a mistake when the player feels themselves become distracted, they need only glance at their wrist for a reminder of what to do. From there, they can reset and get back on track. This style of preparation is important because, if implemented correctly, they direct an individual to task, align them to a game plan and reinforce their confidence through clarity of thought.

This same strategy can be used by anyone who understands their principles of play. Through trial and error, a dentist might have learned that they generally perform to the best of their ability when 1) the first part of the day is spent practising self-care, by stretching, eating right and meditating before setting off for work, 2) they sort their admin as soon as they arrive at the practice, and 3) they take a little time to relax each patient as they settle into the chair. In this case, the trigger words *self*, *sort* and *soothe* will help them to focus on their principles of play. They also work on a personal level. Whenever I go out, I use cue words as a checklist. *Keys. Wallet. Phone.* I now never leave my house without them.

ASK THE QUESTION

Do you have a series of focused processes that you lean into during moments of pressure?

Draw up a list of actions that you could utilise at work or play that might improve your chances of success. When you implement them, make sure to review whether they were successful or not, and then adjust accordingly.

 LIGHTBULBS

- Focused processes can be used by teams and individuals. They direct attention towards the task at hand when looking to apply game-plan execution.
- Using focused processes draws the emotion away from an event. A person only need think about *what they're doing*, rather than any external influences.
- Only through delving into the game-plan's focused processes is it possible to know *why* you're successful *when* you're successful, and vice versa. This then creates consistency.
- Use in-play management to reset or adjust when things aren't going to plan, or to maintain and build momentum when they are. Trigger words make for excellent cues when trying to get a group together on the same page.

CHAPTER FIFTEEN

GAME-PLAN DEBRIEF: PLAN, DO, REVIEW

Whether or not a game plan has been executed successfully, it's important that a team analyse their performance so they can build on the things that went well, and identify and neutralise the things that didn't. Reflection and analysis are at the heart of sport psychology, and as I stated earlier the only way to know *why* a group is successful *when* they're successful is to analyse the focused processes established in the game-plan execution phase. In so doing, it's possible to determine if the techniques and strategies put in place were effective or not. Remember: by concentrating on these areas, rather than the result, it's possible to see the event in performance terms, whether it's a league match, a financial negotiation or a business conference. Moreover, when the emotional highs and lows are stripped out of a discussion, the chances of a constructive dialogue are increased. Of course, it's also important to reflect on the results and examine any differences between the intended outcome and the actual one. But the key is to uncover the cause of the result. That comes from debriefing the focused processes.

In conducting this work, a team can develop a circular process in which they plan, they do and they review. This then allows them to establish which focused processes should be kept, which ones should be tweaked and which ones abandoned. When it comes to planning the next event or fixture, the information can be fed into the updated game plan, and if all goes well the consistency in the team's performances will improve over time. For example, it might be that a boxer and his coaching team establish a game plan in which the athlete 1) puts their opponent under pressure with a powerful jab, 2) traps them on the ropes and 3) dominates them with their superior height and reach. Regardless of the result, these focused processes should be studied after the bout. From there, the team can ask a series of questions, including:

- Were we able to execute our game plan – and why/why not?
- Which processes worked – and why?
- Which ones didn't work – and why?
- Which strategies need to improve – and how?

This is a process that was drilled into me as a young psychologist – a profession where self-reflection is so very important and is regarded as a key ingredient for greater self-awareness and professional expertise. During my training I had to debrief on every completed consultancy session and I often used the Gibbs Reflective Cycle.* After a while, evaluating my performance – and

---

* Developed in 1988 by Graham Gibbs, this model was created to help individuals understand, and learn from, an experience or set of experiences. Their answers and observations enabled them to plan for future events of a similar nature. The Gibbs Reflective Cycle is broken down into six phases: 1) A description of what happened. 2) The thoughts and feelings about what happened. 3) An evaluation of what happened. 4) An analysis of the experience. 5) A conclusion: *What was learned?* 6) An action plan for a similar future event. Each phase carries a series of questions that can be found online and are worth checking out.

looking to see where I could improve – became second nature. (I would also talk to my logical sounding board about my processes, for a 360-degree perspective.) Through this work, I learned that the consequences of *not* conducting a structured performance review were that events or tasks tended to be judged primarily by results. That meant people rarely identified the processes that caused a team, or individual, to be successful, nor did they identify the flaws or mistakes that resulted in failure.

When it comes to the debrief phase, there are two types: the *hot* and the *cold*. The hot debrief takes place in the moment, or immediately after a performance. In military terms it's a battleplan drawn up on the back of a cigarette packet in the middle of a firefight, in business terms it's a breakout meeting in the thick of a tense negotiation and in a sporting context it's a team huddle. These are short, pithy conversations that enable a group to either maximise their momentum (if things are going well), slow play and rethink their approach (if things are going badly), or quickly summarise a performance in the immediate aftermath and move on, knowing it will be debriefed in more detail at a later date. Decisions are made and acted upon immediately.

A cold debrief, on the other hand, is a more considered analysis that is conducted well away from the action, both physically and timewise. For a group of soldiers, this would involve them attending a meeting with their superior officers and analysing their tactics through bodycam footage, maps, drone videos and so on. For a business team, this step might require them to assess their tactics, price points, financial data and presentation skills. In a sporting context, this is a video session reviewing the team or individual's latest performance. Any intelligence emerging from these sessions can be pored over and used for future strategies.

I'd recommend that any team looking to improve their performances in a sustainable manner incorporate both the hot and the cold debrief. I'll now explain how this is done in a sporting context.

THE HOT DEBRIEF

You'll remember from the last few chapters that the Red Roses, under head coach Simon Middleton, had been given a game plan to work from as they moved up and down the pitch. In theory, they knew exactly what to do when operating in the Red, Amber, Green and Gold Zones. However, when the action starts for real, strategies of this nature are much harder to implement. Often when individuals operate in this way, they have to 'play what they see'. In other words, they must react in the moment, being flexible and adapting to what works and what doesn't. Under such circumstances, problems can arise if the players involved aren't clear about how to organise themselves, especially when things go wrong.

The Red Roses staff knew that certain characters would want to take charge vocally in these situations, while others preferred to lead by example, knowledge that had emerged in our personality-profiling sessions. To counteract any potential clashes, and ensure that everyone operated effectively, we looked to devise a hot debrief, or an on-field communication plan, so the team could assess and take action in the moment, while in-play. To get this work started, I joined with another Red Roses sport psychologist, Sophie Walton. Together, we broke the team into four groups according to their on-pitch role.

1. The line-out
2. The scrum
3. The forwards
4. The backs

Sophie and I met bi-weekly with the players in small groups, and during the course of this work we facilitated discussions during which they devised a series of optimal performance strategies for the team during training and matchday scenarios, all while working to Midds's principles of play – *A team that withstands the maximum amount of pressure, while exerting their maximum in the opposition's territory, is more likely to win than not.* It was clear that, under this framework, the players needed to think for themselves from the very first second of a game. That meant they required a fluid method of communication that would enable them to reset and refocus according to how the game was going. Enter: *the team huddle.*

What's great about rugby, from a tactical perspective, is that it's very easy to disrupt the speed of play and slow down a match, and there are also many natural breaks in the game such as during scrum stoppages, while waiting for line-outs to form and when teams decide what they're going to do when awarded a penalty. Whenever there were moments in the game in which the players could regroup and take a moment to think, they huddled on the pitch and asked four key questions of themselves:

- Where is the pressure?
- Is it on them or us?
- What action can we take?
- What's the next step?

In one scenario, the team might have been trailing to a couple of tries early in the game, in which case the conversation would run as follows:

- Where is the pressure? *In our half.*
- Is it on them or on us? *It's on us. We're panicking and kicking the ball into touch.*

- What action can we take? *Take more care with the ball and build momentum.*
- What's the first step? *No one kicks the ball into touch for the next five minutes. We'll run a different pattern of play.*

Just a simple moment of reflection is sometimes enough to shift the momentum in a team's favour.

The Red Roses were a group that was keen to learn quickly. To help them adjust to this tactic, the players implemented their huddle during training sessions, and before long the team was transferring these skills to matchdays. According to the players, their on-field communication improved massively under pressure. This then resulted in a positive performance impact throughout the season and enhanced the group's confidence. Interestingly, our bi-weekly sessions took on a life of their own. The players began arranging *pre-meeting* meetings before they got together with their coaching staff and planned their topics for discussion; they arranged coffee meetings with injured players to keep them in the loop, and a WhatsApp group was set up for the squad to share ideas and feedback.

Given the stop/start nature of sport, tactics of this nature are easy to implement. In a rapidly transitioning game of rugby, football or basketball there are often opportunities to organise team huddles or run through a breakout session on the sidelines with a coach. However, real life can seem more frantic: the office that feels like an arena of drama and unpredictability; the small business with workers pulling in different directions; the boss who delivers mixed messages to their staff. Viewed through this prism, it's easy to see life as essentially chaotic. But the same delaying tactics applied in sport can be used to bring order and structure to the harum-scarum of everyday work. We only need to establish our in-play strategies in advance and take a shared responsibility when bringing them to bear.

- In the meeting where an important team decision is about to be made, a timeout session is arranged. With a moment to breathe, facts are double checked and statements of intent reiterated. The group reassures themselves they are making the correct move. (Or not.)
- When working under pressure to a tight deadline, a team conducts a brief check-in period at certain times during the day. During these moments, they can ensure that everyone is operating as they should and managing the strain.
- While operating in a hectic environment (a supermarket before Christmas; a pub during the FA Cup Final), the staff regroup for a brief huddle. Weak spots are identified, priorities are established and focus processes are recalled.

In some situations there is simply neither time nor space to call for a time-out. Medical staff working at an A&E department at a hospital or traders running the market aren't always able to check in with their colleagues. The work is too hectic and instructions can be misheard and misinterpreted in such a fast-moving environment. The same can happen in team sport, especially when the ball is in play and the athletes are having to reorganise on the move. This problem is exacerbated in a packed stadium when there are screaming fans, and a heightened sense of aggression from the opposition – there's so much that can distort or confuse the way in which members of a team communicate with one another. In these situations it's important that information and instructions are exchanged quickly and clearly. This is particularly important in a team where everybody needs to be on the same page in order to draw an immediate response. The trigger words detailed in the previous chapter come into their own here, so use them.

THE COLD DEBRIEF

The cold debrief is a vital tool in any team's locker because it allows them to step back from a high-paced or dramatic event and take stock, with increased clarity. But it's not simply enough to gather a group of people together and ask them how they thought things went, and why. The conversation must be directed at the game plan and the focused processes that were established during its creation. This is because in doing so, the group can work to maximise their areas of identified strengths and minimise any weaknesses, rather than mourning or celebrating the result. Consistency is a happy by-product of this work. For example, it might be that a team of property developers have bought a series of houses to refurbish and sell at a higher price. They've purchased wisely, so their profit margins are expected to be high. However, if the market crashes due to a political event, there's no point ripping up the playbook and starting again, because – like a poor refereeing decision or a freak goal in sport – certain things will always be beyond their control. The best approach is to review the processes that worked (and why), the ones that didn't (and why), and then plan accordingly.

Even the most successful organisations can overlook this simple point. In comparison with the time spent reviewing their latest performance, teams often spend a disproportionate amount of time planning for the next one. And while post-match reviews often establish what happened and the future impact of those happenings, less effort is often spent digging into why those outcomes occurred in the first place. This is usually because games arrive thick and fast, and there's a desire to move on from one performance and onto the next.

When I first began working with Harlequins, I was impressed with the detailed analysis and foreplanning that took place at the start of every season. This work guided every game on the fixture list. The style of play was ingrained and every game plan was designed to maximise the strengths of the team, while nullifying the opposition's threats. However, I also noticed that team debriefs often focused on the result and the events of the match, rather than the game plan and its focused processes, and whether they had worked or not. After one or two meetings I approached the coaching staff with a suggestion.

'I think we can get a greater level of depth from our reflections,' I said. 'We should build the debrief meetings around the team's focused processes. Currently, it's difficult to determine whether the latest game plan was appropriate or not, and whether or not the players were delivering against it. I think the information that underpins those questions could be really important for us moving forward.'

From then on, the Quins' debriefing process evolved. Matches were assessed through the lens of *why* they had unfolded in the way that they did, good and bad, and how their focused processes could be fine-tuned. A series of questions were asked:

- Did we do what we said we were going to do in defence and attack?
- Did we keep to our mindset focuses for the duration?
- If we were successful, why was that? What enabled us to deliver?
- Where could we improve? And how might we do that?

These discussions then directed the game plan for the following week, and a series of 'work-ons' – techniques to be *worked on* or practised – were established. Elsewhere, the team also reinforced the areas in which they had been excelling. This is a key consideration for any review situation. The tendency in debriefs is to identify what isn't working, even though this can be debilitating to a group or individual's confidence. Instead, the negatives have to be carefully balanced against the positives.

Our revamped debriefing process soon paid dividends. Harlequins advanced to the Aviva Premiership Final in 2012, where they faced Leicester Tigers at Twickenham. I'd only joined up with the club at the start of that season and had very little experience in working with rugby teams. Upon arrival, my brief was to act as a logical sounding board to Conor O'Shea, the director of rugby, and his coaches. Their instructions were clear: *You don't have to change the world. Instead, watch, observe and feedback in what you've noticed. Then figure out what we can tweak, and where we can improve.* Part of this process required me to look at how the team were establishing and reviewing their game plans, as well as their communication style when introducing new tactics, procedures and work-ons.

When doing analysis of this kind, the language we use is so important. New concepts are easily forgotten, subtle tactical nuances can be lost in a blur of jargon. What I've found is that it's important to make new ideas 'sticky' so that they can be easily remembered and taken on board by a player or team. This tactic of using memorable language becomes incredibly powerful when aligned to the psychological profile of a group and its players.

Through performance debriefs with the squad we'd identified Quins' key thoughts, feelings and behaviours throughout the season, both for when they were playing well and when they underperformed. We did this by investigating *why* games had unfolded in the way that they had. Once I'd collated my observations, I was keen to present them to the group, *but how could I make this stuff sticky in a sporting environment?* Dr Mark Bawden, one of the brains behind Mindflick and their Spotlight profiling programme, was my supervisor during my sport psychology training days. He was – and is – someone for whom I have great respect, and I used him as a logical sounding board while working with Quins.

Mark was brilliant at finding metaphors to land new ideas, so I called him and asked for his advice. His response was to suggest the terms Warrior, Thug, Assassin and Robot, as characters to help the team recognise whether they were playing to their strengths, or if their strengths were becoming overplayed and therefore working against them. Under Mark's metaphor system, a Warrior was a disciplined player and a powerful asset on the battlefield. However, if they started to focus on uncontrollable factors, they might become susceptible to being reckless and overly aggressive, and thereby transform into a Thug. Likewise, an Assassin was a cool, controlled killer – they were clinical. When overdone, however, they became overanalytical and constrained by indecision, like a short-circuiting Robot.

The key information I'd collated were listed so that every player could recognise their on-field thoughts, feelings and actions for when they were playing to their optimum and when they weren't. They could also assess whether they were behaving like Warriors or Thugs, Assassins or Robots.

HOW DO WE PLAY?

WARRIOR (DISCIPLINED)	THUG (RECKLESS)
Players sticking to their processes (trigger words)	Considering past/future events
Communication (huddle strategy)	Considering past/future mistakes
Players doing their jobs	Overthinking the scoreline
No silly penalties	Annoyed by the ref/unfair decisions
Enjoyment	Lack of composure
Belief	Concerned by missed chances
Playing for the team	Fear of consequences

ASSASSIN (CLINICAL)	ROBOT (CONSTRAINED)
Focused on team's strengths	Tentative
Focused on non-negotiable behaviours	Fearful of making mistakes
Focused on the next job	Rushed
An 80-minute performer	Focused on uncontrollable details
Plays confident, aggressive, innovative rugby	Fatigued and anxious
Takes chances; plays to win	Plays with fear; aim is not to lose

Mark's metaphors were brilliantly realised. Not only did the players have a selection of relatable identifiers to work with (the concepts of Warrior and Assassin were very much in tune with the image of a skilled rugby player), but the listed characteristics had come from the team's debriefing sessions. The players were familiar with all of them. After they had been named, these identifiers became 'sticky'. The players knew what the game looked like when they were performing to each of the identities, and we developed in-play tactics to help the team course correct in-game where necessary. This work supported them through the season.

By the time the Premiership Final came around, the players were fully in tune with the concepts of Warrior, Thug, Assassin and Robot. So much so, in fact, that in the week leading up to the match I presented them with only two slides during our last preparatory meeting. The first reiterated the characteristics of Mark's suggested identifiers. The second reminded the squad to enjoy the event. These slides were fixed to the dressing-room walls on game day.

'It's just another rugby match,' I said. 'There's a big prize at the end, sure. But you know how to get out there and put your best game on the park. I believe that the greatest travesty in sport is if a person looks back on the moment and realises that they didn't enjoy it because they were feeling stressed and anxious...'

To get to the final, Quins had performed phenomenally well. During the season the squad identified their strengths and super-strengths, and built a clear picture of where they wanted to be, and how to get there. Harlequins' famous stadium, The Stoop, was directly opposite Twickenham, and prior to every home game the team gathered there for their pre-match preparation. They even practised their line-out at the back of the stands. For the final the team followed their same routines, to highlight the sense that this was just another match. Once their prep was completed, the players walked from The Stoop to Twickenham stadium across the road, where their fans lined the streets and created a guard of honour, and then strode into the grand old arena, where they beat Leicester Tigers 30–23 in front of a crowd of over 80,000 fans. The atmosphere was electric; the game went right down to the wire, with Quins resisting a Leicester comeback towards the end. Under extreme pressure they worked as Warriors and Assassins, holding out to win their first ever Premiership title.

ASK THE QUESTION

What does your post-performance debrief look like?

If you don't have one – or if your analysis looks towards results only – establish a set-up that assesses the team's or individual's focused processes (as established in the game plan). Ask questions: *Did we stick to the focused processes? Which ones worked, and which ones didn't? What might we do to improve on the strategies that didn't work and reinforce the ones that did?* Then factor the answers into your next game plan. Your group will soon develop a circular process in which they plan, do and review, all while improving and finding consistency along the way.

 LIGHTBULBS

- Post-performance debriefs are incredibly important. The only way to know *why* a group is successful (*when* they're successful) is to analyse the focused processes established in the game-plan execution phase, and to determine whether the techniques and strategies put in place were effective or not.
- There are two types of debrief – hot and cold. The hot debrief happens during a lull in the thick of the action (or immediately post-performance). A cold debrief is a more considered analysis conducted after the team's performance has been concluded.

- Remember to see the 'match' through the team's focused processes, as well as the overall result. That way, it's possible to see the event in performance terms. Meanwhile, the emotional highs and lows are stripped from any discussions, which increases the chances of constructive dialogue.
- When it comes to establishing game plans, or looking to introduce new tactics, procedures and work-ons, the language we use is key. Use words or phrases that chime with the team's goals or image.

BUILDING BLOCK #4

HOW DO WE WIN?

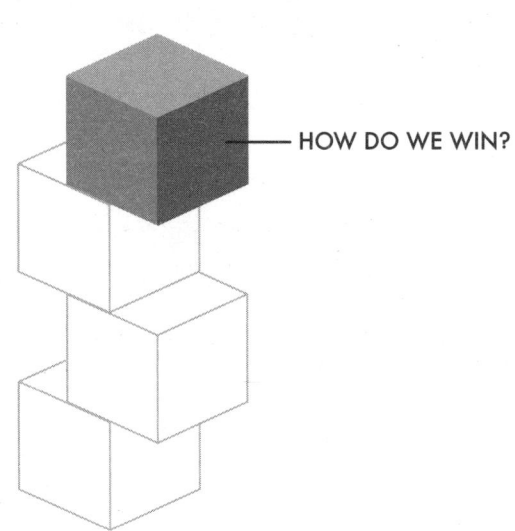

INTRODUCTION

On the eve of the 2015 Boat Race, one or two members of the Cambridge Women's team were visibly nervous. This was understandable given it was the first ever televised women's event and very few of our athletes had experienced anything in the way of media attention before. They were also expecting huge crowds: in previous years, 250,000 people had lined the Thames Tideway, which must have sounded like a terrifying figure to some of Cambridge's rowers when it was first mentioned.

On the morning of the race, one of the women approached me and admitted she was feeling nervous.

'Kate, I don't know if I can do it,' she said.

'Do you think you can try your best?' I said.

'Well ... *yeah*?'

'Because that's all that's being asked of you,' I explained, putting her mind at rest. 'The preparations have been done and the race plan is set. If you can follow the cox's instructions, everything takes care of itself.'

Given the circumstances, the rower's reaction wasn't exactly a shock. A moment of this kind had previously been discussed with the crew, and it had been revisited when a former Olympian visited Cambridge and gave a talk in which they admitted to fantasising about being anywhere else in the world when the moment to compete arrived. Feeling sick on the start line was normal for them. But nerves, when reframed, might also be regarded as excitement, which was an emotion that everyone in the boat could control.

'It's OK,' I eventually said to the rower. 'What you're feeling is part of the process. It doesn't mean you can't race.'

In such circumstances, there's a misconception that pressure can be problematic – *that nerves are bad* – but if a team or individual can normalise them, it's possible to turn that pressure into fuel. From there, a sense of safety can be created, and incredible results will follow.

The fourth building block in this book deals with exactly that process. Throughout the forthcoming pages, I've laid out a series of strategies, or 'stadium skills', designed to help a person function optimally while working under pressure. They're particularly useful for those moments when the hands go sweaty, the heart rate jack-hammers away and even the simple process of breathing can become overwhelming. Among the included techniques are self-talk, breathwork, self-care, visualisation and decompression, and given so many of us operate at the edges of our coping resources there is a universal application for each one, whether we're involved in elite-level sport, the military, career advancement, family drama or even exam hell. That's because a person can only sustain themselves for a short period of time when functioning at maximum capacity, or 'playing in the red zone'. If their stress levels remain too high and for too long, they will become susceptible to all sorts of physical and mental health issues. The skill sets I've listed above help the individual as they operate at their peak, while reducing the risk of burnout. From there, they can increase their chances of thriving over time – again and again.

There's a caveat to this work, though. To achieve success in a crunch event, it's not enough simply to perform a series of breath-work exercises, or to lean into one or two refocusing cues. Instead, a person must first assess their well-being and operate within an environment that's conducive to positive mental health, where, for example, they have room to grow emotionally. Within their role there should be flexibility and adaptability, plus a holistic worldview: the feeling that there's so much more to life than their job, career or position.

In a sporting context, it's my responsibility to support athletes and teams as they build a sturdy psychological foundation. I then help them to develop performance strategies for those important moments when *their* hands go sweaty, *their* heart rate jackhammers away, and *their* breathing becomes laboured and heavy. When this occurs, they move away from stress and unsustainable success and into a zone where goals are smashed and barriers are kicked down. Where people *win*.

Now you can do the same.

CHAPTER SIXTEEN

DON'T ICE A COLLAPSING CAKE

There's a growing belief that an individual, or team, is more likely to perform at their highest levels when they're in a good place mentally. They win gold medals, nail sales targets and create award-winning artistic masterpieces. And while people *not* in a good place can achieve similar results, they're unlikely to sustain that same success over a long period. That's because the mental and physical costs to an athlete, banker or abstract painter working at the limits of their capacity are high. Humans are designed to press the throttle during times of stress and then pump the brakes when that stress dissipates, but the problem for a lot of us is that our limbic system (the fight, flight or freeze mechanism, remember?) can't tell the difference between a life-threatening event, such as an oncoming tsunami, and a tricky deadline. Consequently, a lot of us feel a constant level of ambient stress and we hammer the speedometer to 'survive' at all times, before blowing ourselves out.

So how does someone maintain a healthy life balance while operating in a high-performance environment? The answer: *they don't ice a collapsing cake.* If that sounds like a strange analogy, consider it this way. A person's life can be viewed as a multi-tiered cake, covered by frosting and containing all sorts of sugary goodness. For the cake to remain stable, the base must be solid, because without a strong foundation its upper layers will topple over. *Humans are the same.* A robust base is needed if we're to succeed sustainably, and to stop us from falling off the edge of our coping resources. To set a solid platform for ourselves we must create conditions that are conducive to success by focusing on three important areas:

1. Mental health and well-being
2. Environment
3. Performing under pressure

Too often, people pay insufficient attention to these foundations and instead ice the upper tiers of their cake with coping strategies, quick fixes and psychological hacks. They're then forced to watch in horror as everything collapses around them. However, if they were to mix their cake with the three key ingredients, and balance them out, they would build a stable platform for continued success.

1. MENTAL HEALTH AND WELL-BEING

When discussing the concept of well-being, it's important to remember that a person, or persons, shouldn't be defined by their sport or profession. Their role as an elite athlete, or CEO, or head teacher is *what they do* not *who they are.* (As we'll discuss later, this understanding will help them to transition into a new life or career when the curtain comes down on their old.) While working at the UKSI during Project Thrive (see Building Block #2, Chapter 7), we accepted that a person's well-being and mental health, and how they function and feel, are influenced by several different factors:

- **Physical:** How well do you operate?
  This is an assessment of physical health. It should take into consideration everything from the absence of disease to a person's overall fitness levels.
- **Psychological:** How happy are you?
  Or in other words, how does a person think, feel and behave? The way in which they cope with the stressors of everyday life should be assessed, plus their ability to function well at both work and home as they attempt to fulfil their potential.
- **Personal and professional:** How supported are you?
  If an athlete (or otherwise) is to grow personally and professionally once their career has ended or changed course, they should develop new skills outside of their present full-time role. These will enable them to explore new opportunities and grow.
- **Social:** How connected are you?
  Human beings are social creatures. If we share close bonds with family and friends, enjoy a sense of belonging with a group or groups, and feel supported and loved, we can ensure an excellent level of social health.
- **Financial:** How stable are you?
  There are many dimensions to financial health but essentially it describes the state of someone's monetary affairs and concomitant stress levels.
- **Spiritual:** How in tune are you with something bigger than yourself?
  What does a person believe in? This doesn't have to be religion. It could be a sense of purpose, a shared target or belief.

All sorts of teams, groups and collectives can benefit from conducting a health assessment in these areas. That's because when someone works in an environment that encourages positive mental well-being *alongside* performance, they're being given the tools to thrive, which then enables them to perform sustainably at the highest level. To return to our cake analogy, the base layer becomes less stable when we neglect our physical, psychological, personal and professional, social, financial and spiritual health. For example, sustainable success is much harder to achieve if we drink too much or smoke; if we carry unresolved trauma; if we can't stand our boss; if we're so busy that our friends and family have become an afterthought; if we don't believe in anything bigger than ourselves; or if we struggle to pay the bills on time. But if we nurture our well-being, our performances are highly likely to improve.

I accept that approaching the issues of mental health and well-being can feel a little overwhelming. But a very good first step is to acknowledge that they're a subject for discussion in the first place. These issues should be talked about in the workplace, contributing to our daily narratives, so that they become an accepted part of everyday language. All of us sit on what's known as a mental health continuum – a spectrum of emotional wellness – and we move up and down it on a weekly, daily and sometimes even hourly basis. By simply understanding that reality, it's possible to devise support strategies that will keep us on track psychologically. From time to time, we all face emotional challenges where additional support is needed. Just knowing that help and understanding are available, should we need it, can be enough to create a healthy environment.

Examples of these support strategies might include:

- The small business that regularly checks in with staff, providing a safe space for them to ask questions and raise issues.

- The office culture that encourages people to start on time, leave on time and escape the office during their lunch break.
- And, of course, the international football team that has a psychology department working alongside the players.

I've been lucky in that regard. While you won't have to go far to read an article on the toxic environment experienced by some elite sports stars – where athletes have been worked to the limits of their emotional capacity so that they remain at the very top – that hasn't been my experience. Throughout my career I've operated alongside some incredible coaches, some of whom appear in the pages of this book. All of them had one thing in common: they understood the importance of nurturing the person, as well as the performer, while creating an environment in which people can thrive.

As with most things, balance is key. People often prioritise certain elements in their life over others, which, of course, we all must do from time to time. However, if the pendulum swings too far in one direction it can have a detrimental effect. At first, it's unnoticeable, but an early-warning sign might be that a person considers their thing to be *the only thing*. For example, imagine an athlete whose identity is wrapped up in the fact that they're a successful footballer, runner or swimmer. As far as they're concerned, the job is everything. They don't spend time with friends and family; they fail to look after themselves or process stress properly; they're not out and about experiencing nature; and they're not spending time 'in church' (whatever that church might be – their favourite restaurant, art gallery or hobby). The only thing that matters is their next game or performance, and while this might be fine in the short term, it will likely become problematic if their self-worth is solely being determined by their results on the pitch, in the pool or on the running track.

When I was doing my PhD, I interviewed a very famous athlete who told me about their motivations for getting into track and field, and their reasons for retiring. Unlike many sportspeople, their decision to quit had come easily. One day during training they asked themselves a question: 'Can I genuinely get any faster?' While the individual had it in them to win more medals and take more championship titles, their personal development had stalled. For them, satisfaction came from running as fast as they could. Breaking records, and being the then world record holder, was their thing. But having bumped up against their performance ceiling, they felt as if the time to move on had finally arrived. The athlete went home that day and hung up their spikes. They were able to make this decision because they had developed personally and professionally throughout their track career and had a new vocation that they were keen to explore. It turned out they were very good at that, too.

This transition is vitally important because too many athletes become defined by their identity as an elite performer. The same happens in all industries, and when the day eventually arrives where it's no longer possible for a person to work as an angel investor, a touring musician or a scientist, they can struggle to adapt to a new life. *That's unless they have a purpose to fall back on.* The UKSI, through its Performance Lifestyle programme, tells the athlete that, 'Yes, you're a runner, or a hockey player, or a boxer. You're incredible at it, and that's great . . . *But there's more to you than that.*' The programme has been designed to help the athlete develop multiple identities so that when the day comes when they're no longer picked for the team or are unable to make Olympic qualification, they have another exciting life to step into.

This is an incredibly important process, because when a person's purpose fades away, it's important that they have the resources to find another. The UKSI helps its members to retire from sport in a secure position – it's why so many former athletes write newspaper columns, become sports broadcasters or produce podcasts. Without this process, an athlete can find themselves caught in a trap. If they haven't looked at what drives them, or gained an understanding of their *why* and *who,* once they eventually reach the point of retirement their first thought is: 'Oh, no. *What next?*' This moment, sadly, is inevitable for all of us because jobs change, illness and injuries affect our ability to perform, and advances in technology can kill off industries. But being aware of that fact is a blessing, because it allows us to develop professionally and prepare for the next phase in life.*

For the individual, one way to avoid the stresses of any major transition is to revisit the bigger questions that we outlined in Building Block #1. These could include:

- Who am I and what am I all about?
- What do I value?
- What drives me and what am I interested in?
- And most importantly of all: How might the answers to these questions align to other things?

For a company or team, it's important that the individuals within their care are encouraged to develop and grow, to collaborate and learn. Although most organisations provide personal development

---

* This is especially the case if we're at the end of our working years. According to a study conducted by the Harvard School of Public Health, retirement is a 'transition involving environmental changes that reshape health behaviours, social interactions, and psychosocial stresses . . .' It also noted that those people with a clear sense of purpose, a set of hobbies and volunteer work opportunities were able to settle into a new routine and remain healthy. Those that lacked these things struggled.

courses and leadership programmes, to really help their staff or members it's important they also promote curiosity and encourage their teams to learn from the other people around them. Through personal and professional development, an individual can find out what's important to them. They can then discover a role that might bring them happiness and fulfilment beyond whatever it was they were doing in the first place. This also helps them to feel valued in their current position and is a great way of giving them inspiration. In many ways, a carrot is being dangled. It shows a person that there are different ways of viewing the world. *The mind gets going.* And that can only benefit the group.

When it comes to the consideration of mental health and well-being, sport hasn't always got it right, and this kind of thinking is still evolving. There has, however, been a significant shift in the past 20 years, with the industry moving away from a 'win at all costs' mentality, and more towards a process of 'winning healthily'.

And it all starts with the mind.

2. ENVIRONMENT

When it comes to striving for sustainable success, environment is everything, and the telltale signs of a toxic workplace are easy to spot. People blame one another, they lack autonomy and they're frightened of making mistakes. The individual's point of view is ignored and their requests for collaboration or help are denied. On the other hand, the best environments are those in which the opposite holds true. The team and the individuals within it are allowed to make mistakes and learn from them. They're able to speak their mind and convey their thoughts and feelings. They have autonomy. They can contribute to the decisions being made. *They feel safe, protected and heard.*

One of my greatest lessons in trying to create a positive team environment came from an occasion when I did it badly. I'd just taken on the head of psychology role at the UKSI, and we were about a year away from the 2016 Olympics in Rio. At the time, I felt ready for the challenge. I'd been working in Olympic sport for a long time, with a number of teams and individual athletes, and I'd managed several groups of multidisciplinary staff as well as supervising several other sport psychologists. I was as ready as I was ever going to be at that point, and I went into the job with enthusiasm and excitement. Given that I was familiar with the great work previously conducted by the UKSI and its members, I was eager for them to share their ideas and motivate one another. I also wanted them to be confident in me as a leader.

'Right,' I thought, 'I'm going to take this team on a journey.'

The jumping-off point for this process was an annual conference. During this event, separate groups from within the organisation come together to discuss their findings, share plans and exchange ideas. I saw this as my chance to inspire the team and make a strong first impression, but it turned out to be one of the most important mistakes of my career. I became so excited about what I wanted to expose the team to that I overlooked the importance of developing an environment conducive to success. The upshot was that the space felt hierarchical. *I* had opened the day and presented *my* journey and *my* thoughts for the future. A succession of senior team members then detailed what they'd been working on. Meanwhile, the voices of everyone else in the room went unheard. Rather than it being an engaging and inclusive atmosphere, everything seemed off.

Afterwards, when I spoke individually to the other members of my team, which included several new employees and early-career practitioners, my fears were confirmed. While they'd enjoyed listening to the UKSI's senior figures, at no point did they feel as if they could contribute or ask questions. One member told me that they'd left the conference feeling as if there was a massive gap between the capability of the senior figures in the team and everyone else. My heart sank. Instead of departing the event feeling excited and inspired, their confidence had been eroded, and we hadn't had the opportunity to learn from the diversity of experiences inside the room.

Ultimately, the process was a massive lesson in how *not* to do things and I course-corrected almost immediately. When Project Thrive was launched shortly afterwards, I dismantled the hierarchy within the team and created a new environment where the mechanisms of *how* we did things ensured that everyone's opinions and ideas were heard and explored. Meanwhile, I made it clear that nobody had a monopoly on ideas. Instantly everybody felt involved. We ran multiple focus groups with different staff where the individuals within the team learned from one another; they discovered what had worked in the past and what hadn't. They also gained an insight into what could work in the future by listening to the experiences of other members in the groups, and they were encouraged to be bold with their ideas. It totally changed the way that our team went about their business. Together we were able to create something that couldn't have been achieved without everyone owning the project and playing their part.

There's a common misconception regarding psychologically safe environments, and many people consider them to be 'soft'. But that's not the case at all. As Project Thrive proved, such a space allowed people to make mistakes. They could air wild suggestions and opinions without fear of recrimination or judgement. From there, great ideas often grew. That process must start somewhere, though. After the UKSI conference, I made it my mission to create a psychologically safer workspace by displaying vulnerability; I explained to the team that I didn't have all the answers, and as we spoke I shared my misses as well as my hits, while ensuring that every single person had a voice. This process was accelerated when Covid arrived in 2020, because suddenly the group had to collaborate in a way that was new to *everybody*. When it came to organising working-from-home practices and a nationwide return-to-training programme for our Olympic and Paralympic athletes, there were no experts in the room. This led to an incredibly collaborative project across multiple teams as everyone came together to solve the unique problem of supporting athletes, coaches and support staff during a global lockdown.

The problem-solving process was extraordinary. Remember, at the time there was still a lot of fear and uncertainty surrounding the novel coronavirus. There were no vaccines, home testing was in its infancy and people like me had been cooped up indoors for months on end. We'd been glued to the news, and at times the world seemed to be in a terrifying state. Locked-down athletes and coaches, who had all experienced the pandemic differently, were being transitioned back into training, and that had to be done in a safe manner. As you can imagine, there was a lot of apprehension, particularly among the para-athlete community, which was especially vulnerable.

However, by acknowledging that we were in a brand-new situation and that nobody had ownership of what was the right and wrong way of going about things, several exciting possibilities emerged. One UKSI member, Paul Hughes, started researching 'transitions'. He found that the Red Cross had decades of experience in caring for hostages that had been held in captivity for long periods of time. This was how some people had viewed the emotional experience of a national lockdown, after all. *Talk about a brilliant, but abstract, idea.* We learned how released hostages were reintegrated into society and we studied the frameworks used within the National Health Service (NHS) for when considering psychological responses to crises. Some of these techniques and strategies were applied to the Olympic and Paralympic programmes. Paul gathered a group of practitioners within our own psychology team and set up a project group with multiple other stakeholders, among them medics, performance lifestyle practitioners and mental health experts. Working collaboratively in this way wasn't always easy – it took greater thought, organisation and planning – but it soon become part of the team's DNA.

All of us can benefit from creating a healthy working environment of this kind, whether we're employed by a bank, a business or a hospital. To do so, the group should embrace the following key concepts:

- **Mistakes are lessons.** People should be allowed to take interpersonal risks and be encouraged to assume ownership of mistakes without fear of reprimand. This provides the opportunity for people to ask for help and learn from their errors.
- **There's no such thing as a bad idea.** When individuals speak their mind and convey their thoughts and feelings, great solutions can be found. (See Paul Hughes and the Red Cross.)
- **Autonomy is important.** It creates a sense of control and choice.
- **Everyone should contribute to the decisions being made.** If ideas are always being generated by an expert in the room (self-appointed, or otherwise), the group will fail to

innovate beyond their expertise. However, when everyone is encouraged to have their say, and diversity in thinking is promoted, the group will feel safe, protected and heard as a result.

Of course, introducing practices of this kind can be problematic for some people. A CEO of a multinational company might find it difficult to extend their decision-making process beyond a small group of trusted colleagues. The buck stops with them, after all. There's also a certain self-imposed pressure that can prevent some individuals from asking for help. The CEO's take might be that they're supposed to know all the answers, so they shouldn't display vulnerability by suggesting otherwise – they must instead take responsibility for *everything*. However, by expanding the circle, as we did with the UKSI, it's possible for a CEO to hear new ideas, opinions and perspectives. Leading from the front can be a lonely and vulnerable experience, but when other people are given the opportunity and freedom to communicate and evolve, the responsibility of leadership is shared. It's my experience that the team will become more creative and successful as a result. And as the saying goes, 'It's amazing what you can accomplish if you don't care who gets the credit.'

3. PERFORMANCE UNDER PRESSURE

When it comes to explaining the third and final focus area, I'll keep the details brief because I'll be explaining how to perform when the stakes are highest elsewhere in the book. For now, it's important to know that functioning effectively under pressure lies at the heart of sport psychology. This is facilitated by prioritising well-being and creating an environment beneficial to positive mental health and performance. However, despite having a strong foundation in place, many elite athletes stand on the start line and feel fear, especially if they're in front of a packed stadium, with a world record or medal within their reach. As with those Cambridge rowers in 2015, that doesn't mean they're lacking in confidence; rather, such an emotional state is a by-product of pressure, and the most successful competitors, through training and experience, will have a well-defined strategy in place to handle those very moments. Processes of this kind are the final ingredient in our base mix, but they also make up the icing, frosting and cherry on top of the performance cake. We'll discuss them further in the coming chapters.

 ASK THE QUESTION

Do you have a solid foundation on which you can build a set of stadium skills?

If not, look to improving your ingredients: 1) mental health and well-being, 2) environment and 3) performance under pressure.

LIGHTBULBS

- In any context, a person's performance can be viewed as a multi-tiered cake. For the cake to stand up, the base layer must be well constructed, because without a solid foundation, the higher levels will fold in on themselves.
- Well-being can be assessed by considering the following areas: Physical health (*How fit are you?*). Psychological health (*How happy are you?*). Personal and professional health (*How supported are you?*). Social health (*How connected are you?*). Financial health (*How stable are you?*). Spiritual health (*How in tune are you with something bigger than yourself?*).
- There's more to you than your job, position or role. To become equipped for change – which is a vital part of *winning* – it's important to look at who you are, what you value and the things that drive you. The answers to those questions, and how they align to another purpose or cause, can help you to transition into a different life.
- In a psychologically safe environment, people are allowed to make mistakes and learn from them; they're able to speak their mind and convey their thoughts and feelings; they have autonomy. *They feel safe, protected and heard.*
- Many sportspeople experience nerves before competing. That can be interpreted as fear, excitement and readiness, among other things. What it doesn't mean is that the person is lacking in confidence. An experienced competitor knows that a) they have the skill sets to succeed, b) their emotions are part of the process and c) they'll likely respond positively once the crunch moment arrives.

CHAPTER SEVENTEEN

THE PRE-COMPETITION HEALTH CHECK

In the build-up to any event that we're trying to win, there's no point arriving at the start line (or the business conference or job interview, for that matter) expecting to excel without some form of pre-competition assessment. By that I mean a health check that a team or individual undertakes to ensure that they're fully prepared for the task ahead, and capable of dealing with any unexpected circumstances that might derail their plans. The idea of running an assessment of this kind was first presented to me while I was working at the UKSI. Between the 2012 Olympics in London and Tokyo 2020, a shift in sport psychology took place where a greater emphasis was placed on systemic support: *how*, psychologically, an environment could be facilitated in which a person might excel sustainably, from a personal and performance perspective.

This idea would be tested to the max in Tokyo. The Olympic and Paralympic Games are always a crunch moment, and while the athletes, coaches and support teams have four years to prepare, so much disruption can take place before and during the event. Tokyo was, of course, the Covid Games, a story of extreme restrictions and challenging logistics, given it was being held under the cloud of a global pandemic. There were no crowds in the stadiums, people were banned from travelling around the city, and athletes, coaches and travelling team members were only allowed to move from the accommodation areas to their respective venues, and back again. While working through Project Thrive, an Olympic health check was created so that everyone working under the Team GB banner, from the athletes and coaches to the sport psychology team itself, would have the best chance of performing to their optimum at the Games. Through this, a questionnaire was used by the psychology team that dealt with performance system, performance dynamics, team preparation, individual preparation and psychological well-being.

- **Performance system:** This section focused on a lot of the work conducted throughout the first three building blocks of How to Win. The health check asked the individual to reflect upon team values and behaviour, agreement of goals, role clarity and selection, because it was important that athletes not only had clarity on the selection process but also that they were mentally prepared for a scenario in which they didn't make the team. (It was important too that the sport had a care strategy in place for those athletes.)
- **Performance dynamics:** The focus in this section was on the values of the individuals and their psychological safety. For example: *Did the members within a team setting ask for help, and/or freely give assistance to those people alongside them?* We also looked at some of the logistical details that could sometimes throw an athlete off balance, such as accommodation, transportation and the various rules that needed to be observed when staying in the Athletes' Village. It was important to normalise the uniqueness of an Olympic Games.

- **Team preparation:** The athletes, coaches and support staff representing Team GB had to understand their process-focused goals and what was needed for them to perform to the best of their ability. Elsewhere, it was vital that the language used by everyone prioritised the *process* rather than the *outcome*. When considering team preparation, thought was given to the mindset of first-time Olympians, the shared language used by teams and athletes, and guidelines for dealing with media, both traditional and social.
- **Individual preparation:** *Were the individuals travelling to the Olympics in tune with their individualised plans, pressure responses, and the signs and symptoms that they might be struggling under pressure?* In assessing a person's individual preparation, we were checking that their performance mindset was in place and that they were proactively exploring and managing their expectations, while establishing a strategy to deal with friends and family, which could sometimes be a major distraction during an Olympics, especially when it came to the issues of communication, contact and ticket allocation.
- **Psychological well-being:** Finally, we wanted to assess everyone's mental state during the build-up to what might be the biggest event of their life. It was important that they felt fully supported outside of their sport programme and that there was a plan in place for anyone in need of mental health support. We also asked several important questions regarding personal preparation. For example: *Did the athlete/coach have a logical sounding board? Were they clear about their roles and responsibilities? Had they gone through a personality-profiling programme to establish how their needs might be challenged throughout the Games?*

Meanwhile, it was important that the sport psychologists working at the Olympics didn't sacrifice their own well-being when looking after the mental health of others.*

This work was important because the Olympics is an event like no other – the pressure can be intense, and people at the Games can sometimes do unexpected things. I remember a colleague of mine comparing the event to *The Lord of the Rings* and the character Gollum, who became so obsessed with the One Ring that it deformed his body and twisted his mind. While the Olympics were nowhere near as extreme, some people working towards them noticeably changed as soon as the Olympic logo came into view. They became consumed and behaved irrationally. This transformation sometimes created unnecessary stress within their team, and it was hoped that an Olympic health check would ensure that everyone going to Tokyo avoided such a situation.

The added advantage with assessments of this kind is that they often throw up potential scenarios that might otherwise be overlooked. A classic example was the Opening Ceremony, which was a highly adrenalised event. The athletes were on show and mixing with superstars from around the globe. There were bands, a drone display and incredible visuals. By assessing whether the athletes were suitably prepared, the correct approach could be taken. For starters, the right decisions would be made about an athlete or a team's attendance – with those individuals compet-

---

* The sport psychologists reviewed their sport in relation to these categories using a traffic-light system: *red = poor; amber = needs work; green = good to go.* The priority of each category was ranked according to which ones needed the most attention. This stage was important because the process was designed to facilitate preparation; it wasn't meant to be a 'tick box' exercise and it wasn't necessarily imperative that all elements of the health check were in place in every programme. The purpose was to tailor psychological support.

ing early in the Olympic schedule, there was a question as to whether they should attend the ceremony at all. (*What were the emotional benefits of enjoying the hype versus the physical cost of being on your feet for hours on end, late into the night?*) We also catered for those athletes that hadn't been to an Olympic Games before, and in the build-up to Tokyo we asked several former Team GB members to educate the first-timers about their experiences – they detailed things they wished they'd known before the event and listed their lessons learned. As we've pointed out already, storytelling is an invaluable way of educating people on issues as diverse as time management, the Olympic vibe and pressure.

This approach was vital for Tokyo because it was such a unique environment. Delayed by a year due to the issues posed by the coronavirus pandemic, the Olympic Games became an enormous logistical challenge for everyone involved. Purely on the level of timing, everyone was thrown out of synch. Athletes who'd been building towards the 2020 event were suddenly extending their preparation into 2021, an adjustment that needed careful management. (This shift was particularly demanding for those individuals with one eye on the following Olympics. Given the Paris Games were still set to take place in 2024 their preparation for the next event felt like it was being cut by a full year.) Then there were the issues of isolation ahead of the Games, plus a whole list of Covid-related protocols once everyone had settled in Tokyo. And all this on the back of some of the most unsettling times any of us had ever known.

The good news, judging from the Olympic health check and the exceptional work of many people across the system, was that a lot of people – athletes, coaches and support staff such as myself – had already adapted to the worldwide restrictions. People understood how to work remotely, everyone was used to following rules that might have seemed alien 18 months previously and some of the self-care strategies developed during lockdown were highly relevant within an Olympics scenario. Meanwhile, a number of individuals representing several sporting disciplines had already travelled abroad during the crisis, and we were able to glean tips and tactics from them while establishing mental health first aid kits to help those people travelling to the other side of the world in the middle of a pandemic.

At this point you might be wondering: *How can an Olympic health check have any relevance for my business, project or life?* Well, a thorough process of this kind – and the associated conversations they generally stimulate – could be carried out by anyone facing a high-stress event. This is so that the readiness of a team or individual can be analysed in such a way that they'll know whether or not they're in need of any extra preparation, support or information. All that's needed is for the questions to be tailored to the event. It might be that someone is running a stand at a business convention, a fundraising festival or a village fete. These are occasions that bring their own set of unique challenges, stressors and logistical headaches. A team attending such a function could assess their readiness in advance by asking a list of questions under similar headings to the ones used by the UKSI.

Example: Business convention health check

Performance system
- Is the team clear on its targets for the convention?
- Is there role clarity throughout the team?
- Does everyone understand their process-focused goals?

Performance dynamics
- Does everyone feel valued in their roles?
- Are team members able to bring up problems and discuss troubleshooting options and strategies?
- Logistics: Does everyone have the right passes, parking information and schedule?

Team preparation
- Does the team have a plan for briefing and debriefing during the convention?
- Is there a plan for first-time convention-goers?
- Do we have a strategy for promoting our brand and successes on social media?

Individual preparation
- Does everyone have a personal mantra/reminder to keep them focused?
- Are the team's individual strengths, skills and talents being valued and maximised?
- Is everyone clear on how the expectations of themselves and the team will be communicated?

Psychological well-being
- Does everyone have a logical sounding board?
- Do we have appropriate supervision/mentorship in place for all staff?
- Is everyone willing to embrace personal performance challenges at the convention?

In events with lots of moving parts, like business conventions, networking events, music festivals, fetes, fairs and even the Olympic Games, it's very easy for people to get swept up in the emotion and anticipation of what might happen. A health check or similar document ensures that a team can remain focused, while identifying any gaps in their preparation.

CONTINGENCY PLANNING: ASKING WHAT IF . . . ?

As was evident when working towards the Tokyo Olympics, certainty doesn't exist, so there's no point in looking for it. In the build-up to the Games we constantly asked questions such as: *How do we manage our expectations? Where can we go to learn? How do we maintain the flexibility to cope with any changes that might occur at such an unusual event?* The reality of our situation was that there were no definitive answers. Even in the final weeks leading up to Tokyo, there was still a doubt in some quarters as to whether the competition would even go ahead. In the end we adopted a position of accepting the uncertainty. I remember saying to someone: 'We can plan as best we can, but we won't have the answers to everything . . . And that's OK.' In doing so, we became comfortable in the uncomfortable.

When looking to get an edge, *when trying to figure out how to win*, it's important we accept the impossibility of certainty before taking on the challenge of adapting to any surprise events that might come our way. In an Olympic context this could include a race being delayed due to poor weather, a teammate injuring themselves in the warm-up, an ill coach or a personal situation unfolding at home. In a real-world setting, surprise events can include train strikes, a sick pet, a power cut or a technical glitch in the hours and minutes before an important meeting. While it's impossible to prevent these wildcard events from happening, it is possible to prepare ourselves with a little contingency planning so that we can respond positively, rather than losing emotional control at the worst possible moment.

One way of doing this is to consider the *what ifs . . .?*

This is something that should be conducted well in advance of the event in question. During the preparation for the Olympic Games, for example, a contingency-planning programme was conducted several months ahead of the team's departure for Tokyo. That's because the *what if . . .?* process asks a person to consider their worst-case scenarios. If these seeds of doubt are planted with only a few days in hand, they can cause anxiety and panic; someone who on the verge of taking part in their competition with a mindset of blissful ignorance could begin worrying about issues they hadn't previously considered. Ordinarily, an athlete will have worked for a long time just to arrive at the Olympics. The competition is hugely important to everyone involved. In this context, it's important to throw some *what if . . .?* questions at them early on so they can mentally ready themselves for any challenges that might occur.*

- *What if a close family member is taken ill on the day of the race: do they want to be informed or not?*
- *What if they lose an important piece of kit en route to competition?*
- *What if their coach becomes ill and there's no one to manage them through the Games?*

---

* For a prudent mindset, someone who likes to control threat, this process will come easily as *they love contingency planning*. However, for an optimistic mindset, it's unlikely they'll have considered any of the worst-case scenarios, so a long lead time is very important. It's crucial not to create unnecessary stress, particularly if there isn't time to effectively troubleshoot solutions.

Dozens of different scenarios were discussed with the athletes by me or one of the other members of the UKSI psych team so that they could become comfortable with the idea of chaos, and adapt and be flexible in the face of change. This process also encouraged them to have one or two contingency plans in place, while creating a coping framework to fall back on in case life became messy, which it can do at the biggest event in sport. For example, the subject of an unwell family member came up regularly, as there will always be an athlete who has a sick or very elderly loved one. It was important the support staff knew if, and when, to alert them, should something worrying happen. Our mantra was: *The athlete's well-being always comes first.* If somebody wanted to know about a grandparent's health, it was our job to tell them.

At some point in the contingency planning session, I liked to throw in a curveball suggestion: *And what if . . . the water turns green?*

While this might sound like a completely random scenario, during the Rio Games the water in the diving pool did indeed turn a deep shade of green. While this might not sound like a massive deal to the spectators, it presented a potential problem for the competitors. With the water a different colour, it became doubly difficult for them to spot the surface. This made it harder for a diver to know when to come out of shape and to assess their entry point. Suddenly the field was forced to operate in a totally alien environment because of a situation that nobody could have predicted. See also: a race having to take place in a polluted river; Snoop Dogg turning up at an equestrian event; an athlete losing their wedding ring during the Opening Ceremony. Every Games brings a series of weird and unexpected events, and the trick to surviving them is to expect the unexpected. A solid contingency plan, paired with a person's understanding of their *who* and *why*, can help anyone to adapt and thrive.

Even when the water turns a funny colour.

 ASK THE QUESTION

Have you considered the what ifs . . .? for your next challenge or event?

If not, learn to adapt and be flexible in the moment by imagining how you would cope with a variety of different scenarios that might unfold. A classic example would be the job interview or the make-or-break meeting. *What if there's a train strike on the day? What if it pours with rain and you arrive soaking wet? What if your mind goes blank and you can't think of an example to illustrate an important point?* And so on . . .

LIGHTBULBS

- To increase your chances of performing under pressure, conduct a pre-performance assessment and health check your readiness for the work ahead.
- An Olympic health check was a questionnaire comprising several categories: performance system, performance dynamics, team preparation, individual preparation and psychological well-being. Such a document can be adapted to fit any situation.
- Health checks are also useful because they throw up potential scenarios that are sometimes overlooked in advance of an event. They allow us to plan for them and prepare for any problems ahead of time.
- In events where there are lots of moving parts it's very easy for people to get swept up in the emotion and anticipation of what might happen. A health check or similar document ensures that a team stays focused, while identifying any gaps in their preparation.

CHAPTER EIGHTEEN
STRESS BUCKETS AND SELF-CARE

An athlete can conduct all the health checks and contingency planning in the world, but competitive sport is a highly challenging and, at times, incredibly stressful environment. The same goes for driving tests, product releases and the launch of a new website or service. Everyone feels the pinch of adrenaline when being asked to perform to their optimum. Butterflies are inevitable if we're going for that win. But when the stakes are high, what sets the people who *can* apart from those that *can't* is an understanding of how to control the body's responses under pressure. The foundations for how to do so have been established throughout the first three building blocks of this book. What I'm going to discuss now are the ways in which we can manage our anxieties with some well-thought-out preventative strategies.

Let me introduce you to the stress bucket.

The stress bucket is an imaginary tool that looks like any other ordinary garden bucket. But what goes into it are the hiccups and strains of competitive life. For an athlete at a Rugby World Cup, Ryder Cup or Diamond League race there could be all sorts of stuff swilling around in the metaphorical bucket: time away from family, a niggling injury, the challenges associated with operating in an alien environment and so on. Then there are everyday matters, such as financial stress, relationship issues, work pressure, and physical and mental health. These can quickly add to an athlete's emotional load, but it's important to note that not all things are equal. One person's capacity for enduring stress will be greater or less than the person next to them, so some buckets take longer to fill than others. However, the common factor for everyone is that once their bucket overflows, it makes a terrible mess.

The trick to avoiding such a situation is to reduce the levels inside the bucket ahead of time, before the worst can happen. This is done by leaning into self-care, which is any activity or routine that promotes positive mental health, and is under our control and self-initiated. As I mentioned earlier in the building block, we all move up and down the mental health continuum. Anyone can fall victim to stress, uncertainty or anxiety at any time, but a good self-care plan helps us to minimise their impact. The upshot is that we feel fitter, stronger and mentally prepared for the tests ahead. To not work on strategies for self-care in advance of a challenging moment potentially leaves us exposed to extreme fatigue, diminishing returns in whatever it is we're doing and all the associated symptoms of burnout.

To organise a self-care strategy, we need to take two steps. The first is to ask a simple question: *What do we need to tune out the stress going on around us?* Some people like to read quietly in bed, others like to exercise in nature. Providing the activity doesn't add to a person's ambient stress levels, there are no right or wrong answers here. (For a Lioness in the thick of an international tournament, for example, any self-care programme that involves relaxation and positive focus would be appropriate; anything that requires intense physical activity would not.) The second step needs us to assess any challenges to our self-care plan. Having conducted this work with the British Olympic Association (BOA) staff for the Tokyo Games, and later with the Lionesses in 2022, the individuals involved were encouraged to make sure their strategy was clearly defined and well-rehearsed before being shared with their team leader, coach, manager or logical sounding board.

Once that had been established, a series of follow-up questions were put forward.

- Is my self-care plan sufficient?
- Are there other processes that I could explore?
- What are some of the barriers that might get in the way of me sticking to my plan?
- What are the strategies that will enable me to overcome these barriers?

This analysis was important. Some activities that work perfectly well at home might become impossible to re-create in another environment. I remember speaking to one Olympic athlete who practised self-care by walking along the beach with friends. During these strolls they often discussed their future challenges, associated nerves and general concerns, and it served as a brilliant way of emptying the stress bucket. Clearly this wasn't going to be possible in Tokyo, given that everyone was locked down in their hotel rooms for several weeks except when they were training or competing. Instead, we worked up a schedule of online connections with friends and family, a meditation plan and an 'isolation pack' of the athletes' favourite books, films, music and so on. We then got them to work on their self-care strategies in advance so that they could feel ready and reassured before arriving in Japan. Their self-care plan looked something like this:

Athlete X

What I need
Walking with friends
Change of scene
Switching off from sport
Social connection outdoors

What I'd like to improve
Say 'no' to excessive new responsibilities
Meditate, practise mindfulness
To ask for help when needed
Keeping a journal

What can get in the way?
No/limited access to outdoors
No change of scenery
Friends and family needs
Single rooms

What can I put in place?
Utilising indoor spaces
My isolation packs
Remote friends and family connection
Setting expectations with friends/family

We used this strategy when preparing the Lionesses for their successful European Championship campaign in 2022. As the squad readied themselves, I encouraged the staff and players to plan their downtime and self-care routines ahead of the tournament, knowing this would increase the likelihood of them engaging in energising and connecting activities. As part of this concept, the players were encouraged to think about their own 'personal bubble', an isolated space *inside* the one already designed by Sarina and her staff, such as their bedroom, where the individual could practise self-care and look after their emotional well-being. I then asked them to think about three component parts of their self-care, which I referred to as 'switch off', 'refresh' and 'reconnect', and how they might apply them to travel days, matchdays and stressor events such as birthdays.

1. **Switch off:** The player was asked to disconnect from their football brain (without guilt) so they could take up another

activity for an hour or so. Ideas included watching a favourite film, playing darts, reading, drawing or some other artistic endeavour.

2. **Refresh:** Mindfulness, meditation, sleep and journalling were encouraged so that the player could protect their mental health and maximise their performance. The latter can be particularly useful because by writing down their thoughts on the day, an individual will better process any notable events or connections that might have taken place. Equally, if things had gone well, writing those moments down provided a reminder of where they had been successful. This is particularly powerful should they require a confidence boost later on. The players were even given questions to ponder, were they to find themselves struggling for jumping off points.

Morning thoughts	Evening thoughts
Today's message to myself.	A moment I appreciated today was . . .
Today's goals and priorities.	Something I handled well today was . . .
One thing I'm excited about today . . .	Something I could have improved upon . . .
A challenging situation today could be . . .	What I learned today (that I'll use later)

3. **Reconnect:** Given that the players were being separated from their friends and loved ones for a month, we advised them to stay connected to their usual sources of support and advice – parents, partners, best mates and so on. A big event such as the European Championship can be an emotional minefield. It's not uncommon for people to overreact to otherwise normal situations. To counter this, we suggested a series of reconnection strategies for the

players to utilise in tough moments. Some of them were obvious (calling friends and family), while others required a little work in advance (creating a photo library of good times). There were also activities that benefited the group as a whole, and everyone was encouraged to instigate conversations and social activities with other members of the team. Meanwhile, every single player was given a list of contacts within the set-up should they require any additional assistance.

Elsewhere there were strategies for sleep routines and encouragement for the players to look out for certain types of negative thought processes while they were away, among them black and white thinking (all or nothing), negative bias (focusing only on the bad) and catastrophic thinking (magnifying the negative consequences of an event that might not happen). Planning ahead in this way – and practising the suggested techniques – enabled the players to look after themselves in highly pressurised times and lower the stress levels in their bucket.

SELF-CARE CUES AND REMINDERS

When working with teams and elite athletes, there are a few things I like to impress upon them when approaching an event of a certain magnitude, such as a cup final or a title-deciding fixture. In short, they're reminders to live in the moment and cues for normalising the hectic events swirling around them. While I appreciate that the people I work with tend to be sports stars or coaches, there's nothing to stop anyone else from adopting the following three mindsets. At the very least, they will improve an individual's self-care routine.

1. NERVES ARE NORMAL

All of us will face pressure from time to time, some more than others, because it's unavoidable in life. The key to pushing through the resultant feelings, good or bad, is to normalise them. Yes, we might sleep badly the night before a big day at work or a major life event, in the same way that an athlete might feel sick with nerves while standing on the start line of a major race. *But that's OK.* It's a big stage. Feeling these sensations is totally normal. It's how we react to them that's important, because if we see the butterflies in our stomach as a cue to give in or quit, they can become a problem. However, if we can reframe those same sensations as something positive – a feeling to get excited about or something to trigger action – it's possible to set ourselves up for an optimal performance. Some key phrases for this might include:

- *The nerves are a sign that I'm ready.*
- *The nausea is a reminder that I have a job to do (but I can do it).*
- *That sleepless night occurred due to excitement rather than fear.*

I've found that the individuals who become most unsettled on the eve of a major challenge are often the ones that didn't expect to feel that way in the first place. Having arrived at the Athletes' Village or the team hotel for the first time, with all its distractions and unfamiliarity, they become upended and go into a spin. Then there are the athletes who experience these issues and believe, wrongly, that they're unique to them.

In my experience, a great first step towards re-establishing a sense of calm in both groups is to normalise the thoughts and reframe any heightened emotions as positive indicators. If a person can be reassured that what they're experiencing is in fact quite natural, they'll usually come out of their unsettled state fairly quickly. It then helps to point out the evidence that the preparatory work has been completed, that the hardest miles are behind them, *that they're ready*. Their only job is to stick to whatever focused processes they might have agreed upon for the day. Being familiarised with these facts is often enough to keep a person on track.

2. SELF-CARE UNDERPINS PERFORMANCE

When looking to manage our stress bucket in the run-up to an event of magnitude, it's important to reflect upon and assess our everyday well-being – a catch-all term for a combination of factors that influences how a person thinks and feels *every day*, and, as mentioned in Chapter 16, includes their physical health, psychological health, financial health, educational/professional health, spiritual health and social health. When these areas are all in balance, a person will feel fit, emotionally robust, monetarily stable, in a state of growth and socially connected. But for so many of us, striking that balance can be hard: some of us are fit, but stressed; others are successful at work, but out of touch at home. If we're unbalanced in this way, it's possible to manage the day-to-day events for a while, but over time the cost to us can be great.

To gain an understanding of our well-being, it can be helpful to write a list of the things that are important to us. The areas I mentioned earlier – physical, mental, financial, educational/professional, spiritual and social health – are good starting points. We can gain considerable insight into ourselves by thinking about the things we do well, the things we do poorly and the things we can improve for the future. With a knowledge of what's needed if we're to be at our best, everyone can have a tangible target to aim for. It's also possible to spot any areas that might have been neglected and watch for warning signs that we need to course-correct.

Sure, going on holiday to somewhere exotic might well recharge our batteries once a year. But the reality is that doing lots of little things, and regularly, can make a difference too. Small-but-effective daily strategies could include drinking more water, going for regular walks and cutting down on alcohol or caffeine. On a personal level I can be affected physically and mentally if I sit in front of my laptop all day. I'm more than capable of doing it; I can function from the early hours of the morning until late at night because I've become so engrossed in my work. But I also know there are consequences to my behaving that way: I can become disconnected from friends and family; my body suffers from being hunched over a screen for too long. These have a knock-on effect on my mood and sleep. Knowing all of this, I make sure to schedule phone calls rather than online meetings during the day. I'll try to do them while I'm on a walk, preferably outside. I'm still working, and focused 100 per cent on the job, but by moving and getting fresh air, I'm bringing a little balance to my working day.

3. PRESSURE CAN BE FUN . . . ENJOY IT

Too often we lose sight of *why* we're experiencing pressure. Some CEOs become so stressed that they forget it was once their dream to run a successful company. They reach their target position and feel the need to work 24 hours a day, seven days a week, because they're suddenly running the show. They push themselves too hard, burn themselves out and lose their edge. When the going gets tough, they refuse to accept help or share responsibility, making them susceptible to mistakes. In such moments, it can help the individual to step back and appreciate the fact that they're exactly where they initially wanted to be.

This same situation often challenges athletes. During the writing of this book, I asked the medal-winning diver Tom Daley if he had any regrets from his career.

He nodded. 'Yeah, I wish I'd enjoyed it more back then,' he said.

I fully appreciated Tom's answer, having started working with him following his very first Olympics in Beijing in 2008. Back then, he was a phenomenally talented 14-year-old, but given his age and the fact he didn't yet have a competition repertoire of the same degree of difficulty as his older competitors, he didn't enter those Games with any great weight of expectation. Because of that, Beijing presented Tom with a fantastic learning opportunity, and he received a taste of what to expect in the years to come. Armed with a camcorder, he entered the Athletes' Village, met many of his idols and became a media sensation. More importantly, Tom familiarised himself with the Olympic vibe. But when London 2012 came around, everything changed. There was pressure, some of it self-imposed, and the media attention on him was huge – there were even building-sized posters of Tom around the capital. A lot of people expected him to win, which didn't help matters either. Having then claimed his first Olympic medal, his overriding emotion, unsurprisingly, was relief rather than joy.

Things were very different for Tom by the time he arrived in Paris 12 years later – his fifth Olympic Games. He had a family; there was a newfound perspective on what was most important to him and he was able to relax more easily. Tom's performance resulted in a silver medal in the men's synchronised 10-metre event alongside his teammate Noah Williams. In the last Olympics of his career, Tom was able to enjoy himself by thinking about the other priorities in his life.

Another way of reminding an athlete or team about the *fun* aspect of whatever it is they're doing is to connect them with the people on the other side of fence, so to speak. During the 2022 European Championship, Lionesses head coach Sarina Wiegman encouraged the players to mingle with the fans at an appropriate time during the warm-up – she understood the importance of them relishing such an experience. The Cambridge Women's rowing coach Rob Baker shared Sarina's sentiments and encouraged the same approach from his rowers during the build-up to the Boat Race in 2015.

'You will never have experienced this before,' he said. 'You'll be in the boat house, and then the shutters will go up. *Suddenly you're in the mix.* The fans will be heading to the riverbank and there will be a huge amount of noise. You'll walk out in between the crowds to get down to the river and put your boat out. It will feel huge.'

Rather than scaring them, Rob wanted his team to tune in to the brilliance of the occasion because there was a big difference between rowing on a quiet river and rowing on a waterway lined with hundreds of thousands of spectators. To get everyone's head in the right place, he'd instructed them to bring a set of 'civvies' for race day.

'I want you to get out of your Cambridge gear, put your everyday clothes on and mix with the crowds,' he said. 'Experience it. Feel the buzz. Listen to it. See it. Be a part of the occasion, because most people will never, ever, ever get the opportunity to do what you're doing.'

He then gave them some final words of advice:

> You're as prepared as you can possibly be. This is going to be a moment in time for you that you'll reflect upon, that you'll tell your kids about, that you'll remember for the rest of your life. You get to choose how you want to experience that. *So, get out there and enjoy it.*

ASK THE QUESTION

What prevents your stress bucket from overflowing?

Chances are you'll know, but it sometimes helps to write down a list so you can identify any future problems in your self-care plan. Remember those important life factors: physical health, psychological health, financial health, educational/professional health, spiritual health and social health. Managing these everyday challenges will help you to perform optimally during moments of pressure.

 LIGHTBULBS

1. Self-care is an activity or routine that promotes positive mental health – it's under our control and is self-initiated. We all move up and down the mental health continuum, and can fall victim to stress, uncertainty and anxiety. A good self-care plan helps us to look after ourselves.
2. To devise a suitable self-care plan while working towards a pressurised event, ask yourself: a) What do you need to tune out the stress going on around you? b) What are some of the barriers that might get in the way of you doing this? (And what are the strategies that will allow you to overcome those barriers?)
3. When devising a self-care plan, consider strategies to help you switch off, refresh and reconnect. Switch off: *Disconnect from*

your working brain (without guilt) and take up a fun activity for an hour or so. Refresh: *Protect and maximise your performance, e.g. through mindfulness, meditation, sleep and journalling.* Reconnect: *Check in with your friends and loved ones.*
4. Remember your self-care cues: nerves can be normalised, self-care underpins performance and don't forget to enjoy it!

CHAPTER NINETEEN

PSYCHOLOGY ON THE GRASS

Recently, my daughter came home from school in tears. She'd just auditioned for a role in the school musical, and although her lines had been well-rehearsed, something caused her to trip over her cues when it came to performing for real. She'd learned her part at home by practising in front of the mirror, and much of the work had been done alone (she did, however, sometimes present her performance to the family). What she hadn't anticipated were the conditions for her audition. Rather than simply delivering her lines to one person, she was instead asked to perform in front of four teachers who were sitting side by side on a long desk in the school hall. With the pressure cranked up, her mind went blank.

Yet again, this reaction was caused by the brain's limbic system. Given the four teachers have the power to say 'Yes' or 'No' to a hopeful's ambitions of getting into the school musical, the human mind unsurprisingly views them as a threat. As a result, the fight, flight or freeze mechanism kicks in, overriding the brain's cortex, which is where all the memorised lines from the script are stored. As a parent, my daughter's sadness was heartbreaking; as a sport psychologist, it represented a moment of frustration. After all, it's one thing to deliver a series of written lines at home where there's zero stress. It's an altogether different experience once the stakes have been increased with the addition of four teachers in a set-up not too dissimilar to the judges' table on *Britain's Got Talent*. In the run-up to the audition, I should have introduced my daughter to pressure training or what I like to call 'psychology on the grass' – a process whereby a person or team trains to perform under pressure, rather than simply training to perform.

Ideally, for someone to truly prepare for a moment of pressure, in any context, they must practise in the environment in which they're expected to work and win. Of course, this raises all sorts of challenges. How do you ready an international football team for a high-stakes penalty shootout, where millions of people are watching and the hopes of a nation rests upon a single action? How do you prepare a surgeon for a life-or-death operation? And how do you prepare a pilot to land a passenger jet in a storm? Training will only take the team or individual so far. The answer lies in the definition of pressure: essentially this is when the individual places an increased importance on their ability to perform well in challenging circumstances. In real life, these moments happen with no need for pretence. *If I miss this penalty, everyone in the country will remember my failure. If I get the surgery wrong, my patient might die. If I don't make the runway, the plane and everyone aboard will probably perish.* But mimicking these real-life situations is a whole other story, and the only way to make someone place an equivalent value on their performance is to bring the idea of consequence into play. In other words, to create circumstances where the adrenaline spikes, the stomach churns and the consequence of failure has a personal impact.

This is where psychology on the grass proves invaluable.

PRESSURE-BASED TRAINING: APPLYING EFFECTIVE CONSEQUENCE

While I was working at the UKSI, the psychology team became particularly interested in creating pressure-training environments across all the Olympic and Paralympic sports. As part of this, Mike Stoker, a colleague of mine, completed a PhD in this area and developed an elite coaching framework called 'The Pressure Training Pyramid'.

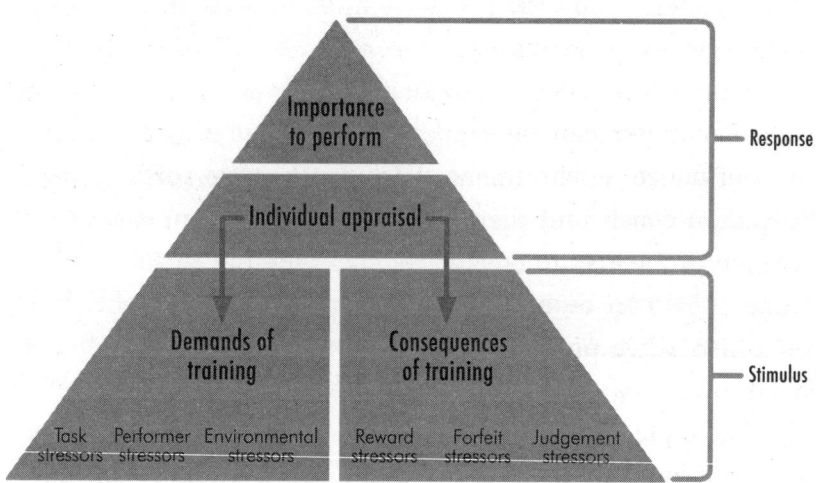

Source: 'The Pressure Training Pyramid' (Stoker et al., 2019)

The pyramid was broken down into two main components:

1. **The demands of training:** This focused on three interacting constraints (stressors) that generally influenced a person's or team's performance: task stressors, performer stressors and environmental stressors.
    - Task stressors: among them, the rules, equipment, opponents, teammates, scoring system and track or field dimensions.

- Individual stressors: for example, height, weight, speed, strength, endurance, knowledge, experiences, emotions, fatigue and attention.
- Environmental stressors: for example, the playing surface, temperature, wind, altitude, and social and cultural factors.

2. **The consequences of training:** The costs and benefits associated with training outcomes (results) and performances (the way in which people play).

Under this structure, what an athlete *does*, and how they do it, can be altered to suit the needs of the individual and the team. Circumstances can be manipulated to make a task harder or more complicated. The types of situations, tactics or mindsets a team might encounter can be replicated so that they can adapt to a performance environment. Within 'The Pressure Training Pyramid', a coach and their support staff design practice tasks in which problems are created for their athletes to solve. Interestingly, this can be applied to all contexts so that autonomy, decision-making, problem-solving and, ultimately, performance all improve.

For example, I once worked with a rugby player (a hooker) who performed their tasks brilliantly during training; at line-outs they hit their mark every time. But when matchday came around, they simply couldn't execute to the same level of accuracy. When I spoke to the player, I asked them to talk me through their process in training. The response was calm and formulaic.

> I get the ball. I dry it on my shirt. I stand there, look for Player X and I make sure I know the call. Then I focus on where the ball has to go – I get my hand placement, stance and set-up right. Finally, I visualise the flight of the ball before release.

So far, so good. But when I then asked the same player to talk me through the line-outs from the previous game, the situation sounded a lot more chaotic.

It was lashing down with rain, everyone's screaming and shouting at me. When I got the ball, I knew there wasn't much time, I didn't dry it properly. I wasn't sure on the call that had been made and I second-guessed myself. I just remember feeling panicked.

It was clear that we needed to bridge what was an obvious gap between the team's line-out training and the demands of a match-day situation. In the next line-out session we re-created more realism by making the play opposed and unpredictable. We also added a time constraint so that the stakes were raised. The hooker soon adapted their pre-throw routine, and by the time the next match came around their mindset had shifted – in moments of chaos they felt more comfortable. Rather than panicking during a line-out when the rain was coming down, time was short and everyone was yelling, they remained calm and stuck to their processes. The player dried the ball, visualised the throw, then looked for a teammate and picked them out with their delivery.

Although manipulating certain training demands was undoubtedly effective, Mike's research revealed one key fact: it had very little impact on the levels of pressure experienced by a team or athlete. This was a problem. If we're going to win, it's imperative we deliver our best performance when the stakes are highest, and the optimal way of preparing for that moment is to practise for it, and with realism. But this isn't always easy. There's no way of precisely re-creating the drama of a World Cup Final penalty shootout in training, in much the same way that it's impossible to re-create the stress of life-or-death surgery in medical school or a high-risk landing in severe cross-winds in a flight simulator. So how do we increase the stakes so that the context feels real and the physiological reactions become visceral? The answer is to create an environment in which the person experiences a very real consequence for not performing as intended. That way, when they place the ball on the spot, pick up the scalpel or set the landing controls in a practice environment, it will feel as if they're doing so for real.

Before deciding *how* to apply pressure in any given context, it's first important to establish *when* to do it. In sport, I've found it's helpful to introduce pressure-based training for one of two reasons:

1. When I have clarity and confidence that an athlete is unable to perform at their best when experiencing pressure.
2. To improve an athlete's capability and confidence. This will help them to consistently deliver at their optimum, even when they're put in a competitive setting.

The purpose of pressure-based training is to gradually expose an athlete to high-stress situations so that they can prepare their emotional responses when performing for real. The intended outcome is not for the athletes to experience less pressure once a crunch moment has arrived, but to help them develop their coping responses and confidence. Pressure can be a launch pad for excellence; stripping it away can be detrimental. However, if a person can harness their emotions in a positive way, their performances will be enhanced. The individual or team can then develop a mindset primed for moments of intensity and stress, while building an evidence-based belief that they can succeed and win, no matter the stakes or the circumstances.

As Mike identified through his PhD programme, there are three ways in which consequences can be applied to an everyday event, or training situation. They are:

1. Reward
2. Forfeit
3. Judgement

When deciding which one to use I generally look to the personality-profiling work conducted in Building Block #1: Who We Are. That's because different people are triggered by different things. Some are stimulated by reward (the optimists among us); others feel threatened by forfeit (those who are more prudent). The trick is to pick the most discomforting circumstances and apply them where necessary. When it came to creating pressure, Mike found that judgement generally had the biggest impact. However, I'll appraise them all individually.

REWARD

Consequences rooted in reward are the carrot being dangled in front of a donkey, rather than the stick spanking its backside. Examples of this would include:

- The child who's rewarded with a pound for every goal they score in their weekend match.
- The work team treated to a day off for passing a course or learning a new process.
- The person in a weight-loss programme who is treated to a spa day for losing the greatest number of pounds that month.

According to research in this area, people that make a poor impression experience more discomfort than those making a good one, which is why a lot of athletes become more susceptible to avoiding a loss than making a gain. So, while it can be emotionally challenging, reward-based consequences don't always create the same high levels of stress as those tasks designed to manipulate forfeit or judgement.

FORFEIT

In this form of pressure-based training, a consequence can be introduced to penalise failure. This is particularly powerful when the forfeit impacts on the trigger points of a team or player. I've heard of Sunday league football sides that practise penalty shoot-outs on the eve of cup games. The person that misses the most kicks must then turn up to the pub wearing the replica kit of their greatest rival – shirt, shorts *and* socks.

Suddenly, with a tangible and stressful consequence attached to missing a penalty, the blood pressure shoots up, the goal seems to shrink in size and the keeper grows an extra foot in height. *The context suddenly becomes more real.* All of this goes some way to replicating the physiological response to a proper penalty shootout. When looking for a non-sporting example, consequence-based pressure training could be applied to an ambulance team that's been asked to implement a new form of technology or treatment to their daily processes. To mirror the stress of a real-life emergency, the person who adapts most slowly to change must donate blood, sing in front of the staff canteen or take the next weekend shift. Suddenly, with a forfeit attached, the job becomes that much harder and the stress of training feels realistic.

This style of work is so beneficial in sport that it amazes me it isn't used more often in everyday life. Imagine, for example, what would happen if school children were prepared for their GCSEs or A-levels by not only training to perform through learning, but also by training to perform *when under pressure*. By teaching kids how their brain works while helping them to develop coping strategies for moments of stress, they would not only be set up for exam season but also for life. This approach would certainly have helped my daughter before her audition, and we now try our best to build practice environments that replicate the tests or challenges she faces at school.

JUDGEMENT

The final way to produce pressure in training is by manipulating a person's judgement stressors, the voice in their head that says: *If you screw this up, everyone will think you're a failure.* I remember this process was particularly useful when preparing a diver for Olympic selection and beyond. The athlete was suffering with performance anxiety, and although in training they were technically proficient, they seemed to struggle in the heat of a competition. After discussing this with the athlete and their coach, we agreed upon a systematic pressure-training protocol.

Everyone is different. We all have our emotional triggers and comfort zones. One person might come alive when performing a skill upon request; another will shrink into themselves. Some people are overly focused on results and consequences; others fear judgement. Having established the diver's timeline, personality and values, we broke down their *hows* and *whys* by examining their thoughts, feelings and emotions across multiple contexts. I encouraged the athlete to reflect on their most confident performances and their not-so-confident ones; on when they felt the most anxious and the most comfortable; on when they enjoyed their diving the most and when they didn't enjoy it at all. This approach was centred around the answers to three critical questions:

1. *What were you thinking?*
2. *How were you feeling?*
3. *How did these show up in your behaviour and performance?*

From there we ascertained that whenever the diver focused on their processes *holistically*, without too much thought, they performed optimally. That's because, once learned, diving is an automatic skill where overthinking becomes counterproductive. If an athlete is so obsessed with the different components of their dive, their automatic skill sets break down. In training, this wasn't a problem for our diver. However, in competitions they became distracted by the perceived thoughts of others, particularly the competitors around them, and the performance director who was ultimately responsible for Olympic selection. This caused them to overthink their take-off, the shape they wanted to achieve mid-air and their entry into the water. Potentially, this would become even more of a problem in an Olympic Games or at any big event where there were crowds, hype and TV coverage. In such a situation, these reactions might prove debilitating.

Think of it this way: walking or running is an activity that can be performed without conscious thought. Now execute that same action, but this time focus intently on all the component parts involved: how high you lift your leg off the ground; the positioning of your knees, feet and back; the placement of your feet on the ground. It's likely that by approaching a routine movement in such a way, your walking or running pattern will suddenly feel more complicated – you might slow down, become less efficient or even stop moving altogether. This is what's known as 'paralysis by analysis', and in a sport such as diving it can prove disastrous.

Instead, through trial and error, an athlete should develop a series of holistic performance cues – words that allow them to focus on the act without breaking down the component parts too much. Examples could include:

- **Height:** where an athlete focuses on achieving the maximum height from the board.
- **Tight:** how they get into shape by moving quickly and cleanly in the air.
- **Clean:** their entry into the water; their hands should be one on top of the other with flat palms to minimise splash.

Having created a series of effective performance cues with the struggling diver, we then developed a 'pressure ladder' so that the athlete (with the support of their coach) could cope with those moments where the attention on performance would be high. This was a scaling system that ran from 0 to 6. The lowest rung in the pressure ladder was a situation that the athlete might consider as being relatively relaxed, like a regular training session at their home pool. The highest rung was an Olympic Games where many people would be watching in the arena and on TV. Between the highest and lowest pressure situations we created several additional rungs.

- RUNG #1: Training.
- RUNG #2: Training a competition list of dives. To be scored by a personal coach.
- RUNG #3: Training the same list of dives but under competition conditions. Training partners will also execute their dive list. To be scored by a personal coach.

- RUNG #4: Training the same list of dives but under competition conditions. The mock event is filmed and shared with the wider diving community.
- RUNG #5: Training the same list of dives but under competition conditions. This time the event is being scored by the performance director responsible for Olympic selection.
- RUNG #6: An Olympic selection event and/or the Olympic Games.

For each rung of the ladder the diver rated their feelings of anxiety, as well as their confidence levels. My job – over several months and with the support of the diver's coach – was to prepare them mentally for each rung. This was done by gradually exposing the diver to more and more pressure while concurrently helping them to build a series of 'stadium 'skills' (we'll discuss these in the next chapter). Having developed a better understanding of their competition mindset, they were then able to normalise the concept of judgement – and as a result their confidence skyrocketed when performing under pressure.

*

One final note on pressure training: *Don't ice a collapsing cake.* As I've stressed elsewhere, it's important the individuals being introduced to consequence aren't ridiculed or exposed in such a way that they become terrified of making a mistake. The purpose of this work is to improve an individual or team's confidence and coping skills so they can perform optimally under pressure. Throughout this process, the athletes must be given the support to appropriately debrief on what's happening. Incidentally, when it comes to devising forfeits, the athletes themselves often come up with the best ideas, and this is an important factor when creating a psychologically safe space, although it's important not to let them go *too* far . . .

 ASK THE QUESTION

Are you capable of executing your most important skill set under pressure, when the outcome really matters?

If not, consider how you might set up a series of practice sessions where you amplify the stakes by applying a reward-, forfeit- or judgement-based consequence. Start small by designing a pressure training ladder as detailed above. Training in this way will re-create the body's physiological response to real life stress. Your performances will improve as a result, particularly if you also bring in a professional to help you develop your stadium skills.

LIGHTBULBS

- 'Psychology on the grass' is a process whereby a person or team trains to perform under increased demand, rather than simply training to perform.
- Pressure-based training amplifies the stress associated with an action, such as putting in golf, by bringing in consequences for failure.
- Pressure-based training should be introduced when you have clarity and confidence that someone can't perform at their best when experiencing pressure, or when you want to provide development opportunities that increase a person's capability to consistently deliver at their optimum when the stakes are raised.
- There are three ways in which pressure (or consequence) can be applied to an everyday event or training situation – reward, forfeit and judgement – the selection of which one to use being dependent on the personality profile of the individual involved. Some people are driven by reward, others are fearful of certain consequences or of judgement. Use the consequence accordingly.

CHAPTER TWENTY
STADIUM SKILLS

For everyone competing at the highest level, there will always be a moment when the crowd falls silent and the watching world holds their breath. Think: Usain Bolt on the start line of an Olympic 100-metres final; Cristiano Ronaldo standing over a free kick in a Champions League match; Tiger Woods preparing to putt on the 18th green at the Masters. In these moments, it's imperative the competitor has a portfolio of psychological tools so that they can maintain composure, focus and control. Known as 'stadium skills', these techniques include 1) breathwork, 2) visualisation, 3) self-talk and 4) a pre-performance routine that incorporates the first three steps, plus a handful of performance cues that aid the individual with their concentration and consistency.

Let me briefly outline each of the stadium skills before looking at them in more detail.

- **Breathwork:** Techniques like box breathing or coherence breathing are used to regulate the body's physiological response to stress. By controlling the rhythm and pattern of their breath, athletes can lower their heart rate and re-engage their parasympathetic nervous system, which brings calm and composure.

- **Visualisation:** This involves mentally rehearsing the performance of a specific action before it occurs. Visualisation helps prepare the mind and body, making the actual execution smoother and more confident.
- **Self-talk:** Negative or disruptive thoughts are part and parcel of performance, especially when the pressure to succeed is high. Being aware of unhelpful thought patterns and directing attention to more useful ones maintains focus and confidence. For instance, instead of thinking, 'What if I miss this shot?' an athlete might focus on a positive affirmation: 'I have made this shot many times before. *I can do it again.*'
- **Pre-performance routine:** These are the specific actions or rituals athletes perform before executing a task. For example, a tennis player might bounce the ball a certain number of times ahead of their serve, or a rugby player might follow a precise sequence of steps before a place kick. These routines help athletes create a sense of normality and focus, while reducing anxiety and enhancing their ability to perform. Generally, an athlete will utilise breathwork, visualisation and self-talk as part of their pre-performance routine.

With the basics covered, let's explore how stadium skills are used in high-pressure environments and the ways in which we can apply them to our own lives.

BREATHWORK

For the sportsperson operating at the edge of their coping resources, breathing techniques are vital for shifting from a state of heightened arousal (such as when taking an important line-out in rugby) to one of calm, enabling them to perform better under pressure. But this process is applicable to just about every walk of life. The UK and US Special Forces train their operators to apply breathing techniques for when working on dangerous missions. Elsewhere, modern-day stress-bombs – work deadlines, financial demands, and the hectic nature of modern life and all its distractions – activate the body's sympathetic nervous system for prolonged periods. This elevated state of arousal, at its most extreme, can cause a range of health issues over time, including heart disease. Breathwork offers a powerful way to counteract these effects, either in the moment or when preparing for (or decompressing from) an event of great magnitude.

I often use breathwork as part of my own stress-management routine and encourage the athletes I work with to do the same, employing several styles (there are tons of different ones, if you want to research them on your own). One simple technique is box breathing, in which a person breaks down their breathing into four stages, like the sides of a box. They inhale for four seconds and hold their breath for four seconds, before exhaling for four seconds and holding again for four seconds. Then they repeat the process over and over again. This rhythmic pattern helps to regulate the heart rate and calm the nervous system, making it easier to manage stress. I've found that the simplicity of box breathing is accessible to anyone, anywhere – from a boxer stepping into the ring to defend their title to someone trying to maintain composure in a tense meeting. If four seconds is too challenging, an individual can start by counting to three seconds. Once someone has grown used to the technique, they can increase the count to five or six seconds.

Another effective method is coherence breathing, which has been taught by several religions and cultures. My mum was a yoga teacher and utilised this slow-based breathwork as part of her practice because it stabilised her heart rate and calmed her brain and body. To achieve this same state it's important to draw in five to six breaths per minute (most people breathe in and out every four seconds or so). This requires us to inhale for six seconds and then exhale for six seconds. If this slow and deliberate breathing pattern is maintained consistently, it eventually signals to our brain that we're not experiencing a threat scenario, so our stress levels will drop and a feeling of control will return. As with box breathing, this technique helps us to improve our focus levels and perform optimally. A javelin thrower can steady themselves in a World Championships event, a learner driver can settle their mind before a driving test and a parent can become calm before breaking some difficult news to their children.

VISUALISATION

When you see a gymnast about to perform or a speed skater at the start line, there's a good chance that they're visualising their future performance by watching a short 'mind movie' of themselves in action – a visualisation in which their required actions are executed successfully. The speed skater gets off to a fast start. The gymnast sticks the landing. But this ritual doesn't just happen as the action begins; many athletes incorporate visualisation into their nighttime routines too. Footballers imagine themselves scoring a hat-trick as they fall asleep, and golfers mentally play their round in a Major championship, even glancing up at the leaderboard as they record a series of birdies and eagles.

This mental rehearsal enables an athlete to build their confidence and reduce anxiety in moments of high pressure. Meanwhile, evidence suggests that when a person imagines themselves performing an action, it activates the parts of the brain that kick in while they're actually performing. As a result, the neural pathways associated with a task, such as putting or ball-striking, are reinforced, just as they would be during physical practice. It's for this reason that visualisation is so useful for injured athletes. Psychologically going through an action or process keeps the neural networks in place, so much so that it's considered to be the second-best thing to physical training.

Diving lends itself perfectly to visualisation, because it's a *closed skill sport* – a self-paced activity that is unaffected by the environment and occurs in a totally predictable situation. One diver I worked with used an incredibly detailed form of visualisation whenever they approached a major competition. If the event's aquatic centre was new or unfamiliar, we'd obtain photographs or video footage of the location so a picture of what the environment looked like could be built up in advance. Then we designed a 'competition script' together, in which we went through the diver's pre-performance routine and identified what focus cues they needed for each of their dives. No detail was spared. It was important the mental rehearsal incorporated all the senses, and in addition to seeing (or feeling) the anticipated performance, the accompanying smells, noises and emotions featured too. From there we visualised the competition from start to finish.

There were multiple benefits to this approach. Whenever the diver arrived at a Commonwealth Games, Olympics or World Championships, they felt familiar with the setting. *They had visualised themselves succeeding there multiple times.* This enhanced their confidence and reduced any anxiety on the day, while reinforcing any physical and technical improvements they might have recently made in training.

Everyone visualises differently. One of the most successful middle-distance runners in the world once told me they imagined battling with their main rival during training sessions. Other people's visualisations are kinaesthetic – they *feel* the movements and motions of their performance. Then there are those that say: 'Oh, I can't do visualisation. *I'm just not wired that way.*' In those circumstances I always ask a simple question – 'Talk me through your journey into work today.' The person will generally tell me about how they picked up their bag and got into the car. They'll mention the route, the traffic and anything they might have seen on the way. Finally, they'll recount how they parked up and walked to their office. In doing so, they've re-created the journey in their head, seeing it all the way.

They've visualised.

Anyone can use visualisation to help them. The vet performing a delicate surgical operation. The skydive instructor bringing their students down safely. The pianist preparing for a recital. By imagining their fingers fluttering along the keys and hearing and feeling the emotion in their music, they're readying themselves for a moment where they'll be expected to perform for real, all while building muscle memory and reducing performance anxiety.

SELF-TALK

We've all had worrisome moments when we've thought, 'What if?' And that's fine if we then used the process as a jumping-off point for self-improvement, as discussed earlier in this building block. However, if we fail to find the solutions to these imagined worst-case scenarios, such thoughts will eventually derail us.

- *What if I sing out of tune in the recital?*
- *What if I false-start in the 100-metres final?*
- *What if I clam up during the presentation?*

and so on . . .

Thinking like this is a natural response to taking part in any event of significance. Our brains are programmed to seek out threats so that we can deal with them and live to fight another day. When people become anxious they're more susceptible to faulty thinking patterns: they convince themselves that because A has happened, B must be true. For example, *I've had a terrible training session, so I must be a terrible player.* Or, *I've made a mistake at work, so I must be bad at my job*. Negative bias encourages them to focus on the bad rather than seeing the event as a blip or learning event.

As a cognitive behavioural psychologist, I know that (*obviously*) everyone thinks differently, and therefore everyone behaves differently when the pressure comes on. Some athletes think, *What if I miss the shot?* And they wilt. Others think, *What if I miss the shot?* And they remember a previous time when they nailed the exact same action under pressure – and there's nothing stopping them from doing so again. With positive self-talk, the doubt is shrugged away. It's my role to help athletes identify their triggers, so they can course-correct with thought restructuring, a process in which a person resets their thinking with positive focus.

The first step in doing this is to find the faulty triggers that might cause an individual to think negatively, such as an unforced error or a poor refereeing decision. From there it's important they become aware of their subsequent thoughts, feelings and emotions, and the impact that these have on their performance. In such circumstances, a thought diary can be a useful resource because it encourages them to dig into their psychological state with a series of questions.

- *What was the thought?* (What was going through their mind?)
- *What was the emotional response?* (Dig into what the person felt and the intensity of feeling.)

- *What was the impact on subsequent thoughts and feelings? (How did the person view their situation afterwards?)*
- *What was the response? (What happened next?)*

For example, it might be that a gymnast admits to feeling unsettled when preparing for a major competition. In their thought diary, they talk about a moment in training where they pictured themselves falling, or landing badly. *An imagined pain ricochets through their body. People in the crowd are laughing. Their coach is furious. Any hopes they'd had of qualifying for the Olympics have gone up in smoke.* Having catastrophised in such a way, they become overwhelmed by negative thinking. *Here we go again. This always happens to me when I'm about to compete – I'm actually no good at doing this stuff.* Finally, the gymnast talks themselves into failure. *Well, maybe I just shouldn't even bother doing this anymore.*

However, if a person can recognise the type of words, processes or environments that tend to set them off, it's possible to halt such a negative reaction. This is done by setting up a circuit breaker, *thought restructuring* – a process of identifying and challenging any irrational or maladaptive thoughts – and it can be done in a series of simple steps.

- Write down the difficult thought. For example: *I always mess up staff appraisals because I lack the confidence to ask for a pay rise.*
- Rate how much you believe in this thought as a percentage.
- List the evidence supporting your fear. For example: *In the last appraisal I felt really nervous. I couldn't think of an example to justify the request so I didn't ask for my salary to be reviewed.*

- List any evidence disproving your fear. For example: *I've had a series of positive meetings with the senior management team over the last few weeks while working on a new project. I was able to articulate clearly and effectively and I demonstrated great leadership. I can perform well in difficult situations.*
- Rate how much you now believe this original thought as a percentage.
- Write down a more useful thought. For example: *I've brought a lot of success to this team and demonstrated my effectiveness to senior leaders, so I'm certainly worthy of a pay rise.*

Unhelpful thoughts are an understandable and very human response, especially when we're being asked to perform in some way. But with self-talk it's possible to normalise the event and improve our response to pressure. For example, a web designer, through their thought diary, has identified that they're prone to negative thinking when nearing the finish line of a project. In the past, they told themselves that they were unlikely to meet their deadlines. After then staring into the crystal ball of doom, they even imagined themselves being dismissed from the job. But having recognised these responses, they can set a circuit breaker for any reoccurrences in the future. At the first sign of a negative thought, they should challenge their thinking by remembering that they've hit plenty of crazy deadlines before. Their next step is to execute the task by sticking to their focused processes and breaking the project down into manageable chunks, recording their latest positive emotional response to pressure in an update to their thought diary. Their self-belief will grow from there.

PRE-PERFORMANCE ROUTINES

Pretty much every elite performer will have some kind of pre-performance routine that readies them for a moment of high pressure. Athletes will have a set ritual just prior to going out into the stadium during a top-flight competition, as will rock stars ahead of taking the stage and politicians before giving a keynote speech. As we established earlier, these are the specific actions to be performed before executing a task. However, it's not enough for a Formula One driver to tap their steering wheel a few times before the start of a race or a quarterback to repeat a mantra in their mind ahead of the snap.

To be effective, a pre-performance routine must comprise a cue, or a series of cues (evidenced through a meticulous process of *plan, do, review*), that settle the mind, ready the body for action and ensure consistency. As with thought-restructuring and visualisation, this isn't a one-size-fits-all stadium skill either. Different people will use pre-performance routines in different ways. Some people might execute them immediately before action (such as the set-up routine used by golfers), others will start their routine several days before competing (a basketball player imagining the perfect game and going through a series of performance-specific drills). A lot will use a combination of both.

One sport in which pre-performance routines come to the fore is diving. That's because a competition can go on for three hours, but within that time it takes less than three seconds for an athlete to execute each one of their five or six dives. The diver might then have to wait 45 minutes before they perform again. Consequently, they need to be able to switch off after each dive and switch on again for the next. Emotionally that's a lot to process, because in the gaps between attempts an athlete will have to navigate plenty of emotional turbulence. This is where a solid pre-performance routine comes into play: it ensures that the individual can arrive at the correct emotional state and execute their skill under pressure. It's just the same with stop-start sports such as golf and field events in athletics (the javelin, shot put, triple jump and so on), or specific actions within more fluid sports, such as penalty kicks in football, conversions in rugby and free throws in basketball.

As I mentioned in Chapter 18, the diver Tom Daley is someone I had the great privilege of working with over several years in a career that saw him win five Olympic medals in four consecutive Games from 2012 to 2024. Over that period he developed a pre-performance routine that enabled him to navigate the stop-start nature of the sport, one that's barely changed throughout his time as an elite athlete.

- At every competition, Tom will jump into the pool and dry off before speaking to his coach for some final words.
- He will then take a drink of water at the bottom step.
- As each diver ahead of him takes their turn, he'll walk up another three metres.
- With two divers to go, Tom waits at the back of the five-metre board with a chamois on his head, before visualising the movements he needs to execute.
- With one diver to go, he stands on the tower and visualises his dive for a final time.
- Once at the top of the steps, he takes ten deep breaths, reminds himself of his processes and then goes.

Over and over. *Olympics after Olympics*. It was the same drill every time, although some of his performance cues changed as the degree of difficulty of his dives increased. Famously, Tom then took up knitting and crocheting because it helped to redirect his attention away from diving during competitions. Making a jumper or a scarf in an Olympic final kept him in the moment, stopping him from becoming distracted by the noise going on around him.

When I first started working in diving I supported several junior divers who were learning how to transfer their training performances into the competitive arena. To set them on their way, I developed an education programme that would facilitate their competition preparation and pre-performance planning. I explained the usefulness of pre-performance routines and detailed how one could be created by using a technique called 'performance segmenting' – a planned-out sequence of events that maintained psychological control and boosted confidence and concentration. This was done in a couple of phases.

PHASE 1

The divers were asked to create a start and finish point for their pre-performance routine. Some of them needed to organise themselves the night before the competition, whereas others preferred to have a 10-minute pre-competition (or even pre-dive) routine and little else. Remember, you can plan for some eventualities during the performance, and you can certainly plan for most eventualities before and after the competition. Therefore, most plans should have the 'before', 'during' and 'after' elements outlined.

PHASE 2

The divers were then asked to list the segments for a competition that were important to them. These segments covered the night before the competition, if required, as well as the journey to the venue and their post-performance routines. For example, it might be that one of them listened to tracks by a particular artist while in the car or on the team bus. This was important and was noted. They were also asked to list the actions they liked to use in the moments before diving, such as visualisation, breathwork and self-talk. An accompanying workbook provided several tips to help them devise their pre-performance routines:

- The detail should be specific to your needs and can be as simple or as complex as you require.
- Try not to use more than three or four aspects to the segments, because too many cues become confusing under pressure.
- The aspects of each segment and the segments themselves may change over time as you add or delete things, based on experience.
- Practising the various parts of your plan in simulated competition during training, and implementing them in low-profile competitions is essential. Don't forget to use the plan whenever you can – following your plan during practice and minor competitions will ensure it's tried and tested for bigger competitions.
- In your post-competition or training evaluation sessions, you should highlight what went well and what could be better in terms of the performance. The aim is to keep hold of and re-create the good, and eliminate the bad, hence each performance becomes a learning situation and we gradually improve our consistency. (It's best to record these good and bad elements in your training diary so they are accessible and form a good reminder when you come to organise your goals for the next training period.)

PHASE 3

I helped the young divers to develop a refocusing routine so they could reset their thinking during the event, if required, especially if there was a long wait between dives. This encouraged them to complete three actions: breathe, focus and act.

- **Breathe:** Concentrate on the movement of the chest, take in a long slow breath, hold for a silent count of three, relax and breathe out slowly. Repeat.
- **Focus:** Use a performance cue word/phrase/picture to get back to the here and now.
- **Act:** Do rather than *think*.

As with their pre-competition planning, the divers were encouraged to practise using their breathe, focus and act cues in training. When put together, a segmented pre-performance routine could look something like this:

SEGMENT 1: NIGHT BEFORE COMPETITION
Things to do:
1. Prepare equipment – check competition gear
2. Relaxation period – listen to music, watch TV, socialise
3. Review strategies
4. Mental rehearsal – best-performance imagery
5. Go-to-sleep strategy

SEGMENT 2: FROM WAKING UP TO ARRIVING AT VENUE
Things to do:
1. Wake-up routine
2. Stretch and mentally rehearse

3. Breakfast
4. Prepare food and drink for day (and between dives)
5. Pack gear
6. Leave for venue

SEGMENT 3: FROM ARRIVAL AT VENUE TO START OF COMPETITION

Things to do:

1. Arrive at venue at predetermined time (i.e. not too long beforehand)
2. Technical checks
3. Relaxation and best-performance imagery
4. Physical warm-up, stretch and keywords

SEGMENT 4: PRE-DIVE ROUTINE

Things to do:

1. Execute pre-dive routine
   - Get wet
   - Chamois
   - Mental rehearsal
2. Breathe – focus – act

SEGMENT 5: BETWEEN DIVES

Things to do:

1. Relax
2. Eat and drink
3. Talk to other people – e.g. coach

SEGMENT 6: POST-PERFORMANCE

Things to do:

1. Highlight good aspects of performance and record in diary
2. Highlight areas of required performance improvement and record in diary

3. Eat and drink (as soon as possible after last dive)
4. Relax and plan evening (e.g. meal/social activities)

*

A pre-performance plan has equally powerful results when applied to a non-sporting context, such as a head chef at a busy restaurant.

SEGMENT 1: NIGHT BEFORE SERVICE
Things to do:

1. Prepare equipment – check knives, pans, etc.
2. Relaxation period - listen to music, watch TV, socialise
3. Review menu – make sure you're familiar with every dish and ingredient
4. Mental rehearsal – best-performance imagery
5. Go-to-sleep strategy

SEGMENT 2: FROM WAKING UP TO ARRIVING AT VENUE
Things to do:

1. Wake-up routine
2. Stretch and mentally rehearse
3. Breakfast
4. Prepare personal food and drink for the day
5. Pack gear
6. Leave for venue

SEGMENT 3: FROM ARRIVAL AT VENUE TO START OF SERVICE
Things to do:

1. Arrive at kitchen at predetermined time (i.e. not too long beforehand)
2. Technical check – surfaces, equipment, ingredients

3. Tactical check – are service staff familiar with menu?
4. Relaxation and best-performance imagery
5. Physical warm-up – check everything is in right place

SEGMENT 4: PRE-SERVICE ROUTINE
Things to do:

1. Execute pre-service routine
   - turn on music
   - check with every chef and every cook station
   - run through visualisation of service running smoothly
2. Breathe – focus – act

SEGMENT 5: DURING QUIET MOMENTS IN SERVICE
Things to do:

1. Relax
2. Play music
3. Check in with other members of kitchen staff

SEGMENT 6: POST-PERFORMANCE
Things to do:

1. Highlight good aspects of performance and record in diary
2. Highlight areas of required performance improvement and record in diary
3. Eat and drink (as soon as possible after last cook)
4. Relax and plan evening (e.g. meal/social activities)

PHASE 4

I encouraged the athletes to consider the *what ifs . . . ?* and asked how they would apply positive self-talk so they might be flexible and adapt to any situation. I remember once hearing the track cyclist and six-time Olympic champion Chris Hoy talking about something similar in an interview. Ahead of the Olympic Games, he considered all the scenarios that could potentially unfold between him competing in the first race and him standing on the podium. One of these was: *What if I have to break the world record to win a gold medal?* It was his way of preparing for every eventuality, and having considered the possibility of it happening, he knew exactly how he'd react were it to become necessary.

 ASK THE QUESTION

Do you have the stadium skills to help you win in high-pressure events?

Consider developing strategies for visualisation, breathwork, self-talk and pre-performance routines, using all the strategies detailed in this chapter.

 LIGHTBULBS

- Stadium skills are psychological tools that help us maintain composure, focus and control when performing under pressure.
- Among these are breathwork (techniques that regulate the body's physiological response to stress), visualisation (a process that prepares the mind and body for action, making the actual execution smoother and more confident), self-talk (inner dialogue used to boost motivation and confidence, reduce

anxiety and direct attention) and pre-performance routines (specific actions or rituals athletes perform before executing a task).
- Some people will execute their pre-performance routine immediately before action, others will start their routine several days before competing. A lot will use a combination of both.
- Pre-performance planning can help us all locate some security through familiarity, while ensuring we focus on the right things at the right time.

CHAPTER TWENTY-ONE
DECOMPRESSING THE RIGHT WAY

There's an interesting fact about the way in which some sportspeople react following high-pressure events. Research has shown that athletes can emotionally struggle when returning from a competition on the scale of an Olympic Games. It's common for some of them to experience a Games hangover or 'post-Olympic blues', which is understandable given that they've worked incredibly hard, with their focus concentrated on a small window in time – and that window is now suddenly shut.

This can leave the individual with an unsettling question of *What next?* (Which is where the work conducted in the *who* and *why* sections of this book is so important, as it helps us to prepare for precisely these moments.) This state can also lead to a decrease in drive and intensity, and declining performance levels. What's most interesting, however, is that this emotional dip isn't influenced by results. The gold-medal-winning sprinter is just as likely to suffer from the post-Olympic blues as the athlete who has underperformed, and the fallout, irrespective of success, can be crushing.

The importance of preparing for the psychological aftermath of an Olympic Games has received significantly more attention in the

UK in recent years, and as a result the concept of decompression has increasingly come to the fore – a process whereby an athlete returns to a more relaxed state after a period of intense stress or psychological pressure. Up until recently, the idea of facilitating a formal decompression process after a global event like the Olympics was relatively unusual. This was an opportunity missed. Elite athletes work in an emotionally charged environment, and not taking the time to assess their psychological state afterwards can lead to a crash that sometimes feels overwhelming.

The performance debriefs that used to take place were generally focused on *what happened* and *why*, rather than processing the emotion of the event per se. When certain Olympians return to relative normality, they find themselves in a completely different environment to the one in which they'd previously lived. Some of them are internationally famous, occasionally becoming social media sensations and even memes. Then there are the lesser-known athletes who return to normality after competing at the highest level, sometimes in front of crowds numbering tens of thousands and TV audiences in the millions. Understandably, a lot of them struggle to adjust. This situation is often exacerbated by the reality that, upon returning, they feel misunderstood by the people around them. They're Olympians; some of them gold medallists with the world at their feet. *So, what right do they have to feel unhappy?*

This has long been a complaint of high achievers everywhere, even astronauts, who can feel profoundly unsettled after having travelled into space. After all, what do you do for an encore once you've been to the moon? But it's the same for everyone. We all experience moments of high stress that require periods of decompression, whether that be a work project, a physical effort such as a 10k or marathon, or an emotional challenge, like a birth, death or marriage. These events – and the emotions attached to them –

need to be acknowledged and processed thoroughly before we can fully rest and recuperate. Only then can we effectively ready ourselves for the next challenge, because without a period of acknowledgement, people will always find themselves in the dark. Unprocessed emotions can simmer, often subconsciously, vital lessons are missed and wounds take longer to heal. In such moments it's important we explore the emotions attached to an experience, to help us make sense of it and its impact on our present and future reality. Because I can guarantee that, 99 times out of a 100, if there are any negative emotions swirling around, they won't be connected to the medal, the moon landing or the amount of money raised for charity. Their origin will be something much deeper and more profound.

When attempting to understand the stressors being experienced by many of our athletes and staff when returning home from the Olympic and Paralympic Games, the UKSI psychology team investigated how other institutions dealt with similar moments of emotional upheaval. In doing so, we learned that the British Armed Forces had previously sent their troops to a sunny location for a few days so that they could blow off steam after a long period of service abroad. It was believed that this 'halfway home' approach helped the troops to re-enter the 'real world' more comfortably because they were being given some time to process their experiences with the people who understood them most. *Their colleagues.* For many of the athletes (and staff) striving on the world stage, there hadn't been the time to fully and comprehensively process their experiences. They'd trained hard for years. They'd competed. Then they disappeared on holiday without fully processing what had happened to them. Before long, they were back into training (or competing in yet another event), with varying levels of emotional aftercare or decompression to help them.

Following this realisation, the question facing the UKSI sport psychology team was simple. *How could we do it better?* The first stage was to accept that our sportspeople (both athletes and staff) would likely benefit from a period of decompression before – or even during – their reintegration into their home lives and normality. This would then help them to avoid an emotional hangover. A processing phase was also important because, as with the British Armed Forces, it would allow the individual to discuss, analyse and learn from their experiences with the people who understood them best. An event such as the Olympics, like war, can be a sensory and emotional overload. Sure, a table-tennis final or fencing gold medal match isn't a life-or-death event, but the brain will often treat it as such, and the feelings attached to the experience can impact on a person afterwards if they're not resolved properly.

In working out our next steps for the Tokyo Olympics and Paralympics, the UKSI sport psychologists Danielle Adams Norenberg and Sarah Cecil were integral to leading the creation of an athlete-friendly period of structured decompression, comprising four key phases.

- **Phase 1: *The hot debrief.*** It was agreed that every athlete should have the opportunity to discuss their experiences and make sense of what had happened immediately after the Games have concluded. This might be with their sport psychologist and/or key members of their support team.
- **Phase 2: *Time zero.*** A designated period in which the athlete goes on holiday, reintegrates back into normality, while mixing with people who aren't athletes (and who won't talk to them about personal bests, medals and training schedules).
- **Phase 3: *Process the emotion.*** A secondary debrief takes place in which the athlete digs deeper into their experience.

The feelings connected to their Olympic or Paralympic journey are discussed rather than recounted step by step. The purpose is to process the emotions, while assessing the strengths and skills that can be utilised moving forward.
- **Phase 4: *Performance debrief.*** Having competed successfully or not, this stage is an in-depth analysis of the performance. In this phase, the athlete, team or sport can build on the things that went well, and identify and neutralise the things that didn't.

Psychologists in every sport were encouraged ahead of the Games to plan decompression sessions for their athletes and staff once the competition was over. This allowed for a period of psycho-education in preparation for the weeks and months immediately afterwards, and while we wouldn't 'predict' an episode of low mood, it was possible to prepare an individual for any thoughts and feelings that might rewind negatively to the past or fast-forward to the future. We even suggested they make the four-phase decompression process a fixture of their athlete-development programmes going forward.

We found that staff and athletes across sports in all different disciplines were able to vocalise their immediate thoughts and feelings before rushing off to holiday, or pre-season training (or, for those athletes facing retirement, a post-sporting life). Decompression following the four-phase structure is so important because without it, feelings are buried or kicked down the road, with this emotional suppression possibly causing psychological turbulence later in life. Sometimes physical problems can occur too, especially if there are unprocessed feelings of confusion, anger, distress or even euphoria. A person can withstand all sorts of emotions, good and bad, but until they're processed those emotions can build up and create pressure, like steam in a kettle.

DECOMPRESSION AND EMOTIONAL CLARITY: 'PROCESS THE EMOTION'

Generally, people are too quick to skip over their successes and achievements without really processing what has happened to them on a deeper level. Sure, the mountain climber who has scaled their first ever 'death zone' 8,000-metre peak in the Himalayas might have a phone full of photos to remind themselves of the experience; there might have been some brief discussions with friends and families on *what happened* and maybe *how it felt*. But without a structured process of effective decompression, so much of what they learned, or how the event might have shaped their worldview, can fade with time. This is a waste, because any associated thoughts and feelings can act like road signs – some of them warn us of impending danger, others provide clues of where to go to next.

After the Tokyo Games had concluded, the UKSI conducted hundreds of sessions with the athletes and staff, across all sports. Developing their work on the 'Four phases of decompression', Sarah and Danielle had evolved a debrief formula for Phase 3, 'Process the emotion', with the help of the wider psychology team. By working through it, an individual, alongside a sport psychologist or a logical sounding board, could come to terms with their psychological state following a major event. In doing so, they acknowledged the emotions associated with their experience before resetting themselves for any challenges ahead. This provided a healthy reset for those individuals struggling to adapt to their new normal as medal winners, or the people simply coming down from the excitement of working at such a life-changing event.

Given there were so many athletes, and only a limited number of UKSI psychology practitioners to go around, Sarah and Danielle also led an educational programme that the psychology team delivered to upskill staff across the system and to facilitate 'Process the emotion' conversations with those under their care. Clear guidelines were provided on what questions to ask, and what answers to look out for:

- **Step 1: *Contracting*.** At the start of the discussion, agreements were made on a) the purpose of the interaction, b) the athlete or staff member's aims for the sessions, and c) who the information was going to be shared with (this could be a coach or manager, should the athlete/staff member agree).
- **Step 2: *Timeline sharing*.** The facts were collected on the individual's experience and ordered into a timeline of events, with the start date beginning at a point of the individual's choosing. The points collated on the timeline had to be meaningful to the individual.
- **Step 3: *Emotional responses*.** Once a timeline was established, the emotions attached to each noted event were recorded. Follow-up questions were asked of the individual so that a deeper response could be recorded: *Why was it meaningful for you? What emotions did it evoke in you? Who experienced that with you? How did that match up to what you expected?* and so on.
- **Step 4: *Recognising the impact of those emotions*.** At this point, the sport psychologist or logical sounding board should dig even deeper into the individual's responses. What's important here is that the individual gained a more profound understanding of themselves through the events

and their emotional responses to them. They were then asked whether their usual coping and self-care strategies had worked, while acknowledging any strengths that had been demonstrated and the strategies utilised.

- **Step 5: The next steps.** *What was the individual going to do with the information gathered from their experience and their emotional responses to it? How could they utilise their learning to move forward? And what might that look like?* It was also important that the athlete or staff member identified a new target, so that they had something positive to work towards.
- **Step 6: The first next step.** At this stage the individual committed to taking a first step towards their new goal. It might be something as simple as identifying a target for the forthcoming season with their coach or manager. Ticking that target off delivered an immediate sense of progression. Momentum could build from there.

All of us can benefit from conducting a decompression process of this kind with our logical sounding board after an emotional or significant event, whether that be in work, play or life. For example, it's quite common for people to feel despondent when they have been made redundant or if a business they were working with closes unexpectedly. They might experience feelings of rejection, failure and embarrassment, even in situations where the redundancy decision was made over company finances rather than personal performance. An overwhelming question of *what to do next* looms large. In such circumstances the individual could conduct a 'Process the emotion' check with their logical sounding board:

- **Step 1: Contracting.** The individual agrees that in the session they'll discuss the events of the redundancy and

beyond. This will help to process what has happened to them. They'll explore the emotions attached to their experience, and evaluate their coping skills and strengths.
- **Step 2: *Timeline sharing.*** The facts about the individual's experience are collected and a timeline of events is written down, beginning with the moment the company announced its decision. The discussion points collated on the timeline might include their last few weeks in the job, the way in which their skills were utilised and any career opportunities or offers that might have opened up.
- **Step 3: *Emotional responses.*** The feelings attached to each event are recorded and follow-up questions are asked. For example: *In the final few days in the office the individual felt agitated and uncertain. They had a few sleepless nights wondering what might happen were they to struggle finding new employment.*
- **Step 4: *Recognising the impact of those emotions.*** The individual's feelings regarding the redundancy have brought up a range of emotions, from fear (for the future), sadness (a number of friends were also leaving the company) and loneliness (they're unsure of who to turn to for help). There's also excitement (the opportunity to open a new chapter and have a change of pace) and fulfilment (reconnecting with friends and family outside of work, and spending more time on hobbies). Processing these emotions has provided the opportunity to re-evaluate what's important and connect with the individual's *why* and *how*.
- **Step 5: *The next steps.*** The individual agrees to take a few weeks off to rest before applying themselves to the job-finding process, reassuring themselves that any negative emotions are a natural side-effect of such an unsettling event. Meanwhile, they're aware that any future life changes going forward might also create a similar response, and they

recognise those emotions as being normal. They're excited about the next step.
- **Step 6: *Closure and the first next step.*** They plan to draw up a list of potential job possibilities, educational options (such as retraining) and personal projects.

Decompressing in this way means we can acknowledge the associated positive and negative emotional responses that emerge during any major life event, work deadline or personal challenge. In doing so, it's possible to capitalise on our strengths and learn from the events that caused us to react badly. Personal growth generally follows these exploratory discussions, and this approach should be utilised by anyone who experiences any periods of intense stress or psychological pressure (spoiler alert: that's all of us). By working in this way, we're controlling the pressure that's impacted upon us during events of great importance. That enables us to thrive in a sustainable manner – and win.

And then win again.

 ASK THE QUESTION

Do you have a period of decompression planned for your next major challenge?

How could you plan one with your workmates, family or friends, while working through some of the 'process the emotions' guidelines laid out in this chapter?

LIGHTBULBS

- People returning from an event of great magnitude, such as a wedding, a high-pressure business project or the Olympic Games, can aid their psychological recovery through decompression.
- There are four stages to an effective decompression plan: 1) The hot debrief – an immediate chat about what happened; 2) Time zero – a holiday or break, with people not associated with the high-pressure event; 3) Process the emotion – an in-depth exploration of the associated feelings; 4) Performance debrief – an analysis of the performance.
- It's not enough to simply go on holiday after a period of stress. To win and thrive in a sustainable fashion it's vital our timeline of recent events, and any associated emotions, are processed.
- Exploring our emotions in the aftermath of a moment of great pressure enables us to grow, learn and prepare ourselves for future events of a similar magnitude. *We can win in a sustainable manner.*

ENDNOTE

Welcome to the end of the book – or maybe it's a beginning, where the 'building blocks of success' can be viewed as a race starter's pistol or a launchpad. They've already helped a long list of elite athletes and teams to reach their full potential, all of whom have grown in some way, with certain individuals even going beyond what they initially thought was possible in their respective fields. By working through the process, Olympic stars have discovered *who they are*; football, rugby and rowing teams have clarified exactly *why they were there*; coaches and managers have communicated to their teams exactly *how to play*; and top-tier athletes have embraced stadium skills that showed them *how to win*.

Now you can do the same.

Human beings are fallible. We make mistakes and get things wrong. My aim through the pages of this book is for you to find confirmation that our failures don't necessarily need to define us, and instead can be used as an opportunity to learn and grow. Our lives are continual works in progress, so return to the chapters that fit your situation most closely and make sure to chart your gains as you make them, as well as those of your team. Simply implementing the four building blocks in full will absolutely move you on from your starting point, but repeating the work will help you to grow and achieve in a sustainable way.

Every team and individual is wonderfully unique, and what works for one may not yield the same positive results for another. But we all have to start somewhere. More than anything, I hope you use this book as a conversation piece with your teammates, work colleagues and the people closest to you. The greatest success stories begin with a wild idea, and by discussing the theories, tactics and case studies I've presented throughout, I hope you come up with your own creative genius to kickstart a period of improvement. In so doing, you will evolve the building blocks of success yourself. Dysfunctional collectives can find new ways to come to together and win, and already successful groups can streak ahead of their competition. Remember: when bringing the building blocks concept to life, first present them to the people that are alongside you for the journey. Then open a debate by asking the very first question in this book: who are we?

That is how *you* win.

AFTERWORD BY TOM DALEY

HOW TO WIN: THE BUILDING BLOCKS IN ACTION

I first started working with Kate just after the 2008 Olympic Games in Beijing, where I was diving in the 10-metre platform and synchronised-10 metre platform competitions. I was 14 years old, and at first the pair of us talked about performance strategies, pre-performance routines and game-plan execution – all of which have been detailed in *How to Win*'s four building blocks. I'd arrived at my first Olympics with the attitude that I wanted to learn; I certainly didn't think I could medal, although that had always been my dream. However, I wanted to be on the podium at London 2012.

All athletes dream of gold medals, particularly when the Games are being hosted at home, but Kate was great at helping me to focus on the things that were important, which in this case were the routines and processes that would give me the best chance of staying in the moment and performing on the day. By extension I'd have a greater chance of getting the outcome I wanted. I secured bronze in 2012 in the 10-metre platform competition, and again in Rio 2016 in the synchronised 10-metre platform. When Kate later left British Diving after the Rio Games, I still called her for advice because she was somebody I trusted, *she knew me* and together we had crafted all my competition routines. They would eventually result in my Olympic gold medal in 2021.

During my career, I've used a lot of the processes that make up the four building blocks of this book in one way or another. They've been applicable to all aspects of my life, and I'd like to explain how some of them have been put into practice.

LESSON #1: DON'T BECOME OUTCOME FOCUSED (AND AVOID MAIN CHARACTER SYNDROME)

When I started working with Kate, our first action was to step back from my dream outcome. When she asked me about my goals, I told her it was to win an Olympic medal. I honestly couldn't think of anything else I wanted more. At that time, I was able to win events with a low degree of difficulty because a) I was diving consistently, and b) the other athletes in the field were making mistakes. That obviously wasn't going to get me through an Olympics, where the degree of difficulty was much higher, so the question became: *What did I have to do to be in a position where I could compete for those medals?*

The answer was to focus on the processes that would lead me to the desired outcome, particularly trying to be in the moment as much as possible, but that was very hard as a young athlete. I found it difficult to trust myself because I hadn't yet experienced the ups and downs of a big competition, and it was difficult to navigate an event of the magnitude of the Olympics. But that was exactly the point: by shutting out the noise, and only looking to my processes, I'd get to where I needed to be.

From 2008 onwards I worked with my team on my approach from a technical, tactical, psychological and lifestyle perspective, and went from there. When I competed in the 2009 Diving World Championships in Rome and won gold, I hadn't expected to come out on top, but everything aligned. Rather than simply accepting the result, we reviewed my processes and my competition mindset, and how we could use that approach to maximise the chances of winning again. But I didn't simply stick to the same game plan. I adapted it. *I had to.* If an athlete is going to win, and in a sustainable way, there are so many things to take into consideration. For example, these days I couldn't replicate my training schedule from 2008. I'm not strong enough, I don't have the same mobility and I wouldn't be injury-free. I have different tools in my arsenal now.

Over time, I've changed with my age, I've changed with my ability and I've changed with my training levels. I've also changed my attitude. One of the things I've learned through working with Kate is that I don't have to let diving define me. The journey to the 2012 London Olympics was so emotionally turbulent that it became very difficult for me to focus on the actual diving (although having said that, thinking about diving every single day has never been healthy for me). Back then there was a lot going on with my education. I was doing my GCSEs and working out what I wanted to do with my A-levels. I also had to change schools because I was being bullied, and my dad passed away in 2011. I had so many distractions that diving became my place of refuge. I felt happy in the pool. I could enjoy myself, judgement-free. But that changed whenever I thought about the pressures to win a medal.

Too many athletes have outcome-focused goals. They allow themselves to be defined by what happens in the pool or on the field of play, but through working with Kate as a logical sounding board I was able to see that I was so much more than my achievements. *We all are.* This wasn't an easy point to reach, as I'd tortured myself through the London and Rio Games. Like I said, it had been my dream to get there, but having finally made that leap, I stressed about not performing to the best of my ability and I worried about screwing up. As a result, I couldn't enjoy it. I struggled to remain present and to show off all the training I'd put in.

And then Covid happened.

Talk about a penny-drop moment! The pandemic made me realise that anything could change at any time. One minute you had control of *everything*; the next you had control over *nothing*. By the time Tokyo came around in 2021 (because of the global lockdown, the event was postponed by a year), I felt so lucky that we were even competing that the Olympics felt like a bonus. I was grateful just to be in the room. Then I learned the greatest trick of all: I gave myself something to look forward to beyond the Games, a reward to enjoy once all the hard work was done. For some people that might have been a holiday, a shopping trip or a party with friends and family. I stood by the pool, looked down at the water and thought: *Oh well, I'm going to have cheesecake after this anyway, so it doesn't really matter.*

I won gold at the Tokyo Olympics in the synchronised 10-metre platform event, but it wasn't the be-all and end-all because I was so much more than my medal. I was a father. I was working as a mentor for young divers. I had TV commitments, I had social media commitments, I had all these things that were going on outside of diving that my self-worth wasn't being judged in relation to my Olympic performances. I was able to let go of that, knowing that my family were going to love me regardless. I'd got to the point where I enjoyed diving for the sake of diving, and because there was so much going on elsewhere in my life, it wasn't going to make me or break me.

But with age comes the beautiful realisation that other people's opinions don't really matter. I stopped caring about what the world thought, and I focused on doing diving for me. That's because I knew that nobody really gave a shit about another person's performance in an Olympic Games. We're all guilty of falling into main character syndrome, a condition where a person believes, wrongly, that all eyes are upon them. The truth is that we're all *supporting characters*, and if we can learn to live like no one's watching, it's possible to free ourselves from embarrassment and fear. This attitude allows to me to do whatever I think is best for success.

LESSON #2: PROCESS IS EVERYTHING

Pre-performance and pre-competition routines are such a big deal for me when I'm competing, although they've changed massively over the years. As a kid I used to turn up to the pool, do my thing and not really think too much about nutrition or recovery. These days, my pre-competition routine begins a lot earlier, especially in the build-up to big events, and more and more things have been added, among them: a tart cherry juice, an ice bath, a strict sleeping schedule, and appropriate moments of refuelling with the right amount of carbs and proteins. I have a plan for what I need to do once I've woken up and how long I want to be awake for before I begin diving. I use a TENS machine to fire up the nerves in my body and I regulate my caffeine intake. I also have a set strength and conditioning programme to prime my body in the build-up to most competitions.

Every single night, without fail, I'll visualise an Olympic competition. It's the last thing I think about as I fall asleep. I'll lie in bed, close my eyes and run through the event in my head. Even if I'm preparing for a World Championships, I'll visualise the Olympic Games. I see the rings, the colours, the logos and the spectators.

Most importantly, I make a concerted effort to see my optimal performance every single time, and picture my scores being enough to take first place. That only really began at Tokyo. Prior to 2021, I imagined my performances being good enough to win a medal, whether that be a bronze, silver or gold. I didn't see myself taking first spot outright. By the Tokyo Games I'd run through this pre-performance routine so many times that I didn't see myself doing anything else other than winning gold.

This was weird because I'd been focusing on synchro at the time and was working with a new partner, Matty Lee. During the run-in to the Games, we didn't know how we were going to do, but there was little doubt that our consistency was improving. We had momentum. On the morning of the synchronised 10-metre platform event, both of us woke up with the same thought. *We were winning it.* It was surreal. I opened my eyes and just knew. It was the right time, everything had fallen into place and we had that competition flow. I can't think of another occasion where I've woken up and my first thought has been, 'Well, today's the day I get gold.'

On the day of a big event, my pre-competition routines have changed too. I used to be very superstitious, but I now try to retain a sense of flexibility in case the day doesn't pan out as I'd hoped. No matter how much I plan, no matter how many times I go through the *what ifs . . .?*, there will always be something that catches me off-guard, so I've learned to let go of the things I can't control. Still, routine is everything. It enables me to wake up, knowing exactly what it is I need to do. For example, I'm a big believer in lists, so whenever I travel abroad I'll write down the things I need to pack in advance, such as stuff for my physical recovery, tools for mindfulness, my knitting equipment, resources for breathwork and so on. As Kate says, consistency is king, especially during the build-up to an Olympics. But it's also important to remember that getting to the start line is often the hardest part of an athlete's journey. Waiting for the starter's pistol, or the first dive: that's the easy part. At that point, if an athlete's still worrying about whether they've done enough in preparation, they've probably messed up.

That said, there's still work to do. Once I'm at the pool for, say, an Olympic final, my pre-performance routine will remain consistent. In fact, a lot of my process has remained fairly unchanged since I was 15, although there have been one or two tweaks over the years. When I first started competing I relied on a playlist downloaded to my iPod Shuffle, and my compilation of songs grew over a couple of years. With my headphones on, I always enjoyed watching the competition – I felt like I was a spectator rather than a competitor. I also felt the urge to know what was happening with the scores, and who was doing what, because that brought the best out of me. It fired up my competitive spirit.

Later I learned to knit and crochet, and as I waited between dives at the Tokyo Olympics, I zoned out by keeping myself busy with stitchwork. Knitting was mindfulness, and it helped me to take my mind off what I had to do over the course of a diving competition. This was particularly helpful when it came to handling nerves. I always experience them, but as the years have gone by they've calmed a little bit. When I first started, the butterflies began before training. Even then, I worried about what might happen. Over time, I've come to see those flashes of anxiety as excitement. They showed up because I was eager to prove myself. The knitting helped me to dial back the adrenaline, without over- or under-cooking my performance, and I was able to home in on what it was I needed to do.

When it's my turn to dive, I act in pretty much the same way I did when I won the 2009 World Championships in Rome. I'll have a drink of water at the bottom of the step. As each diver goes by, I'll walk up another three metres. Once I've arrived at the five-metre mark, I place a chamois on my head and visualise the dive. At seven metres, I physically run through the required movements, imagining myself as being *inside* the dive, rather than simply watching it in my mind in a TV-style action replay. Once at the top of the steps, I take ten deep breaths, step to the board and go.

I'm so well grooved in this pre-performance routine that distractions now bounce off me. At Tokyo, I remember climbing the steps to the board, and as I stepped up, a Games official was standing there. They were trying to figure out a way of moving some towels so the cameras could get a better view of the board. I stopped for a chat.

'Oh, is everything OK?' I said. 'Do you need me to get something?'

In that moment, I felt so content. That had everything to do with creating a tried-and-tested pre-performance routine, while carrying a *why* that wasn't wrapped up in diving. Plus, I knew that if the worst came to the worst, there was always cheesecake.

LESSON #3: MAKE DECOMPRESSION A HABIT

When I first started diving, I didn't really understand the concept of decompression. I finished my first Olympics in 2008, and because I didn't really know the difference between that and any other competition, I couldn't wait to get back into the pool. The Junior World Championships were just around the corner, and I wanted to prepare straightaway. Everything changed after London

2012. I'd spent five years building up to that moment, and once the party was over, I had no idea what to do with myself. I hadn't looked beyond it. So, when I won bronze and the hype died down and the world went back to normal, I was left with an overwhelming feeling of emptiness. 'Now what?' I thought. I had no idea of what my next goals were, or how to achieve them.

For a while I struggled with the concept of getting back into the pool. Even the idea of wanting to dive again felt alien and abstract. I think I only had about six days off before training began for the Junior World Championships and I was soon wrestling with a tricky dive known as a back twister. I was also struggling with my sexuality, having just met my partner Lance. I'd shared the news with some close friends, but I worried how it would affect my diving, and how it might affect my everyday life, were I to keep it a secret. I was overwhelmed. I felt down. Because I was the only member of the GB diving team that had won a medal, I didn't think there was anyone I could talk to about it. I imagined them not understanding. When I thought about how a conversation would go, I saw the other person looking at me and saying, 'Well, you've got a medal. Like, what are you down about?'

The big change came when I started to understand the importance of recognising main character syndrome (see Lesson #1), but also when I embraced the concept of decompression. With Kate's help, I learned that it was vital to relax after every major event so that I could process the associated emotions attached to whatever had taken place: euphoria, sadness, frustration, excitement, numbness, anger and so on. After my experience in 2012, I made sure to go on holiday after every major championship and hang out with friends and family. I also escaped the pool. I've heard a lot of nonsense, usually from motivational speakers, that focuses on the idea of *never having a day off*. Or of the importance of *not resting* (because somebody else is out there working much harder than you). That's bullshit. I don't work in an endurance sport, but I *understand* endurance. The most important thing in life is to feel like you're enjoying the challenges ahead, because if you're not and you're hating them, it's unlikely you'll make good decisions going forward. I'm not saying you shouldn't work hard. I'm just echoing Kate's advice that balance is key.

Decompression brings that balance. Without it, I zone out at training. I stand at the end of the diving board and stare into the middle distance without really focusing on anything. In the past I often ended up training for the training's sake, without getting anything from the experience. It was just another day ticked off on the training schedule. These days I listen to my body. If I'm down to train Monday to Sunday and my body feels tired, I'll take a rest day without feeling bad about it, knowing I'll work much harder once I'm fully recovered. One bad training session isn't going to break me. But a balanced schedule, where I'm decompressed and physically ready, will put me in the right headspace for any competition.

That's how *I* win.

Tom Daley, 2024*

---

* Tom Daley announced his retirement from competitive diving in August 2024. Tom won five Olympic medals: one gold, one silver and three bronze.

ACKNOWLEDGEMENTS

I'm incredibly grateful for the support I've received from so many people in writing this book. The FA have been supportive from the very beginning, and I'd like to extend a special thank you to David Gerty, Joanna Manning-Cooper and Anja van Ginhoven for being my critical friends in the process.

Having an idea and turning it into a book isn't easy, and would have been impossible without my writer Matt Allen, who helped bring my ideas to life. Thank you for your brilliance, your experience and living this project with me. I will be forever grateful to you. Thanks also to our agent The Blair Partnership and the team at HarperCollins for making this happen.

This book exists thanks to many years spent collaborating with fellow psychologists, support staff and coaches in a quest to learn 'How to Win'. A special mention goes to Professor Ian Maynard for the faith you put in me and the support you provided me throughout my MSc, PhD and early career. To all those I've had the opportunity to lead, be led by or work alongside, I'd like to say thank you for your wisdom, creativity, collaboration and time: Mark Bawden, Conor O'Shea, Rob Baker, Cath Bishop, Kevin Currell, Danielle Adams-Norenberg, Kate Ludlam, Mike Stoker, Paul Hughes, Lara

Barrett, Jonny Riall, Danny Kerry, Helen Richardson-Walsh, Simon Middleton, Greg Retter, Sarina Wiegman, Arjan Veurink, Tom Daley. I've loved problem-solving with you and sharing such joy in the process. Thank you for giving permission for your (team) stories to be told, and for ensuring they were captured appropriately.

While there are many people that form 'the team behind the team', far fewer step out in front of the bright lights, cameras and thousands of fans to deliver a performance under the utmost pressure. Those that do deserve a special mention. I'd like to give my heartfelt thanks to all those athletes I've been privileged enough to work with over the years. I have the utmost respect for anyone that navigates the uncertain world of high performance, and I have learned something from every one of you. If I have played a small part in your journey, then know that I hold the memories very dear – thank you.

Finally, I'd like to thank my husband Ian for always backing me, encouraging me and going on this journey with me; my parents-in-law Pam and Mel, who are the team behind our team, continually supporting our family; and Shaun Canning for once again being there when I needed some help. Above all, I want to thank my parents Jane and Alan Hays for the unconditional love and support I've always received and felt. Thank you.